HTML5 Mastery: Semantics, Standards, and Styling

Anselm Bradford

Paul Haine

friendsof

DESIGNER TO DESIGNER™

an Apress® company

Credits

To my parents, Harda and Stuart, for showing me that tornadoes and gusty winds can both describe the same storm.

—Anselm Bradford

Contents at a Glance

Contents

About the Authors

■ **Anselm Bradford** is a lecturer in digital media at the Auckland University of Technology (AUT) in New Zealand, where he researches interactive media, web media, and visual communication. His experience with Internet-related development stretches back to 1996, when he hand-coded his first website. He may be found on Twitter @anselmbradford, and he occasionally blogs at AnselmBradford.com.

■ **Paul Haine** is a London-based web designer. His personal blog is joeblade.com.

About the Technical Reviewer

 **Jeffrey Sambells** does what he loves. He is a father, designer, developer, author, and entrepreneur, among many other things. He started dabbling in the Web more than a decade ago and has turned it into a passion, pushing the limits of what's possible. With an expertise in creating slick end-to-end user experiences, Jeffrey is always on top of the latest technologies, especially when it comes to mobile devices.

You can probably find him writing something interesting at http://jeffreysambells.com or possibly catch him working on a stealth project via Twitter's @iamamused.

About the Cover Image Artist

 **Corné van Dooren** designed the front cover image for this book. After taking a brief hiatus from friends of ED to create a new design for the Foundation series, he worked at combining technological and organic forms, with the results now appearing on this and other books' covers.

Corné spent his childhood drawing on everything at hand and then began exploring the infinite world of multimedia—and his journey of discovery hasn't stopped since. His mantra has always been "The only limit to multimedia is the imagination"—a saying that keeps him constantly moving forward.

Corné works for many international clients, writes features for multimedia magazines, reviews and tests software, authors multimedia studies, and works on many other friends of ED books. You can see more of his work at and contact him through his website, at www.cornevandooren.com.

Acknowledgments

Like all we will do in life, the road toward a body of work starts long before any book comes hot off the press. Looking back, I'd say my road toward writing this book started from two directions. There is one path that built the body of knowledge needed to fill a book, and there is another path that led to the process of communicating with a publisher and having this book actually materialize.

For the first path, I am indebted to numerous people through my life that have allowed me to develop my web authoring skills. I could go further back, but my direct curiosity of the Web began as a teenager living in Vermont. In 1996 I built a website for *Rainbow Organic Fiber Mill*, an organic cotton fabric company started in North Bennington, Vermont, by Bryant Rayngay. And although it never went live, it was the first time I hand-coded a complete website from scratch, and my interest was forever piqued. In the years after my skills developed, particularly with the help of Sean Murphy, webmaster at College of the Atlantic. I owe many thanks to Sean, who during my undergraduate college years allowed me tremendous opportunity and free reign to explore and develop my skills as his assistant webmaster on `http://coa.edu` and eventually opened the door that allowed me to design and implement the appearance of the site for many years. Thanks also to Jared Vorkavich and Taeil Kim, who allowed me space to develop my visual design, interactive, and web authoring knowledge during my time in graduate school. These people and more indirectly and directly created the steps that allowed me to build my web knowledge to what it is today.

The other path that brought this book into existence began many years ago when I lost the opportunity to be a technical editor on a book to my adept friend Eric Kramer, who scooped up the position we both applied for. But as the project got underway, another editor was needed, and on Eric's recommendation I was brought into the project as well. This was a book by Rich Shupe for O'Reilly Media, and since that first book, I edited two more books by Rich, who requested me as reviewer. Thanks to Eric and Rich, because without them I likely wouldn't have become involved in publishing as much as I have. Reviewing technology books with a discerning eye and seeing the process of producing a book gave me the confidence that I could do it myself. These projects also led to book editing opportunities with Peachpit Press and last but not least, Apress.

Thanks goes to Ben Renow-Clarke of friends of ED, who got the ball rolling on this book, and Jennifer Blackwell and the rest of the Apress team for their patience and guidance as this book got underway. Thanks to my technical reviewer, Jeffrey Sambells, who pleasantly surprised me with his astute error-finding skills. Also, thanks to Paul Haine for laying the groundwork for this book with his authorship of *HTML Mastery*.

Thanks to my colleagues at AUT University, who created the opportunities for me to both further develop my web skills and write about it at the same time. Specifically Gudrun Frommherz, who helped structure my teaching schedule to give me more time to write, and Abhi Kala, who kept the Digital Media department alive during many nights of writing (also thanks to Abhi for shooting my author photo for this book). Thanks also go to the numerous people behind the helpful pseudonyms that popped up on the WHATWG IRC channel and answered questions when I was confused about something in the HTML specification.

Special thanks goes to Whitney Traylor for putting up with my distraction and preoccupation as I began writing this book, and, lastly, thanks to my brother, Orson, for always being enthusiastically interested in talking about and sharing web development knowledge.

—Anselm Bradford

Introduction

Unless you have been off on a digital-free holiday, you've heard a lot of chatter about HTML5. As a web professional, it is apparent that having an understanding of HTML5 is not only beneficial—it's essential. The future of the Web has radically changed course in the last few years from XHTML to HTML5, which means there are new concepts to learn but also outdated coding practices to unlearn.

At times HTML5 can seem enigmatic and ambiguous in what it encompasses, and threshing out a definition for HTML5 can lead you in many directions. This book will comprehensively cover the state of HTML5 and give you a solid foundation in the technologies it covers. Fundamental concepts are briefly covered before diving into specifics, with an emphasis on gaining a solid grounding in HTML. There are many new elements and attributes to cover, in areas such as web forms, multimedia, and improved website semantics. There are also a handful of elements and attributes that are now obsolete, which as a professional web developer you will absolutely never use ever again (right?). The correct usage of the current HTML elements, new and old, is shown in clear easy-to-follow summaries. CSS and JavaScript are the next topics on the table, and both are discussed and explored through their relationship with HTML.

Also, in order to give you the theories and practical knowledge that will take your web practice higher, related foundational topics, such as digital color, media formats, responsive design, and even trigonometry, will be covered as relevant to HTML5.

While HTML5 will be molded for years to come, you will find that it has laid the foundation for many next-generation web applications to be built today—web applications that might just be built by you!

Who is this book for?

HTML5 Mastery is aimed toward anyone with a working familiarity with HTML, CSS, and JavaScript, who is interested in gaining a deeper understanding of the specifications that define these languages. The HTML5 specification is very large. Approaching it through the pages of this book will quickly get you up-to-speed and serve as a launching board to take your HTML knowledge to new heights.

HTML, CSS, and JavaScript may feel familiar and easy to you, but you are sure to find hidden gems that will surprise you. Learning about these subtleties will go a long way toward making you a master of HTML5. You will walk away equipped with foundational knowledge and the wherewithal to seek out higher-level concepts in order to follow the trends of modern web development.

How is this book structured?

This book begins with a discussion of the surprisingly convoluted history that led to HTML5 becoming today's hottest web development trend. For those newer to HTML, fundamental terminology is covered before running through the highlights of HTML5 and what's changed since HTML 4.01. After this high-level view of the state of HTML5, subsequent chapters dive deeper into specific areas of interest, providing a comprehensive overview of the HTML elements and related technologies.

The first third of the book will give you a solid grounding in what is available to you in HTML5 and help you organize and build better web pages for today's Internet. In Chapter 2 you will learn about the global attributes present on all elements and the new content model categories of HTML5 that organize each HTML element into a set of overlapping groups. The elements are then explored in-depth across the next two chapters. Special attention is given to semantically structuring your pages. After gaining a broad understanding of all the elements in HTML, the second third of the book will dive deeper into the elements of web forms, followed by the elements for embedding multimedia into your web pages.

The last third of the book goes into concepts that are used closely with HTML but are separate from the HTML elements used to structure a page. Beginning in Chapter 6, HTML's relationship with CSS3 is discussed. Fundamental CSS concepts are also shown, and examples of key new features of CSS3 styling are demonstrated. Next, concepts from the HTML5 JavaScript APIs are introduced. A small template for exploring JavaScript within the web browser is constructed and demonstrated through specific practical examples. The book finishes up with the road ahead into web development for mobile devices and ends with a summary of upcoming and evolving HTML5 technologies and, lastly, coverage of technologies that aren't part of HTML5 but are commonly used and associated with it (such as the Geolocation API).

This book can be read from cover to cover or kept by your computer as a reference for particular elements and concepts. To get the most out of this book, I recommend you follow the wisdom of the (WHATWG) HTML specification, which, when talking about how a document should be read to get the most out of it, puts it this way:

"[It] should be read cover-to-cover, multiple times. Then, it should be read backwards at least once. Then it should be read by picking random sections from the contents list and following all the cross-references"

Lastly, the book has an accompany website at `http://html5mastery.com` where you can find related information and links.

Conventions used in this book

This book uses a couple of conventions that are worth noting:

- Unless otherwise noted, *HTML5* and *HTML* refer the most recent implementation of the HTML language.
- *Modern browsers* are considered to be Google Chrome 11 or newer, Mozilla Firefox 4 or newer, Safari 5 or newer, Opera 11 or newer, and Microsoft Internet Explorer 9 or newer.
- Individual HTML elements may be referred to with and without "element," for instance, `pre` and `pre` element, both refer to the HTML `<pre>`.
- Unless shown or implied, it is assumed that all the HTML examples in this book are nested in the body of a valid HTML5 document.
- Unless otherwise shown, any CSS and JavaScript code is assumed to be within an external style sheet and external script file, respectively.

- Code snippets that are contained in a larger piece of code may include the ellipsis character (…), which is used to denote that there is code not shown that continues before and/or after a particular code snippet. Here's an example:

```
...
<body>
        <p>The head area and the rest of the body aren't shown, but they should be
there if you wrote this code yourself.</p>
...
```

- Lastly, it should be noted that the JavaScript examples shown have variables and functions that are created in a global scope for the sake of brevity and clarity. This likely will be fine for most uses, but in a truly professional best practice environment, the scope of a particular set of JavaScript variables and functions would likely be placed inside a custom object to prevent naming conflicts between different scripts running on the same page.

With the formalities out of the way, let's begin this road to HTML5 mastery.

Getting Started: Transitioning to HTML5

HTML5 is the first major update to the HTML specification in more than a decade. A decade! And what an update it is! Exciting new features such as multimedia support, interactivity, smarter forms, and better semantic markup are present, but the slate is not being wiped clean and started from scratch. The HTML you know and love is still there for you to play with, as is XHTML. With HTML5, you are free to code your pages in (almost) any way you are familiar with, but mastery of your craft comes from understanding the history, conventions, and semantics (meaning) of what you are coding and from creating informed decisions that drive your authoring style.

This chapter will untangle the foundations of HTML5 so that you can see where it has come from; this is followed by an overview of fundamental HTML terminology and concepts. Next, the major changes of HTML5 are summarized, and the state of XHTML is explained. Finally, some tools for using HTML5 features today are summarized, followed by a listing of other web developer tools.

HTML5 = HTML • HTML5

What does HTML stand for? "Hypertext Markup Language." This is likely not new to you. Well, what then does HTML5 stand for? "HyperText Markup Language, version 5" sounds reasonable. It's a reasonable assumption indeed, but HTML5 has a convoluted history that makes the term not as clear as it first seems. It may mean the most recent draft of the HTML specification to some, a stable snapshot of a larger specification to others, or a label to describe a whole suite of new and not-so-new technologies that aim to make the Web a richer, more engaging place to interact with.

Before HTML5

Remember Web 2.0? The term that rose to prominence in the mid-2000s became synonymous with a transition from a read-only mentality toward the Web to one that allowed active participation in its content: the read/write Web. As the term popped up at more and more conferences and elsewhere, eventually becoming a common catchphrase in mainstream media, its exact meaning became less than defined. Companies such as YouTube seemed to have it, yet undoubtedly web developers the world over were presented with the headache of explaining to confused clients that the old and antiquated HTML of their websites could not be supplanted with Web 2.0. The term became largely symbolic of what was possible, what was hip, and what was new. In practice, it encompassed old technologies that were repackaged in new ways, such as the asynchronous loading of content with JavaScript and XML (which became known as Ajax). In actuality, the ability to interact with a website in a read/write context had been around for years.

Perhaps more than anything, this period signified the desire to bring new life to the Web. The World Wide Web Consortium (W3C), the organization behind the direction of HTML at the time, had not released a recommendation for the HTML specification since 1999, when HTML 4.01 was released. For years after, the W3C was busy at work on XHTML 1.0 and then XHTML 2.0, a reworked XML-based flavor of HTML that sought to implement a stricter, more consistent coding practice. Since XHTML was based on XML, web page authors needed to adhere to the specification exactly; otherwise, the page would not load when it was not valid. The hope was the world's website authors would adopt this new standard, flushing the Web of malformed markup. But there was one problem. The world didn't switch.

Why XHTML 2.0 died and HTML5 thrived

By the time *Web 2.0* was coined, there was mounting criticism toward the use of XHTML. In an effort to accommodate browsers that did not support XHTML, web page authors were writing XHTML markup but continued to serve the pages from their web servers using the Internet MIME type "text/html," instead of the proper "application/xhtml+xml," which would tell the browser it was viewing XML. The authors would build what they thought were valid XHTML pages, yet without delivering the pages as XML. They would not see any coding mistakes materializing in the browsers they were building against. The point became lost. The XHTML syntax did not matter if it was not being checked as such. In 2004 a group formed named the Web Hypertext Application Working Group (WHATWG), which aimed to evolve good old HTML instead of focusing on XHTML, as the W3C was doing at the time. The WHATWG began developing a specification named "Web Applications 1.0," which would eventually become HTML5!

The WHATWG philosophy

The WHATWG took a different approach from the W3C in developing the HTML specification. Instead of pushing what some saw as a draconian overhaul of web standards, the WHATWG aimed to evolve HTML incrementally, maintaining backward-compatibility with previous versions of HTML. This made sense because web browsers did not operate on a versioning approach to rendering HTML; they attempted to render whatever HTML was thrown at them, independent of which version of the specification the web page author attempted to adhere to (HTML 3.2, HTML 4.01, and so on). The WHATWG developed a specification that was largely driven by what was practically in use—what web browser vendors were implementing and what web page authors were using. In 2007 three web browser manufacturers, Mozilla Foundation, Apple, and Opera Software, requested that the W3C adopt the work of WHATWG as a starting point for further development of HTML. Soon after, the W3C took the suggestion, and after nearly a decade of keeping HTML in hibernation, the next version, HTML 5 (with a space), was underway. In 2009, after eight Working Drafts and no Release Candidate, the W3C decided to bring XHTML 2 to a close and concentrate on HTML 5 (which was eventually shortened to HTML5). (Refer to Figure 1-1 for a chart of this convoluted history.) Additionally, XHTML lives on as XHTML5, which adheres to XML syntactic rules, as opposed to the HTML rules. Bits of XML syntax are permissible in HTML syntax (trailing slashes on empty elements, such as `<br />`, for instance); however, these are not true XHTML documents unless they are explicitly delivered from a server as such using the MIME type "application/xhtml+xml" or "application/xml" (more on this later).

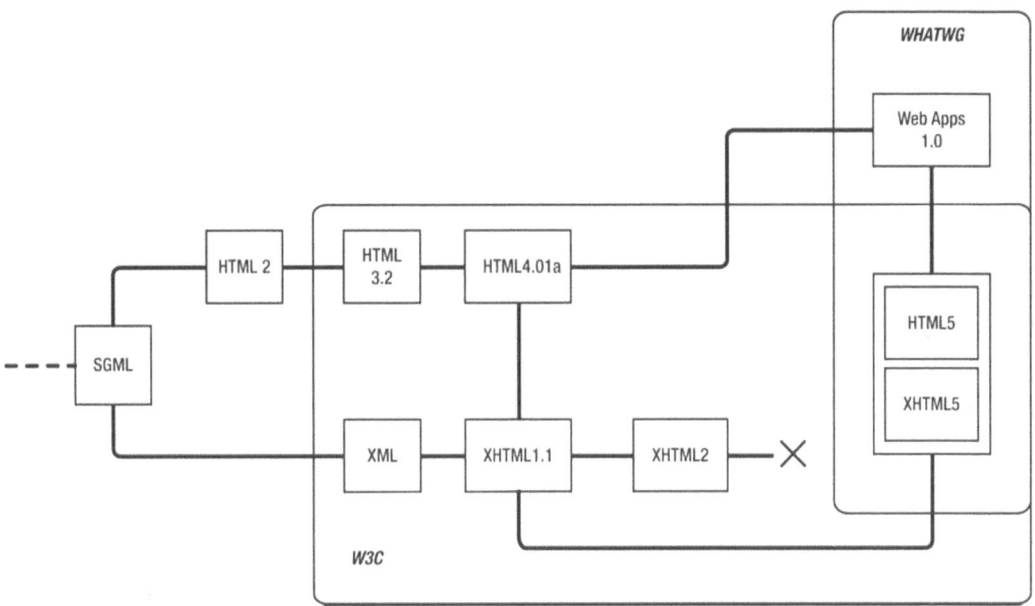

Figure 1-1. The convoluted evolution of HTML. Note that the HTML2 specification appeared prior to the formation of the W3C.

The current state of HTML5

"The specification is never complete because it is continuously evolving."

WHATWG FAQ

Is HTML5 done? No! Is it ready to use? Yes! The WHATWG and W3C continue to develop the HTML5 specification in conjunction with each other; however, WHATWG no longer refers to its specification as HTML5 (and you just thought you were wrapping your head around the history!). In addition to focusing on codifying what is already in practice, another philosophical difference between the WHATWG and the W3C HTML Working Group is that the WHATWG will no longer be developing a version of HTML that will at some point be closed for further revision. The W3C treats each version as a "snapshot" of the current state of development, while the WHATWG aims to have one specification for HTML that gets updated as needed. This reflects a move away from developing web applications that rely on the features of a particular version of HTML and instead relies on checking for support of the features directly, regardless of the "version" of the HTML specification used.

In the eyes of WHATWG, the W3C HTML5 specification (`http://w3.org/TR/html5/`) is a snapshot of the most stable features of the "living specification" WHATWG is overseeing. This specification is simply named HTML (`http://whatwg.org/html/`). The HTML specification is nested further as a subset of Web Applications 1.0 (Figure 1-2), which includes specifications related to web development that are separate from HTML, such as Web Workers (concurrent JavaScript threads), Web Storage (used for storing data in a web application), and others. You can view the full Web Applications specification at `www.whatwg.org/specs/web-apps/current-work/complete.html`.

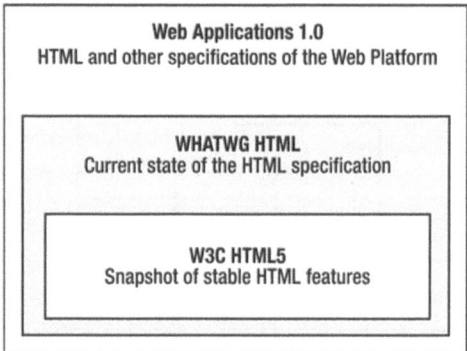

Figure 1-2. How HTML/HTML5 fit together

This brings me back to the beginning of this trip through HTML's history. What is HTML5? Depending on the context:

- It is the most recent version of the HTML specification.

- It is a stable snapshot of an earlier version of the HTML specification.

- It is a label used to describe the contemporary state of open web technologies.

As far as the meaning of HTML5 referred to in this book, what is covered here is by its very nature a snapshot of the current specification. This means it may be ahead of W3C's HTML5 specification but will likely be behind the WHATWG's "living specification" by the time this goes to print. That is the nature of the Web. It's continuously evolving. For what is covered in this book, the third bullet point shown earlier possibly works the best. This book is a look at the contemporary state of web development. HTML5 is the new hip state of the Web, like the Web 2.0 that came before it. Where appropriate, associated APIs and technologies are included, regardless of the exact specification they draw from, but the overarching framework they work under is the next version of HTML—HTML5! (Or however you want to refer to it.)

Anatomy of an HTML5 document

Now that you are sufficiently versed in the path toward HTML5, let's look at a simple document so you can see how things have changed. Open your preferred code editor, create a new HTML file, save it as `index.html`, and type the following:

```
<!DOCTYPE html>
<html>
        <head>
                <meta charset="utf-8" />
                <title>HTML5 Apprentice</title>
        </head>
        <body>
                <p>Hello World</p>
        </body>
</html>
```

Surprise! You will notice that this document is not only familiar but also simpler than the HTML you may have seen before. Pretty clean and compact, huh? OK, feel free to open this in your preferred web browser to see that the text *Hello World* will in fact display on your page. If you can name every term in the previous code, feel free to skip the next section; otherwise, read on to get a refresher on fundamental HTML terminology and concepts.

HTML terminology and concepts

To avoid confusion on what is being referred to within this text as well as what you may read or hear spoken elsewhere, it is important that you know some fundamental terminology and concepts. Using the correct terminology is important both to avoid confusion and to aid your own and others' understanding.

Three fundamental building blocks make up an HTML document: elements, attributes, and text (content). Consider the following HTML code snippet for creating a link:

```
<a href="about.html">About Us</a>
```

The **element** is the **a** (which stands for *anchor*) element, which generates a clickable link to another HTML page or other resource. The element is composed of two **tags**: the **starting tag** (`<a>`) and the **ending tag** (`</a>`), which are also known as the start and end tag or the opening and closing tag. The **attribute** is the text that appears inside the starting tag as a name/value pair. Finally, the text content (which appears in the web page when this code is viewed in the browser) appears between the opening and closing tags (see Figure 1-3).

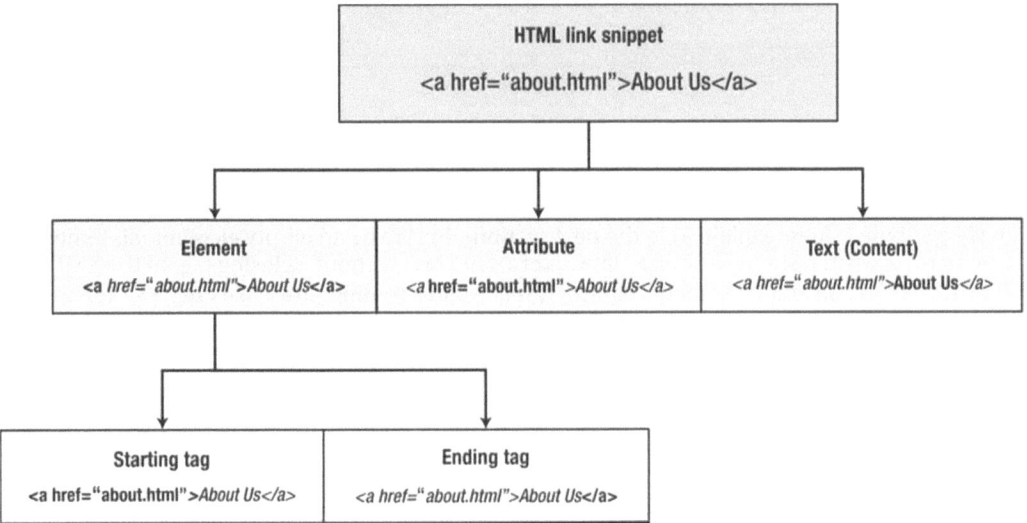

Figure 1-3. Fundamental components of a typical HTML snippet showing element, attribute, content, and tags.

Elements

Elements are the *M* in HTML; they are the markup instructs a web browser on how to handle some content. Each element has a keyword, such as `body`, `p`, `a`, `img`, and so on, that defines what it is (body element, paragraph element, anchor element, and image element, respectively). Different elements define different types of behaviors, such as creating links, embedding images, and so on. You may hear of an element being referred to synonymously with tags, but elements and tags have slightly different meanings. Tags are *part* of elements, as Figure 1-5 shows. The majority of elements consist of an opening tag, some content, and a closing tag, but depending on the tag, one or more of these three components may be absent. Many elements can contain any number of further elements nested inside of them, which are, in turn, made up of tags and content. The following example shows two elements: the `p` element, which is everything from the first opening angle bracket (`<`) to the very last closing angle bracket (`>`), and the `em` element, which encompasses the opening `<em>` tag, the closing `</em>` tag, and the content in between.

```
<p>Here is some text, some of which is <em>emphasized</em></p>
```

Notice that the `<em></em>` element is entirely enclosed in the `<p></p>` element; it would not be proper syntax to nest them any other way, as follows:

```
<p>Here is some text, some of which is <em>emphasized</p></em>
```

There is not a clear hierarchy of what is inside of what, which is problematic when a web browser is deciding how to display this text. A web browser will still parse and attempt to display this code, but it is not code that conforms to the HTML specification.

Empty elements

Not all elements contain text content. For example, the `img`, `br`, and `hr` elements insert, respectively, an image, new line, and horizontal rule into the page. What they don't do is modify some content on the page, beyond taking up space for themselves. Such elements are not container elements—that is, you would not write `<hr>some content</hr>` or `<br>some content</br>`. Instead, any content or formatting is dealt with via attribute values (explained in the next section). In HTML, an empty element (also known as a **void** element) is written simply as `<img>`, `<br>`, `<meta>`, or `<hr>`, without a closing tag. In the XML form of HTML, XHTML, an empty element requires a space and a trailing slash, like `<img />`,[1] `<br />`, `<meta />`[1], or `<hr />`; these are referred to as **self-closing** tags. Because of HTML5's flexible syntax, either form is acceptable to use. I tend to lean toward the XHTML syntax because the presence of the slash makes it clearer that the tag is an opening and closing tag merged together.

Attributes

Attributes appear within the starting tag of an element. A particular element often contains a mixture of attributes that are unique to that element along with attributes that are valid on a broad range of different elements. They are used to modify the behavior of the element in some respect. They can be thought of as key/value pairings, like `key="value"`, where a particular element will have a number of defined attributes (the key) that can be set to some value. For instance:

---

[1] In practice, the img and meta elements will have attributes as well.

```
<a href="contact.html">Here is some text that links to a contact page.</p>
```

The attribute `href` appears in the opening tag and is set to a custom value that changes the behavior of the HTML element. Depending on the attribute, it may contain multiple, space-separated values. Other attributes you may have already encountered might include `alt`, `src`, and `title`, but there are many more attributes. As with elements, HTML5 supports both HTML and XHTML syntax when writing attributes; in HTML syntax they would not need to be in quotes, so `<a href=contact.html>` would be acceptable, but, as with elements, I believe the XHTML syntax is clearer, because the quotes let you know the value is a custom value, like a quotation of something you have said. An exception to the clarity of XHTML syntax may be the way it handles certain attributes known as **Boolean** attributes. Boolean attributes provide an effect solely based on their presence or absence within an element. In XHTML, which requires that each attribute have a value, their value either is left empty or is set to a text string that is the same as the attribute name. For instance, the `video` element contains an attribute called `autoplay`; in XHTML syntax, this would look like `<video autoplay="">` or `<video autoplay="autoplay">`. However, in the more forgiving HTML syntax, this could be written as `<video autoplay>`. In this case, the HTML format is clearer. Since HTML5 supports either syntax, which way you write it is up to you!

DOM

With the descriptions of elements, tags, and attributes safely behind us, let's turn our attention to another concept related to HTML that you should know: the DOM. The **Document Object Model** (DOM) is a term that crops up particularly when discussing JavaScript's relationship to a page, and as a web designer/developer, it is an important term to be aware of. What is it? It is a standard way of representing a document, in this case an HTML page, as a treelike data structure composed of connected nodes. The nodes represent the elements, attributes, and text content in the page. Through its branching, tree-like structure, the DOM describes how the nodes are nested inside of each other.

The DOM and the nodes it contains are represented in JavaScript as **objects**, which describe what a particular node contains and can do. Using JavaScript, individual components on the page can be accessed using **dot notation** to traverse the tree structure. If you are not familiar with dot notation, it simply means that one node in the DOM tree that is nested inside another can be accessed through its containing nodes (known as objects in this context) by supplying the node (object) name separated by a period. For example, the HTML page is represented in the DOM as an object named `document`, which contains the actual HTML page contents. Since the HTML page contains a head and a body, there is a `head` and a `body` object inside the `document` object. So, to access the HTML page's `body` element, the following would be written in JavaScript: `document.body`. This won't actually do anything; the `body` element is just being accessed from JavaScript, but it isn't being processed in any way. The point is that the structure of the page is represented by nested objects, each of which can be accessed using a dot (period).

Once you get down to the specific HTML elements, the commands get more generalized, because it is unknown in advance what elements are on your particular page. JavaScript contains a number of commands that can be used for accessing the contents inside the body of the HTML page, for dynamically updating content, for responding to events, and so on. For instance, to access the first HTML element shown on the page, you would use `document.body.firstElementChild`. To access the first attribute of that element, you would use `document.body.firstElementChild.attributes[0]`. The zero in brackets just refers to the number of the attribute to access; 0 refers to the first of the attributes in the HTML element, 1 to the second attribute, and so forth. Lastly, to access the contents of this element, you would use the following: `document.body.firstElementChild.firstChild`.

Figure 1-4 shows the structure of a simple web page with only a link in the body area. Looking at this diagram, you'll notice an extra object at the top, called `window`. While the DOM is accessible through the `document` object, `document` is actually contained in this `window` object, which represents the web browser window the page content is contained in. Technically, accessing the DOM would be done through the `window` object first, which is the "root" object through which all other aspects of the web page are accessible from JavaScript. Accessing the page's body, for instance, could be done with `window.document.body` or `document.body` (in which case, a reference to `window` at the beginning is implied).

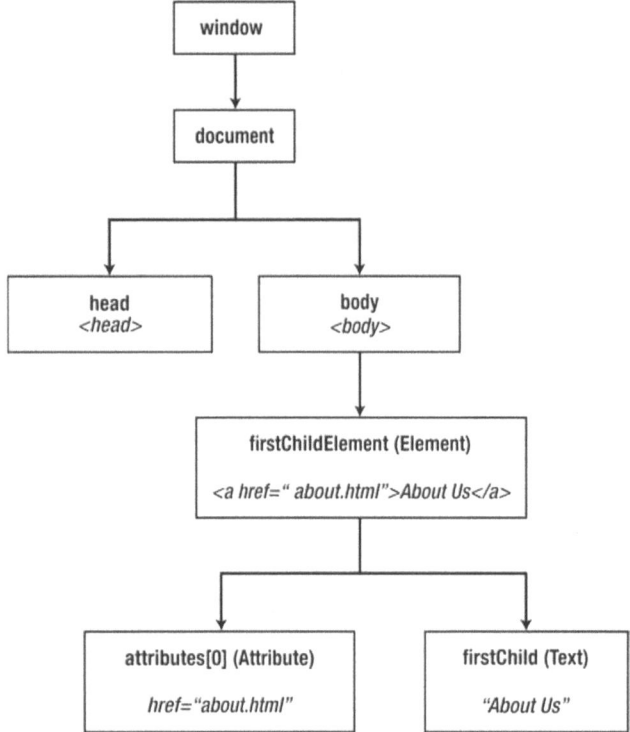

Figure 1-4. Accessing the DOM through the document *object reveals the inverted tree-like structure of a simple web page (which in this case, only contains a link in the body)*

What's new in HTML5?

At this point, you may be asking yourself, "What, really, is new in HTML5?" To begin with, it's worth noting that HTML was originally conceived of as a markup language for presenting text documents, not as an application development platform. However, over time, more and more functionality has been squeezed into the web browser. HTML5 has first and foremost attempted to consolidate, document, and add to the features added to the language over the past decade. Some of the main changes are described in the following sections.

Backward-compatibility

HTML5 is compatible in most cases with previous forms of HTML syntax and tags. How is this new? Well, for years a "standards-based" approach to web authoring was emphasizing a transition away from HTML syntax toward XHTML syntax. As discussed in the history section, HTML5 has moved the emphasis away from a syntactically "pure" XML-based approach and instead moves the emphasis toward better documentation of the practices already in use.

Error handling

While web page authors may write documents any way they are familiar with, pretty much, a major change in HTML5 has been directed toward user agents (web browser manufacturers), not authors. Web browsers attempt to render HTML code, whatever it may look like. Because of the flexibility of HTML in practice, the code can be ambiguous in its structure at times. In the past, web browser manufacturers approached ambiguous code differently and implemented different algorithms for how to handle the ambiguous HTML (termed **tag soup**). This led to inconsistencies in appearance across different browsers. One obvious approach toward solving this issue is to make the language stricter so web page authors are forced to structure their pages a certain way. This was the thought and effort behind XHTML1.*x*; however, another approach is to standardize how errors are handled on the browser implementator's side. This is what HTML5 seeks to do. It seeks to finally document how variations in syntax should be handled. Web browsers have two choices when dealing with a parsing error: either implement the rules specified in the HTML5 specification or abort processing the document at the first error. The idea is that different browsers will consistently handle the same errors, and those that do not implement the error-handling behavior will stop parsing the HTML, thus notifying the author of an issue with their syntax.

Obviously, it will be apparent to the web developer that something is wrong if the page does not render, but it will be far less apparent if the page renders fine, even if there is an error the browser is handling. In such situations, the page is being handled, but it is considered nonconforming with the HTML5 specification. This is why it is of utmost importance that web developers are familiar with what has changed in HTML and which elements and attributes they should not use (see the "Obsolete Features" section later in this chapter). If in doubt, however, there are conformance-checking services such as `http://html5.validator.nu` or `http://validator.w3.org` that will check supplied HTML code against the HTML5 specification.

Simplified doctype

HTML often begins with a doctype declaration. In the past this has looked something like this:

```
<!DOCTYPE HTML PUBLIC "-//W3C//DTD HTML 4.01 Transitional//EN"
"http://www.w3.org/TR/html4/loose.dtd">
```

or

```
<!DOCTYPE html PUBLIC "-//W3C//DTD XHTML 1.0 Strict//EN"
"http://www.w3.org/TR/xhtml1/DTD/xhtml1-strict.dtd">
```

A doctype declaration provides an indication as to what Document Type Definition (DTD) you're going to be writing your markup against. A DTD is basically a page detailing the rules and grammar of the markup. So, the difference in the two lines of the code listed earlier is that they are specifying a DTD for different versions of (X)HTML, one HTML 4.01 and the other XHTML 1.0. Wait a minute! This heralds from a worldview of HTML that sees it as broken into different versions. Since we are talking about HTML5, which is backward-compatible with previous versions of the specification, all that needs to be done is say the page is displaying HTML. Therefore, the doctype has been simplified to the following:

```
<!DOCTYPE html>
```

How's that for simplification of the doctype? It really couldn't be any simpler. Well, actually it could; it could be absent, and your HTML page will still load if it is omitted, but don't erase this line from your web pages just yet!

Doctypes in HTML serve two important purposes. First, they inform user agents and validators what DTD the document is written against. This action is passive—that is, your browser isn't going and downloading the DTD every time a page loads to check that your markup is valid; it's only when you manually validate a page that it kicks in.

The second and, for practical purposes, most important purpose is that doctypes inform browsers which parsing algorithm to use to read a document. Web browsers commonly have three ways they can parse an HTML document:

- No-quirks (or "standards") mode

- Quirks mode

- Limited-quirks (or "almost standards") mode

To render documents in one mode over another, the browser depends on the presence, absence, or value of the doctype string. This is known as **doctype switching**, and it was included in browsers as a way of determining how to render a document. The assumption is that if an author has included a doctype, then that author knows what he or she is doing, and the browser tries to interpret the strict markup in a strict way (in other words, standards mode). The absence of a doctype triggers quirks mode, which renders the markup in old and incorrect ways; the assumption here is that if the author hasn't included a doctype, then he or she probably is not writing standard markup, and therefore the markup will be treated as if it has been written in the past for buggier browsers. Whether no-quirks or limited-quirks mode is triggered is subtler and depends on the doctype chosen as well as the browser the document is viewed in.

■ **Tip** Do you want to convince yourself that the browser switches parsing modes based on the presence or absence of the doctype? If you open a page in Mozilla Firefox 4 and select Tools ➤ Page Info, under the General tab you will see a Render Mode listing that will show the current mode being used to view the page. If you add and remove the doctype declaration from a web page and check the Page Info during each state, you will see that the browser is triggering different parsing modes. Alternatively, if you are familiar with JavaScript, insert the following script into the head section of an HTML page:

```
<script type="text/javascript">


        alert(document.compatMode);


</script>
```

When loading the page, this will show a pop-up with either "CSS1Compat" or "BackCompat." The former means the mode is set to no-quirks mode; the latter means it is set to quirks mode.

One last note in regard to doctypes: in order to be compatible with legacy systems that generate HTML code and therefore require the doctype syntax to look more like it previously has, the following alternative doctype declaration for HTML5 is acceptable:

```
<!DOCTYPE html SYSTEM "about:legacy-compat">
```

This is provided only for systems producing HTML, so it is unlikely that you, as a web page author, would use this declaration unless you wanted to give your fingers an additional workout or show your friends that you are a master of the smallest nuances of HTML5.

Simplified character encoding

The HTML you type is text, right? Well, to you it is, but to the computer it is stored as a series of bits: 1s and 0s. Therefore, a particular character is actually stored as a particular binary number. A computer program (such as a web browser) reading a text document needs to know two things fundamentally:

- That what it is reading is supposed to be text
- Which convention is being used to map the bits it reads to the representation of a particular character of text

This second point is referred to as the **character encoding** for the document. Think of it as like the old telegraph system of communicating, where messages were sent as Morse code and subsequently translated into letters and words. To successfully transmit text using Morse code, the sender and the receiver both need to know how the clicks being sent map to particular letters. The character encoding tells the computer how to translate the bits and bytes it reads into letters for display or other purposes.

The HTML5 specification strongly recommends that all HTML documents have a character encoding set. The recommended way is to have the server send this as part of the response headers, in the *HTTP Content-Type* header, but if this is not possible, the meta HTML element can be used in the head section of the HTML document. The most widely used character encoding system in use on the Web is UTF-8, which can encode more than 1 million characters covering most written language scripts in use around the world.

In HTML 4.01, the meta element looked like this:

```
<meta http-equiv="content-type" content="text/html; charset=UTF-8">
```

This is still supported in HTML5 for backward-compatibility, but the preferred syntax is shorter and includes a new attribute, charset:

```
<meta charset="UTF-8">
```

Ahh, this is much more succinct! Remember, you don't need this at all if your server sends the character encoding as part of its HTTP response header.

New content model categories

A **content model** is used to specify the kinds of content that specific HTML elements are expected to contain. Different HTML elements that can contain the same kinds of content can be grouped together into categories. Traditionally, HTML elements have fallen under two categories: block and inline. In HTML5 these have been significantly expanded to seven major categories:

- Metadata content

- Flow content

- Sectioning content

- Heading content

- Phrasing content

- Embedded content

- Interactive content

The block category roughly corresponds to "flow content," while the inline category corresponds to "phrasing content" to make a distinction between this category and the `display:inline;` property used in CSS. These will be explored further in the next chapter.

New elements

HTML5 introduces a large number of new elements to help give greater meaning (semantics) to the structure of your web pages. New elements such as `header`, `nav`, and `footer` describe areas where the title and logo of the page may appear, where the main navigational menu appears, and where the copyright and legal information would be found, respectively. This standardizes the common practice of creating these areas of a web page using elements such as a `div` element with an `id` attribute. For example, previously a footer section might have been created with this:

```
<div id="footer">copyright 2011</div>
```

Using the new section tags, this could be rewritten as follows:

```
<footer>copyright 2011</footer>
```

Using these new structural tags is clearer and standardizes the identifier for this tag, since an `id` attribute could be written "page-footer," "thefooter," and so on, by different authors. The "Semantic Web" aims to provide clearly defined content that is readable by machines for better data mining/search purposes. The old format makes it impossible for a machine to pick out the footer consistently on several different web pages, while the HTML5 syntax makes it totally predictable—assuming, of course, the author in fact was using the footer tag for the appropriate section of their web page.

In addition to new structural elements, there have been major upgrades to the element types available in web forms, introducing new input types for entering dates, URLs, e-mail addresses, phone numbers, and so on. Also introduced is a number of new elements for embedded and interactive content, such as the `video`, `audio`, and `canvas` (a scriptable drawing surface). There have also been changes to existing elements, such as redefining the meaning (semantics) of the `b`, `i`, and `small` elements so that they are no longer presentational in nature. The new elements and changes to existing elements will be explored in greater detail in upcoming chapters.

Microdata

This new addition is based on the idea of annotating HTML elements for the purposes of adding metadata to the page's content so that it may more easily, and in a standardized way, be processed by external applications, aggregators, and search engines. This idea isn't new. Microformats and RDFa are two formats for annotating HTML for this purpose, but HTML5 introduces a third format: Microdata (itself based on RDFa). Microdata uses a set of global attributes that may be used to add additional semantic structure to the content on a page.

Embedded MathML and SVG

Mathematical Markup Language (MathML) and Scalable Vector Graphics (SVG) are both XML-based markup languages that are described in different specifications than HTML. As the name implies, MathML is for describing and presenting math equations using correct mathematical notation. SVG is used for describing interactive and static (noninteractive) vector-based graphics. Neither of these languages is new, but since HTML5 may include XML-style syntax, both of these languages can be embedded within a regular HTML page. These will be touched on further in Appendix A.

APIs

In the spirit of creating a platform for web application development, HTML5 introduces a number of scripting application programming interfaces (APIs). These include additions to the JavaScript API that allow elements to be selected via their classes. For example, using array syntax, the first element on a page with the `class` attribute set to `aClass` could be retrieved via JavaScript with the following:

```
document.getElementsByClassName("aClass")[0]
```

Also added are APIs associated with the new elements, such as a means to control video and audio playing within the new `video` and `audio` elements. Additional functionality added includes handling drag-and-drop user interaction, getting access to the web browser history state, and storing web page data in a cache for later retrieval in an offline state. There are also a number of related APIs that work with HTML5 but actually fall under separate specifications. A notable one in this category is the Geolocation API, which provides a means to handle location data within a web context. Later chapters will explore these APIs in greater detail.

No longer SGML conforming (again!)

Well, frankly you are unlikely to notice this change at all. HTML in its purest form originally developed from Standard Generalized Markup Language (SGML), a much older markup language. However, the HTML implemented by web browsers did not fully comply with the SGML specification, and HTML5 has simply codified that fact. HTML5 has syntactic elements borrowed from SGML, HTML, and XHTML1.x, making it an amalgamated language distinct in its own right.

Obsolete features

There is a bit of a catch-22 in HTML5, in that it must remain compatible with old features of HTML, while discouraging the use of certain elements that are no longer considered acceptable to use. For instance, HTML contains certain markup that is presentational in nature, meaning the effect it has on its content is to stylize its appearance in some way (the `font` element, for example). Presentational markup has long since been usurped by Cascading Style Sheets (CSS), so the majority of these features have been deprecated. Authors should not use these elements any longer, even though they still appear in the HTML specification. These elements are not simply removed from the specification so that user agents (web browsers) will know how to handle them when they are encountered (such as in older web pages); however, such pages are said to be nonconforming. The web browser will render them, but they do not adhere to the current HTML specification. Table 1-1 shows the list of obsolete elements and the alternatives to their use.

Table 1-1. Obsolete elements

Element	Alternative
applet	Use embed or object.
acronym	Use abbr.
bgsound	Use audio.
dir	Use ul.
frame	Use either iframe or CSS.
frameset	
noframes	
isindex	Use a textfield input type inside a form.
listing	Use pre or code.
nextid	Use globally unique IDs created by other means.
noembed	Use object as a fallback for embed.
plaintext	Use the "text/plain" MIME type.
rb	Provide the Ruby base directly in the ruby element.
strike	Use del if the element is marking an edit; otherwise, use s.
xmp	Use code, and escape < and > characters as < and >, respectively.
basefont	Use CSS.
big	Use h1, strong, or mark, depending on the meaning of the content.

blink	Use CSS or more appropriate elements.
center	
font	
marquee	
multicol	
nobr	
spacer	
tt	Use kbd, var, code, or samp, depending on the meaning of the content.
u	Use em, b, or mark, depending on the meaning of the content.

In addition to the deprecated elements, many attributes have been filed under obsolete as well, and many are presentational in nature and are easily emulated using CSS. See Table 1-2 for a list of attributes that have been marked obsolete in HTML5. They should not be used.

Table 1-2. Obsolete attributes

Element	Obsolete attributes
a	charset, coords, datafld, datasrc, methods, name, rev, shape, urn
area	nohref
body	alink, background, bgcolor, link, marginbottom, marginheight, marginleft, marginright, margintop, marginwidth, text, vlink
br	clear
button	datafld, dataformatas, datasrc
caption	align
col	align, char, charoff, valign, width
div	align, datafld, dataformatas, datasrc
dl	compact
embed	align, hspace, name, vspace

fieldset	datafld
form	accept
h1 – h6	align
head	profile
hr	align, color, noshade, size, width,
html	version
Iframe	align, allowtransparency, datafld, datasrc, frameborder, hspace, longdesc, marginheight, marginwidth, scrolling, vspace
img	align, border (except if value is 0), datafld, datasrc, hspace, longdesc, lowsrc, name, vspace
input	align, datafld, dataformatas, datasrc, hspace, usemap, vspace
label	datafld, dataformatas, datasrc
legend	align, datafld, dataformatas, datasrc
li	type
link	charset, methods, rev, target, urn
menu	compact
meta	scheme
object	align, archive, border, classid, code, codebase, codetype, datafld, dataformatas, datasrc, declare, hspace, standby, vspace
ol	compact
option	dataformatas, datasrc, name
p	align
param	datafld, type, valuetype
pre	width
script	event, for, language

select	datafld, dataformatas, datasrc
span	datafld, dataformatas, datasrc
table	align, background, bgcolor, border (except if value is 1 or ""), cellpadding, cellspacing, dataformatas, datapagesize, datasrc, frame, rules, summary, width
tbody	align, background, char, charoff, valign
td	abbr, align, axis, background, bgcolor, char, charoff, height, nowrap, valign, width
textarea	datafld, datasrc
tfoot	align, background, char, charoff, valign
th	abbr, align, axis, background, bgcolor, char, charoff, height, nowrap, valign, width
thead	align, background, char, charoff, valign
tr	align, background, bgcolor, char, charoff, valign
ul	compact, type

Is XHTML gone?

Short answer: no. It is now known as XHTML5. However, the HTML5 specification states that XHTML must no longer be served with the MIME type "text/html," as was commonly done with XHTML 1.*x*. A major reason this came into practice was that Internet Explorer would not parse a page served as XML and would instead attempt to download the page to disk instead of displaying it. This was not the only reason, however. XML is very strict in its syntax, and the smallest validation error would cause the web page to break and become unusable, with the error visible for the entire world to see. So, XHTML syntax was often used but still delivered as HTML as a precaution.

What's all this noise about MIME types?

Multipurpose Internet Mail Extensions (MIME) types, also known as the **media type**, tell a web page what kind of data it is receiving. Obviously, the web browser would want to handle an image vs. a text document very differently, so it is important to have the means to tell it what kind of data it is being sent. Since XHTML and HTML look very similar, the web browser needs to be told which it is dealing with. If it is XHTML, it needs to parse it using an XML parser that adheres to the XML specification; if it is HTML, it needs to parse it using an HTML parser that adheres to the HTML specification.

Before I continue, let me clarify the major difference between XHTML and HTML. Although they share a common vocabulary, XHTML has several theoretical advantages over HTML, including the following:

- XHTML that is not well-formed will be immediately spotted, because browsers will refuse to display the page and will display an error instead.

- XHTML provides a guarantee of a well-formed[2] document.

Neither of the preceding points is true, however, unless the pages are serving XHTML with a MIME type of "application/xhtml+xml" or "application/xml." If your web server is serving your web pages with a MIME type of "text/html," then you will not be taking full advantage of XHTML.

Deciding between HTML and XHTML

So, which should you use, HTML5 or XHTML5? It depends on your syntactic preferences and how important the guarantee of well-formedness in your documents is to you. XML-style syntax can still be used in HTML, but don't expect it to have the implications of XHTML unless it is served as such. Ultimately, it's a judgment call entirely dependent on your own circumstances. Just don't make the mistake of thinking that by serving a page as XHTML you've done all you need to do to create a professional, well-structured, semantically meaningful document.

Web browser support

Whichever syntax you use, let's turn to how you see the fruits of your labor. As features of HTML5 become stable, they are—in a perfect world—expected to appear in the latest version of your preferred web browser. But how do you know which features are actually supported and which are not? Testing code in the browser you are developing against is the surest option, but there are also websites such as `http://caniuse.com` available that give you an idea of what your preferred browser supports. Another site, `http://html5test.com`, detects whether certain features are available in the browser used to visit the site (Figure 1-5). Use a different browser, and you may see a different score and summary, highlighting that not all features will work on all major browsers.

---

[2] I should point out that "well-formed" does not mean the same as "valid." For instance, a tag with an attribute mymadeupattribute="true" is well-formed but still invalid.

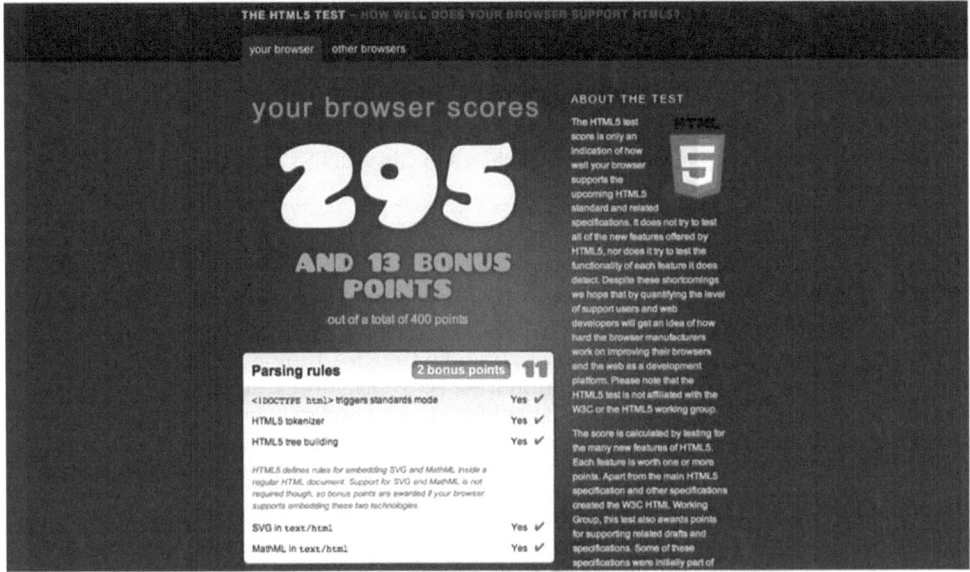

Figure 1-5. http://html5test.com *results for Google Chrome 11*

Since not all features of HTML5 are supported on current web browsers, it is a good idea to detect for support of any features that do not fail gracefully. Modernizr (`http://modernizr.com`) is a JavaScript library that is worth investigating for this purpose. The library detects the availability of HTML5 (and CSS3) features, whose presence or absence are stored as Boolean values in a JavaScript object the Modernizr library creates.[3] These values can be checked using conditional JavaScript code to add functionality if the features are present or, otherwise, handle the page if they are not. For example, to detect whether the audio element is supported, you could write the following in your page's JavaScript code:

```
// Check Modernizr object for audio Boolean value of true
if (Modernizr.audio) {
        // Enable functionality on page for audio controls
}
else
{
    // Handle lack of audio element support on the page
}
```

---

[3] If you want to know more about creating custom methods of detecting HTML5 features, check out Mark Pilgram's excellent summary at http://diveintohtml5.org/detect.html.

■ **Note** Paul Irish (`http://paulirish.com`) is a lead developer on the Modernizr project, as well as a project called the HTML5 Boilerplate (`http://html5boilerplate.com`), which is worth checking out as well. The Boilerplate provides a default bare-bones starting template for HTML5 web projects. It includes the Modernizr and jQuery JavaScript libraries, as well as a default web page structure and attached CSS style sheet.

Web browser developer tools

Each web browser uses software known as a **layout engine** to parse HTML and CSS and render it on-screen. Unsurprisingly, these are often different for each (though Google Chrome and Apple's Safari both use WebKit), which explains the differences in support of HTML5 features, even among the most recent releases of different web browsers. Since they are different, it's good to have a solid in-browser developer tool in order to explore and manipulate the HTML/CSS. Each browser has a set of tools for aiding web development in this regard. Typically, these tools, when enabled, allow content on the page to be right-clicked, and an "Inspect Element" or similar option will be present in the contextual menu. Inspecting the HTML element will reveal its structure and CSS styling, which can be explored and manipulated (nonpermanently) in the browser. These tools also feature some sort of "console" where JavaScript code can log commands using the code `console.log("message");` or similar. See Table 1-3 for a list of major browser's respective layout engines and developer tools.

Table 1-3. Browser layout engines and developer tools

Web browser	Layout engine	Developer tools
Chrome	WebKit	Google Chrome's Inspector
Firefox	Gecko	Firebug[4]
Opera	Presto	Opera Dragonfly
Safari	WebKit	Web Inspector[5]
Internet Explorer	Trident	Developer Tools (since IE8)

---

[4] Visit http://getfirebug.com to download this Firefox extension.
[5] Enabled through the Develop menu, which is enabled by checking the box in Preferences... ➤ Advanced.

Summary

It's been a convoluted road—years in the making—that now brings us HTML5. More and more new features are finding their way into web browsers, and certainly the majority is here for us to use today! Now that you have gotten your head around how HTML5 fits into the larger picture and explored what has changed and what has stayed the same, it is time to head off into the details of how to most effectively use the new features. You have only just scratched the surface!

CHAPTER 2

Using the Right Tag for the Right Job

With HTML5, web developers are given an even wider palette of HTML elements with which to paint meaning into their pages. Many new elements have been introduced to more precisely mark up, define, and organize content. Understanding when and where to use the many elements within HTML is integral toward creating logically structured, specification-conforming, semantically rich web pages.

This chapter will provide an overview of the elements available in HTML5, both newly added and those inherited from HTML 4.01. That's a possibly daunting task, you might think! After all, there is an 800+ page specification that covers them all (the current length of the full WHATWG HTML specification, as of July 2011). To make tackling the longish list of elements easier, we'll examine the elements in sets and will devote separate chapters to further examine groups of elements of particular interest. The elements in HTML can be loosely grouped together in the following sets:

- **Root element:** The `html` element rightly stands alone, because it is the only element that contains all the other elements in a document.

- **Document metadata and scripting elements:** The `head` element contains metadata for the document, as well as CSS styles and JavaScript in many cases.

- **Document sectioning elements:** The body element encloses the content of the page, and new semantic sectioning elements define the header, footer, articles, and other sections on the page. These will be discussed in detail in Chapter 3.

- **Content grouping elements:** The content in a specific section of the web page may be organized into paragraphs, lists, block quotes, figures, and so on.

- **Text-level semantics elements:** Individual runs of text may have words or sentences marked up to provide fine-grained control over the content's meaning, such as separating time, abbreviations, and superscripts from adjacent content or providing emphasis, importance, or other differences to the normal prose. These will be discussed in detail in Chapter 3.

- **Tabular data elements:** Data that would be appropriate to display in a spreadsheet would likely be marked up using the rows and columns of the `table` and related elements.

- **Form elements:** These include the text fields, drop-down menus, check boxes, and other elements for gathering user input in web forms. These will be discussed in detail in Chapter 4.

- **Embedded content elements:** These include external media embedded into a web page such as video, audio, a bitmap drawing surface, or third-party plug-ins such as Adobe Flash content. These will be discussed in detail in Chapter 5.

- **Interactive elements:** These include inherently interactive elements that require no further scripting.

Before diving into these groups, we'll cover two areas that apply to all the elements: the global attributes that apply to all HTML elements and "content model categories," the often overlapping grouping that the HTML specification uses to categorize elements relative to each other. Let's get to it!

Global attributes

Becoming familiar with the attributes that are found on all HTML elements (Table 2-1) provides powerful tools for utilizing the core functionality available in HTML, such as integration with CSS and JavaScript as well as the new editing and drag-and-drop APIs.

Table 2-1. *Global attributes found on all HTML elements*

■ NEW in HTML5	Attribute	Purpose	Value
	accesskey	Used by web browsers for creating a keyboard shortcut for activating or bringing focus to the element	One or more keyboard characters, separated by spaces; e.g., **o** or **j q**
	class	Category assigned to an element that is accessible from CSS and JavaScript	A set of space-separated identifying characters; e.g., **home link**
■	contenteditable	Specifies whether the content can be edited within a web browser	**true**, **false**, or **inherit**
■	contextmenu	A contextual menu associated with the element	A unique ID of a **menu** element
	dir	The directionality of the text, that is, whether the text should go from left to right or right to left	**ltr**, **rtl**, or **auto**
■	draggable	Whether the user can drag the element	**true**, **false**, or **auto**
■	dropzone	Specifies when dragged items are dropped on this element	**copy**, **move** or **link**; also needs to be

			told the kind of data to accept, such as `s:text/plain`, `f:image/png`, `f:image/gif`, or `f:image/jpeg`
■	`hidden`	Hides the specified element	Boolean attribute (presence of attribute determines value) or `hidden`
	`id`	Unique identifier for the element so it may be accessed from CSS, Javascript, or as the target of hypertext anchors	A set of characters unique on the page (a word typically); e.g., `logo`
	`lang`	Specifies the language used in the content of the element, such as English, French, Japanese, and so on	A language code;[1] e.g., `en` or `fr`
■	`spellcheck`	Whether the element should be checked for spelling and grammar by the web browser	`true` or `false`
	`style`	An inline CSS style applied to the element	Any CSS styling rules, separated by a semicolon
	`tabindex`	Specifies the order in which elements are active when the Tab key is pressed	The number 1 or higher
	`title`	Additional text for the element, which appears on mouse hover, for instance	`Some text`
■	`data-*`	Custom data attributes	`Some text`

---

[1] See www.iana.org/assignments/language-subtag-registry for a list of language codes; the "subtags" shown are what you would use.

> ■ **Note** There is an additional set of global attributes that apply when microdata is used, which allows additional markup to be added to the elements on a page to make it easier for machines, such as search engine algorithms, to parse and use the content. Microdata will be discussed later in the book.

Accessibility

The **accesskey** and **tabindex** attributes provide access to elements on the page using the keyboard, which may be helpful for users with limited mobility. When set on an element, the **accesskey** attribute allows a key (or keys) to be pressed on the keyboard that activates the element. It could be used for following a hyperlink using the keyboard, for instance. Unfortunately, this accessibility upside has a downside. A keyboard combination is often needed to activate the access key, such as pressing the Ctrl or Alt key in combination with the set access key. Precisely which keyboard combination to use varies by browser and operating system, degrading the usefulness of this feature. Additionally, the keyboard combinations used could interfere with existing keyboard shortcuts—most critically those used by screen readers for visibility impaired web users. Lastly, having multiple access keys set on a single element (which could be helpful if the website is viewed from two types of devices) does not enjoy wide browser support. All of these factors make using access keys rather discouraging.

One last note before we move on—Opera Software's Opera web browser offers a nice feature in regard to access keys. By pressing the Shift key and the Esc key at the same time, a menu pops up over the web browser window that shows all access keys available on the page and where they link to (if the attribute is set on anchor elements; "null" is shown otherwise). See Figure 2-1 for an example.

Figure 2-1. Opera web browser showing access key and associated links available on the company homepage

The next attribute, **tabindex**, is possibly more useful. Press the Tab key repeatedly on your keyboard while on a web page, and you'll see different page elements become highlighted. This is a common way to access elements of a web page using the keyboard, which may be particularly familiar when filling out a web form. The **tabindex** attribute, when set on a number of different elements (beginning at 1 and incrementing by 1 on each element), determines the order that presses of the Tab key will move through the different elements, with lower numbers accessed first, for example:

```
<ul>
    <li><a href="first.html" tabindex="1">First Item Active</a>
    <li><a href="third.html" tabindex="3">Third Item Active</a>
```

```
    <li><a href="second.html" tabindex="2">Second Item Active</a>
</ul>
```

On presses of the Tab key, the first item in the list would be activated, followed by the last item and lastly the middle item. Obviously, in a list such as this, it would make more usability sense to have them activate in the same order as the list, but this demonstrates how the order can be customized using `tabindex`.

Metadata

The `title` attribute provides advisory information for an element. Often this is seen in the form of a tool tip when hovering over a link, form input field, or abbreviation or acronym. Here's an example:

```
<a href="http://w3.org" title="World Wide Web Consortium">W3C</a>
```

This will show a tool tip that shows "World Wide Web Consortium" when hovering over the link text "W3C" (Figure 2-2).

Figure 2-2. *The tool tip effect of the* `title` *attribute being set on a link*

The next attribute, **lang**, specifies what language the text within an element is written in. This is used by some elements to render text differently based on differences in language scripts, such as the type of quotes used. For example, the following code snippet from the top of a web page would specify that the whole HTML page is written in the English language:

```
<html lang="en">
```

Lastly, the **contextmenu** attribute was added in HTML5, but at the time of writing has yet to be implemented in any released major browser. The idea is that a **menu** element can be associated and displayed with a particular element by setting the element's **contextmenu** to the **id** attribute of the menu. For any more insight into how it works, you will have to wait for the browsers to catch up with the specification!

Identification

The **id** attribute is used for assigning a unique identifier to a specific element on the page, which can subsequently be accessed using CSS or JavaScript for styling or scripting purposes.[2] It is a unique name you can assign to one of your HTML elements, which you can then use to reference the element. The **class** attribute is used in a similar fashion; however, unlike the **id** attribute, the same class value may be

---

[2] The id attribute may also be used as the target of hyperlinks. Using the id attribute for this purpose is discussed in the "Hyperlinks" section in Chapter 3.

applied to multiple elements on the page for the purposes of specifying that they have something in common (such as a particular CSS style). To summarize, the main differences between the **id** and **class** attributes are as follows:

id

- The value may appear once and *only* once per page so as to identify a single element.

class

- The value may appear multiple times per page.

- A particular **class** attribute value may contain multiple class names, each separated by a space.

To illustrate these differences, consider the following code snippet:

```
<p id="about-text" class="homepage popup">
```

This code contains the unique **id** attribute of **about-text** and two classes: **homepage** and **popup**. The **id** attribute of **about-text** would not be able to be used anywhere else, while both **homepage** and **popup** could be used on other elements. Note that elements do not need to have both an **id** attribute and a **class** attribute assigned to them; they could have one or the other, or neither. Also, to avoid problems, don't begin an **id** or **class** attribute with a number, and definitely don't include spaces (use dashes or underlines instead) in the name.

SENSIBLE ID AND CLASS VALUES

It can be very tempting to assign values based on how you want the element to look, rather than what it is, but it is best to avoid doing so. For example, instead of values such as this:

```
<div id="topBox"> <strong class="redText"> <p class="big">
```

you should instead use values such as this:

```
<div id="notificationBox"> <strong class="important"> <p class="introduction">
```

Why? Simply because one day you may find you need that **strong** element to be blue instead of red, or you may want to move this box of content from the top of the page to the bottom—and when that happens, your **id** or **class** value will be misleading.

Both these attributes are used extensively in web development, so it is essential you are familiar with them. We will work with CSS and JavaScript where appropriate to illustrate the features of HTML5, but briefly, if you want to reference and style these attribute values from CSS, you type the value and then prefix IDs with a hash sign (**#**) and classes with a period (**.**), like this:

```
#about-text { background: blue; }
.homepage { color: white; }
```

To reference these attribute values from JavaScript, you would typically use the command **document.getElementById("about-text")** from within your JavaScript, where **about-text** is replaced with whatever the actual ID is of the element you want to gain access to. A similar command is available for retrieving all elements with a particular class value: **document.getElementsByClassName("homepage")** (where **homepage** is replaced with the class value you are referencing).

Editability

The **contenteditable** attribute is used in the new Editing APIs, well new as in HTML standards new. The Editing APIs, which allow in-page edits of page content, have had the attribute **contenteditable** since Internet Explorer introduced it in 2000, but it took until now to get the attribute into the HTML specification. The idea is to allow elements of HTML to be edited so that rich-text editors for web forms and the like can be more easily created (for creating marked-up text for a blog entry using a web application interface, for instance)[3].

Spell-checking

The **spellcheck** attribute, as the name implies, is for specifying whether an element should be spell-checked. Web browsers often have a spell-checking feature that checks for spelling and grammatical errors as the user types into, for instance, a web form's input fields. Sometimes it's desirable to disable this spell-checking feature on certain elements on the page. For example, you may not want to check for spelling errors on an e-mail address typed into a web form, so the browser could be informed to ignore an e-mail address form input control using the **spellcheck** attribute. The values for the **spellcheck** attribute are **true** or **false** (or an empty string of text **""**, which maps to the true state). Naturally this fits quite well with content that can be edited.

Hiding elements

The **hidden** attribute, is for hiding and showing HTML elements. This is equivalent to using the CSS property and value **display:none**. While using CSS for hiding elements is a common practice, it is actually discouraged by the HTML5 specification in favor of using the **hidden** attribute. The **hidden** attribute adds additional semantics to the affected element. Its presence means that the element is not relevant at this time. This could be used by screen readers, for instance, which may otherwise pass over any hiding applied through a CSS display rule.

The following HTML and JavaScript snippet shows how to use the **hidden** attribute to show and hide content. The HTML part shows a definition list with a fox's common name and its Latin name:

```
<dl id="fox">
    <dt>Red Fox</dt>
    <dd id="latin" hidden>Vulpes vulpes</dd>
</dl>
```

The JavaScript part adds the functionality to show and hide the Latin name of the red fox when rolling on or off of its name. Since the **hidden** attribute is a Boolean attribute, it can be set to **true** or **false** using JavaScript, which leads to showing and hiding the element in question:

```
function toggleLatin(){
    var entry = document.getElementById("fox");
```

---

[3] For an example of using contenteditable, refer to the "Web Storage" section in Appendix A.

```
    var latin = document.getElementById("latin");
    entry.onmouseover = function(){
        latin.hidden = false;
    };
    entry.onmouseout = function(){
        latin.hidden = true;
    };
}
window.onload = toggleLatin;
```

Drag-and-drop

The **draggable** and **dropzone** attributes are two attributes that really exemplify the move of HTML toward building applications, as opposed to documents. These require some setup and JavaScript integration (which we'll discuss in Chapter 7), but when functional, these attributes allow HTML elements to be dragged from one part of the page and dropped onto another element (though as you will see, you will likely only use **draggable** for making this happen, as **dropzone** has yet to gain much browser support). What happens next is governed by JavaScript events.

Style

The **style** attribute provides a method of applying CSS styles directly to an element. Any styles applied in this way will override styles set on the element elsewhere. Although this can provide a quick way to apply styles to an element, it is best to avoid this attribute altogether and provide the styles for your page in an external style sheet. Having a clear separation between CSS and HTML code within your website provides organizational and flexibility advantages, because it is far easier to find and disable CSS rules when they are contained in a CSS file, instead of being spread between CSS and HTML.

Text directionality

The **dir** attribute controls which way text flows. Text normally flows from left to right, but if a language is used that flows the other direction, such as Arabic, the text needs to go that way as well. The **dir** attribute provides this ability. If an entire block is in a right-to-left language, use the value of "rtl" for right-to-left languages and "ltr" for left-to-right languages on the container element, which will flip the alignment of the text and punctuation:

```
<p dir="rtl">When rendered by a browser, this paragraph will appear aligned to the right.</p>
<p>While this paragraph will not because it lacks a <code>dir</code> attribute.</p>
```

A value of "auto" can also be given, which seeks to automatically determine the text directionality based on the enclosed text.

___

■ **Note** The CSS **direction** property provides this same functionality and takes the values **inherit**, **ltr**, and **rtl**. However, this CSS should <u>NOT</u> be used as this information should be embedded into the page itself so that the directionality of the textual content can still be determined even if the associated style sheet is disabled.

___

Custom data

The **data-*** attribute is a bit of an odd one. It is the catchall of attributes, allowing any attribute name to be added for the purposes of storing custom data in HTML elements for the use of, for instance, JavaScript applications. The ***** in the attribute name is not the actual finished attribute; it can be replaced with any text to create custom attributes. For example, **city** could be added to create the attribute **data-city**. Or **score** could be added to create **data-score**, which might be used on a web page listing high scores for a game. Take the following HTML snippet, for instance:

```
<button id="show-score-button">Show Scores</button>
<ul>
        <li data-score="3200">Top Blaster Tom</li>
        <li data-score="2250">Middle Range Merv</li>
        <li data-score="1100">Last Pop Louis</li>
</ul>
```

A JavaScript function could then be written that replaces the user name with the winning score when clicking a button:

```
function showScore(){
    document.getElementById("show-score-button").onclick = function(){
        var entries = document.getElementsByTagName("li");
        entries[0].innerHTML = entries[0].dataset["score"];
        entries[1].innerHTML = entries[1].dataset["score"];
        entries[2].innerHTML = entries[2].dataset["score"];
    }
}
window.onload = showScore;
```

■ **Note** The dataset property in the previous code allows access to **data-*** attributes as key/value pairs. However, only the custom part of the attribute is needed, so the attribute **score** is looked up in the dataset, not data-score.

This permits a lot of flexibility in what can be stored in an individual element but at the same time is backed by a specific specification. How paradoxical! The intention is that these attributes are used only within a particular site, and they are not utilized by software residing outside of the website's domain. On this, use these with caution and only when absolutely no other solution will work!

Content model categories

As stated in Chapter 1, originally, elements in HTML could be roughly divided into two categories: block and inline. The **content model** of one category or the other defined what kind of content could be placed inside a particular element. For instance, inline elements could not contain block elements. As

HTML5 developed, these two types of content did not adequately describe the behavior of the available HTML elements. The WHATWG replaced block and inline with a larger set of categories,[4] which group elements based on their similar characteristics. Elements in each category have a similar content model and must abide by the rules defining what kind of content it can have. There are now seven major categories, listed in Table 2-2.

Table 2-2. Major content model categories

Category	Description
Metadata	Elements that set up the presentation, behavior, associated documents, or metadata of the rest of the content.
Sectioning	Elements that define the scope of sections of content.
Heading	Elements that define the header of a section of content.
Flow	Most elements that are used in the body of document.
Phrasing	The text of the document, as well as elements that mark up that text at the intra-paragraph level. Runs of phrasing content form paragraphs. (Note that most elements categorized as phrasing content can only contain elements that are themselves categorized as phrasing content, not any flow content.)
Embedded	Elements that import another resource into the document, or content from another vocabulary that is inserted into the document, such as using MathML inside an HTML document.
Interactive	Elements that are specifically intended for user interaction.

Even these seven categories do not fully cover all elements within all contexts. For instance, an element may not fit into any of these categories (the **html** element, for instance) or may be referred to as **transparent**, meaning it inherits the category of its parent element. Many elements fit into more than one category, in which case they are said to have a **hybrid** content model.

---

[4] See http://blog.whatwg.org/content-model-overhaul for a description of the impetus behind this change.

■ **Note** There are actually a further seven minor categories that group elements within specific contextual scenarios, such as when they are part of a form. To view the additional categories, browse the category reference in the HTML specification at `http://dev.w3.org/html5/spec-author-view/index.html#element-content-categories` or `http://whatwg.org/specs/web-apps/current-work/#element-content-categories`.

Root element

To begin looking at the elements in HTML, it makes sense to look at the beginning—well, almost the beginning. We talked about the doctype declaration in the previous chapter, which is the first element to appear in an HTML document. However, following the doctype declaration is the **html** element, which serves as the element that encloses all other HTML elements in the document, otherwise known as the **root element**.

The root element is one of a handful of elements whose tags are optional (see Table 2-3 for a list of other elements that include optional tags). Although the tags may be optional, the element is not omitted. Optional elements will be implied if they are left out (the **body** element being an exception, which will be omitted if no page content is provided). For example, the following is a perfectly valid HTML5 document:

```
<!DOCTYPE html><title>Tiny HTML5</title><p>This is a valid HTML5 page!
```

In this case, the missing tags of the **html**, **head**, **body**, and **p** elements are added when parsing the document. It could even be shorter without the inclusion of the doctype declaration, but that would trigger quirks mode in the web browser (for a discussion of quirks mode, refer to the doctype section in Chapter 1).

■ **Note** For an easy way to check the validity of your documents against the current HTML5 specification, visit `http://html5.validator.nu` or `http://validator.w3.org`, both of which provide web-based services that validate supplied website URLs, uploaded HTML files, or directly input HTML. For the validator housed at the W3C, ensure you set the document type in the validator drop-down menu to "HTML5 (experimental)" to be certain you are checking it against the most current specification.

Table 2-3. *HTML elements with optional start and end tags*

Element	Start Tag	End Tag
body	Optional	Optional
colgroup	Optional	Optional

dd	**Required**	Optional
dt	**Required**	Optional
head	Optional	Optional
html	Optional	Optional
li	**Required**	Optional
optgroup	**Required**	Optional
option	**Required**	Optional
p	**Required**	Optional
rp	**Required**	Optional
rt	**Required**	Optional
tbody	Optional	Optional
td	**Required**	Optional
tfoot	**Required**	Optional
th	**Required**	Optional
thead	**Required**	Optional
tr	**Required**	Optional

Although the preceding code snippet is handy for infuriating your XHTML-devoted friends, it is a good idea to include the optional tags anyway, if only for clarity's sake. While HTML5 can seem like it's bringing back coding practices from the 20th century, it is important to remember that it is documenting what has been used in practice, not necessarily what may be the best practice to do.

Attributes of html element

In addition to the global attributes, the **html** element has one new attribute, **manifest**, which is used in a new API for creating offline applications. When you utilize this attribute, the essential functional components of a web application (the JavaScript, for instance) can be cached in the browser so that the page will still function if the user goes offline and reloads the page.

■ **Note** The html element also has an attribute, xmlns, used to declare an XML namespace, which describes the markup language that is being used. This attribute should be present in valid XHTML documents. It has only one supported value, the text http://www.w3.org/1999/xhtml. It is applicable only to XHTML and has absolutely no meaning in HTML, other than to make the transition between HTML and XHTML easier in a document that may cross over between the two.

Document metadata and scripting elements

After the opening root **html** tag, the **head** element's opening tag appears, which contains the document metadata elements that specify such page properties as the title for the document as it appears in the browser window, a default URL address for elements on the page, character encoding information, and linked and embedded CSS style sheets, if they are utilized. Table 2-4 lists the relevant elements along with their content model categories.

Table 2-4. Content model categories for document metadata and scripting elements

NEW in HTML5	Element	Description	Major Content Model Categories						
			Metadata	Sectioning	Heading	Flow	Phrasing	Embedded	Interactive
	title	Document title	●						
	base	The default URL and/or the default target for all elements that include a URL	●						
	meta	Text metadata, such as character encoding	●			●[5]	●		
	link	Linking to an external resource, such as a CSS stylesheet	●			●[6]	●		

---

[5] Fits in flow content category only if the itemprop attribute is present, which is part of the microdata specification available in HTML5.

[6] Like the **meta** element, the link element fits in the flow and phrasing content category only if the **itemprop** attribute is present.

style	Embedded CSS style rules	●			●[7]				
script	Embedded script	●			●	●			
noscript	Fallback content for when scripting is disabled	●			●	●			

Web page information: title and meta

As demonstrated in the minimal HTML5 example shown earlier, **title** is the only compulsory element within the head section. The text between the opening and closing **title** tags will be displayed in the browser window title bar. The document title is an oft-neglected area of the document; you've surely seen pages with the title "Untitled Document" before. This is unfortunate, because given the proper care and attention, the document title can provide you and your users with many benefits:

- **Better search engine ranking.** Search engines will factor in the page title when determining the relevance of your web page to a particular topic, as well as when determining what to display on a search results page.

- **Better convenience.** Should your users bookmark the page, the page title will be used by default for the bookmark name.

- **Better usability.** Identification of both the website and the page in the same location can help to identify a particular page's association to a particular website. For example, "Semantic Web – W3C," which is the title of the main semantic web page on the World Wide Web Consortium's website, clearly identifies the topic of the page as well as the website it is a part of.

■ **Note** As an example of the importance of meaningful titles in a web page, try opening several "Untitled Document" windows and then switch between them after minimizing them—can you tell which is which before

---

[7] Fits in flow content category only if the **scoped** attribute is present.

switching? Or try opening the same pages as tabs in a single web browser window. Can you see at a glance which page is which?

Also note that if the name of the website is included in the title, the website name should appear after the page topic title. A similar problem to this can occur when a company or website name is placed before the actual page title, because the title may be cropped right to left if it is too long to display when minimized or in a tab, leading to the actual page topic title being cropped from view.

The meta element

The previous chapter introduced the **meta** element as being commonly used to set the character encoding for the page, but it is also commonly used to set up a series key/value pairs of metadata information and instructions. For instance, it may be used for defining a summary description of the web page or for defining a set of keywords for content on the page. In creating the "key" in the key/value pairing, the **meta** element uses one of two attributes, **http-equiv** or **name**, and the "value" part is set using the **content** attribute. Here's an example:

```
<!-- defines a set of keywords for the page's content -->
<meta name="keywords" content="html5, css, javascript, semantic web, web apps"/>

<!-- refreshes the page every 15 seconds -->
<meta http-equiv="refresh" content="15" />
```

■ **Note** Historically, search engines used keywords, but today many do not use them because it is easy to mislead a search engine that depends on this feature for the purpose of spamming the search results. However, if used properly, there is no harm in including them, although it would be important to update the keywords to reflect changes in content on a document that was edited frequently, which may create an extra step of maintenance without substantial gain. The choice is yours!

Some uses of the **http-equiv** attribute (known as a **pragma directive**) provide tasks such as setting cookies, specifying the character encoding, and so on, which are redundant to better approaches available. Consequently, several of the values are not recommended in the HTML5 specification. Specifically, the **content-language** and **set-cookie** directives are non-conforming and should not be used (the **lang** attribute should be used for setting the language of the content, and real HTTP headers should be used for setting cookies). The other official pragma directives from the HTML5 specification are **content-type**, which is an alternative form of the **charset** attribute; **default-style**, which is for setting the default CSS style sheet for the page (explained in Chapter 6); and **refresh**, which refreshes or redirects the page after a number of seconds, as shown in the code sample earlier.

▪ **Note** To redirect the page after a pause, a URL is added to the **content** attribute when using the **refresh** pragma directive. After the specified number of seconds, the page is redirected to the URL. A redirect would look like so:

```
<meta http-equiv="refresh" content="3; URL=homepage.html">.
```

The full list of proposed values for the **http-equiv** and **name** attributes is large, so you are best to consult a resource such as the WHATWG PragmaExtensions and MetaExtensions wikis at **http://wiki.whatwg.org/wiki/PragmaExtensions** and **http://wiki.whatwg.org/wiki/MetaExtensions**, respectively. In addition to the values listed at those web addresses, the HTML5 specification also includes **application-name** as a value for the **name** attribute. This value allows for a title to be given to a web application (not a standard web page but an actual web application with scripted functionality added), which may be seen as an overarching title that is independent or supplementary to the page title (set using the **title** element). This is provided since the page title may change while using the application to reflect operations that are occurring, such as loading additional content, and so on.

▪ **Note** Possibly more useful is the meta name keyword **robots** that instructs web crawlers (the automated programs that Google and others use for indexing web pages) on how to index the page. Information on this name value and others is available on the aforementioned WHATWG MetaExtensions wiki at **http://wiki.whatwg.org/wiki/MetaExtensions**.

Links, styles, and resources: base, link, and style

Only one **base** element may be used per document. It should appear in the head before any other elements that include a URL in their attributes. The idea is that the **base** element can prevent redundant typing of the same root URL over and over again when adding links throughout the page. Its two attributes, **href** and **target**, specify the URL to use and the default target (where applicable). **target** tells, for instance, whether a link opens in a new window or the same window. For example, if this appeared inside the head section:

```
<base href="http://example.com/portfolio/" target="_blank" />
```

and this appeared in the body section:

```
<a href="photographs.html">Photography</a>
```

then clicking the link would open a new browser window and connect the user to the URL **http://example.com/portfolio/photographs.html**.

The link element

The **link** element has the attributes **href**, **rel**, **media**, **hreflang**, **type**, and **sizes**, as well as the global attributes. Of these, at very least **href** and **rel** are commonly set. The **href** specifies the address (URL) of the linked resource, while **rel** specifies the *type* of resource. The following code is how you will most likely use this element, because it is commonly used for linking style sheets to your pages:

```
<link rel="stylesheet" href="main.css" type="text/css" />
```

However, the **rel** attribute can be used to provide additional related information about the page. The nature of this attribute can be a little tricky to grasp, so let's consider an example. In addition to style sheets, you may have encountered **rel** before when using the **link** element to reference an RSS feed in the head of your web page, like this:

```
<link rel="alternate" href="http://example.com/feed/" type="application/rss+xml" />
```

The preceding code means that "an alternative version of this document exists at **http://example.com/feed/**," and user agents can spot that and find the RSS feed—most modern browsers will display a feed icon in the browser address bar, allowing the user to select, view, and subscribe to the feed.

The **alternate** value can also be used with the **hreflang** attribute if the alternate version is a translation. It can also be used with the **media** attribute if the alternate version is designed for a different medium.[8] It can also be used with the **type** attribute to indicate the linked document is a version of the page in a different file format, such as a PDF version of the page. For example, a link that referred to a printable PDF version of the document that was also in French might look like this:

```
<link rel="alternate" href="alt-fr.pdf" type="application/pdf" hreflang="fr" media="print"
title="French version PDF for printing" />
```

The HTML specification lists more than a dozen predefined types for the **rel** attribute (Table 2-5).

---

[8] The **media** attribute has a number of valid values such as **screen**, **tty**, **tv**, **projection**, **handheld**, **print**, **braille**, **aural**, and **all**, which are aimed respectively at computer screens, terminals, televisions, projectors, handheld devices, printed pages, Braille tactile feedback devices, speech synthesizers, and all of the above. Of these, you are most likely to use screen and print and possibly handheld. Opera uses projection when in full-screen mode, so if you have specified a screen type for your main style sheet, you may want to consider including projection: **<link media="screen, projection" ... />**.

Table 2-5. The link *element* rel *attribute values and descriptions*

rel value	Description
alternative	Designates that the link connects to an alternate version of the document
author	Designates that the link connects to the current document's author page
help	Refers to a help document that should relate to the website or web page—for instance, a collection of "further reading" links or an explanatory document listing FAQs
icon	Imports an icon used to represent the current document. The new **sizes** attribute can be used in conjunction with this value to specify the width and height of the linked icon image resource
license	Links to a copyright license that covers the current document
next	Indicates that the linked document is the next document in a collection of documents
pingback	The address of the server that handles pingbacks to the current document
prefetch	Identifies a target resource that should be cached
prev	This value is similar to **next**, except it indicates the previous document rather than the next document in a collection
search	Links to a resource that can be used to search through the current document and its related pages
sidebar	Links to a document that is intended to be shown in a secondary browsing context, such as a sidebar (if it has one). This value is usually ignored
stylesheet	Imports a style sheet. You can use this in conjunction with **alternate** (as in **rel="alternate stylesheet"**) to specify a range of alternative style sheets that the user agent can allow the user to select from (Note that the global **title** attribute needs to be set when specifying an alternative stylesheet. See Chapter 6 for more details on importing style sheets.)
tag	Creates a tag (identified by the value in the **href** attribute) that applies to the current document. Tag-aware services and aggregators can

> determine that your page belongs in a certain category and that the resource indicated can be considered as part of a collection of related pages

The **type** attribute specifies the MIME type of the resource being linked. It is purely advisory to the browser (for example, the user agent won't solely rely on the value specified here to determine the resource type) and can be omitted for style sheets since they are the most commonly encountered type of file used in the **link** element.

The style element

The **style** element allows CSS style rules to be embedded directly into an HTML document, which may be a quick and convenient way to add style rules when creating a page, but as with the global **style** attribute, the CSS styles for a document are best provided through linking an external style sheet into the page using the **link** element. One new attribute is the **scoped** attribute, which (in theory) allows a piece of generic CSS to be applied to a specific block of HTML. However, at the time of writing, the current releases of major web browsers do not support this attribute.

Adding behavior and fallbacks: script and noscript

The **script** element is like the **style** and **link** elements combined, because it supports writing embedded client-side JavaScript code directly in the HTML document *or* allows a script to be loaded as an external file. As with CSS, unless it is unavoidable to embed the code in the HTML, it is best to place JavaScript in an external file (or files) that is loaded, like so:

```
<script type="text/javascript" src="js/menu.js"></script>
```

The previous code snippet shows the general appearance of the **script** element when linking in an external JavaScript file (in this case named **menu.js** and residing in a directory named **js**). Note that when linking in an external script, the element should not contain any content between its starting and ending tags.

HTML5 defines a new attribute named **async**, which in combination with another attribute, **defer**, can be used to control when an externally loaded script is parsed. These are both Boolean attributes, so their presence and absence can affect the loading of external scripts in various ways (Table 2-6).

Table 2-6. *Effect on parsing of client-side code when different combinations of the async and defer attributes of the script element are set*

async attribute	defer attribute	Effect
Present	Absent	Script executes concurrent with the parsing of the page. If multiple scripts are present, they may execute out of the order they appear in the source code, depending on which finished loading first.

Absent	Present	Script executes after the page has finished being parsed. Scripts are guaranteed to execute in order.
Absent	Absent	Script executes immediately when encountered, and parsing of the rest of the page waits for script execution to finish.
Present	Present	Same effect as having only the **async** attribute present.

SCRIPT: AT THE TOP OR AT THE BOTTOM?

It is important to note that the `script` and `style` elements do not need to appear in the head of the HTML document; in fact, the Yahoo! Developer Network published a list of 35 best practices for performance gains that stated the `script` element should be placed at the bottom of the web page (see `http://developer.yahoo.com/performance/rules.html`). (Conversely, the `style` element should appear at the top, in the head area.) Additionally, the HTML5 Boilerplate (`http://html5boilerplate.com`) mentioned in Chapter 1 places all scripts (except Modernizr, because it is needed earlier) at the bottom of the page, before the closing `</body>` tag. Arguably this practice, while offering a performance boost, has semantic issues, because it moves metadata about a page into the body area, instead of the head where it belongs. Ideally as the `async` and `defer` attributes gain wider support, the location of the `script` element within a page will become a moot point.

Lastly, the **noscript** element is for surrounding content that is shown only when scripting is disabled or not supported in the browser. If the **noscript** element is placed in the head of the document, it can contain only the **link**, **style**, and **meta** elements; otherwise, if it is in the body, it can contain all the normal elements that would appear in the **body** element, except another **noscript** element. It's also worth noting that the syntax of the **noscript** element is such that it is only applicable in HTML documents and has no effect in XHTML documents. **noscript** is one of those elements that had an uncertain future when XHTML was being pushed by the W3C, and it retains a bit of a crude and dirty reputation—a hackish—way of handling a disabled script. A better approach is to write a script that converts the content of a page from a static to a dynamic nature on the fly, because it's possible a script could fail even when scripting is enabled, and in that case the contents in **noscript** would not show up. For instance, consider the following code (which is embedded in the HTML for brevity's sake):

```
<div>
    <p id="fall-back">Script disabled</p>
    <script type="text/javascript">
    var fallBack = document.getElementById('fall-back');
    var fallBackParent = fallBack.parentNode;
    fallBackParent.removeChild(fallBack);
    fallBackParent.innerHTML = "<button id='alert-button'>Show Alert!</button>"
    var showAlert = document.getElementById('alert-button');
```

```
        showAlert.onclick = function(){alert( "script worked!" );}
    </script>
</div>
```

A paragraph (with an **id** set to **fall-back**) is provided with some default static content. A **script** element follows, which removes the default HTML and replaces it with a button that has the functionality to show an alert box when clicked. The advantage here is that, not only is finer-grained control provided for converting a static page to a dynamic one, but this will also work in XHTML.

Document sectioning elements

Following the closing **head** tag is the opening **body** tag, which can contain any non-head-specific markup, typically the content that would be expected to appear in the web browser window content area: paragraphs, lists, images, and so on. The **body** tag traditionally had several presentational attributes: **background**, **text**, **link**, **vlink**, and **alink**, which were used to set the document's background color, text color, link color, visited link color, and active link color, respectively. All of these attributes were depreciated in HTML 4.01 and have been labeled obsolete in HTML5. Their effects should be created with CSS instead. The CSS **background-color**, **color**, **a:link**, **a:visited**, and **a:active** properties and pseudoclasses (discussed in chapter 6) are appropriate.

The closing **body** tag is followed immediately by the closing **html** tag. That's an HTML document in its entirety, albeit devoid of any content. The rest of the elements we'll look at in this chapter and the subsequent ones will primarily be the content elements—the ones that would appear in the body to mark up and organize content in various ways.

Semantic sectioning elements

The first set of elements likely to appear in the body would be those involved in organizing content into different logical sections. These are shown in Table 2-7, which also lists the content model categories for each. You'll notice almost all are new to HTML5. You'll also notice their names imply common components of a web page, such as headers, footers, navigation bars, and so on. The semantic nuances of these elements deserve their own close attention, so for the time being just be aware that there are new elements in HTML5 for giving content finer-grained meaning than **div** and **span** elements are traditionally able to do. We will explore these new sectioning elements in more depth in Chapter 3.

Table 2-7. Content model categories for document sections elements

NEW in HTML5 ■	Element	Description	Major Content Model Categories						
			Metadata	Sectioning	Heading	Flow	Phrasing	Embedded	Interactive
■	section	Generic section, separate from other types of content on the page		●		●			
■	nav	Section with navigational links		●		●			
■	article	Self-contained syndicatable or reusable composition		●		●			
■	aside	Sidebar to tangentially related content		●		●			
	h1, h2, h3, h4, h5, h6	Heading within a section			●	●			

▪	hgroup	Heading group			●	●				
▪	header	Introductory or navigational aids for a page or section				●				
▪	footer	Footer for a page or section				●				
	address	Contact information for a page or section				●				

Content grouping elements

Inside a particular section of content on the page, the various components of that section are broken into paragraphs, lists, figures, and the like. The elements for paragraphs and so forth group content into smaller units than sections do. Except for **figure** and **figcaption**—which are new in HTML5—the elements in this group are all likely quite familiar to you. See Table 2-8 for the content model categories and descriptions of these elements.

Table 2-8. *Content model categories for content grouping elements*

NEW in HTML5 ▪	Element	Description	Major Content Model Categories						
			Metadata	Sectioning	Heading	Flow	Phrasing	Embedded	Interactive
	p	A paragraph of content				●			
	hr	Thematic break				●			
	pre	Block of preformatted text				●			
	blockquote	A section quoted from another source				●			
	ol	Ordered list				●			

	ul	Unordered list				●			
	li	List item for **ul** or **ol** element							
	dl	Name/value description list				●			
	dt	Legend for **dd** elements (found inside **dl** element)							
	dd	Description for **dt** elements (found inside **dl** element)							
■	**figure**	A figure with an optional caption				●			
■	**figcaption**	Caption for the **figure** element							
	div	Generic division of content				●			

The inevitable paragraph: p

Perhaps the markup you've used most often when writing web pages is **p**. There isn't much to be said about **p**: it is simply used to mark up a paragraph. Yet this humble element is often abused by WYSIWYG (What You See Is What You Get) web authoring software as a quick and dirty spacer for adding padding between content. You have likely seen markup such as the following, where an author has pressed the Enter key a few times in their editor:

```
<p> </p>
<p> </p>
<p> </p>
<p> </p>
```

This is a prime example of (X)HTML being co-opted into acting in a presentational manner. We find here multiple, pointless paragraphs, with a non-breaking space entity inside (because of some browsers not displaying empty elements), but the effect should really be achieved with CSS. A quick way of adding some space beneath your content is to add a class to the relevant content:

```
<p class="section">Your content here.</p>
```

and then style the class with CSS to add padding on the top or bottom:

```
.section { padding-bottom: 3em; }
```

■ **Note** Use of ems has traditionally been the preferred unit of measurement by professional web developers, because it is a relative unit of length, and will resize proportionally if the page is scaled up or down by the user (or developer). However, preference for ems has become less pronounced in recent years as web browsers have become better at handling resizing of absolute units (such as pixels). There is considerable debate over whether to use ems or pixels for sizes. An em may be less intuitive to use, while a pixel won't accommodate cascading size changes. It generally would not be a disaster to choose one or the other, so go with whichever you feel more comfortable using. At the end of the day you should be testing your pages under a variety of scenarios anyway, so issues should reveal themselves pretty quickly.

Break in thought: hr

The **hr** element, or horizontal rule, has historically been a presentational element, but it has been redefined to represent a thematic break between one piece of content and another. The **hr** element came with several attributes—**size**, **width**, **noshade**, and **align**—but all have been declared obsolete in HTML5, so CSS must be used for the horizontal rule's style, as it should be.

Retaining formatting: pre

Now, what about **pre**? The visual effect caused by the **pre** element is to preserve the whitespace (that is, the tabs, spaces, and line breaks) in your markup, so if that whitespace is important in understanding the content, such as in computer code samples, then use **pre**. Alternatively, the effect can be replicated with the CSS **white-space:pre** property and value, and this may well be a more viable option to use in cases where another element could be used that better describes the content in question. For example, in the case of marking up computer code, the **code** element along with the **white-space** CSS property could be used to preserve the formatting as well as convey the meaning of the content for situations where the formatting may be lost (such as if it were read by screen-reading software, for instance).

Quoting text: blockquote

blockquote is an element that has historically been used for its presentational effect rather than its semantic meaning or structural relevance, but it should be viewed as enclosing content that is quoted from another source, regardless of how it will be presented. The **blockquote** element has a **cite** attribute, which allows the author to reference the source of the quote (usually in the form of a URL, but it can be any form of citation, such as the name of another author or the title of a movie).

■ **Note** For inline quotations that appear in a paragraph, for instance, there also exists the q element, which is listed in the text-level semantics section in Chapter 3.

Lists

Three list types are available in the current HTML specification: unordered lists (**ul**), ordered lists (**ol**), and description lists (**dl**).

The differences between the list types are fairly minimal and straightforward:

- An **unordered list** should be used when your content is (as you would expect) not in any particular order.

- An **ordered list** should be used when your content is in an order of some kind: alphabetical, numerical, and so on.

- A **description list** is designed for associating names or terms with values or other data—any items that have a direct relationship with one another, such as a glossary of terms.

Unordered and ordered lists: ul, ol, and li

Unordered and ordered lists consist of an opening **ul** or **ol** tag, respectively, followed by any number of list item—**li**—elements, and then finally a closing **</ul>** or **</ol>** tag. The opening and closing tags can contain only list items, but list items can contain any flow elements, including paragraphs, **div**s, headers, and yet more lists. So long as they're all contained within a single list item, it's perfectly valid and well-formed markup. As far as differences between HTML/XHTML go, in HTML you don't have to close list items with **</li>**, but in XHTML you do.

Unordered lists do not have any attributes other than the global attributes. Ordered lists, on the other hand, have three additional attributes: **reversed**, **start**, and **type**. The first, **reversed**, determines what direction a list should be ordered. It is a Boolean attribute, meaning its presence or absence determines its behavior. If this attribute is present, the list will be descending (9, 8, 7, 6, 5...); otherwise, it will be ascending (1, 2, 3, 4, 5…). Unfortunately, at the time of writing, this attribute had poor browser support.

■ **Note** As mentioned in the attributes section in the previous chapter, Boolean attributes either can be included without any value when using HTML syntax or, if XHTML syntax is used, can be given a value equal to their name. In this situation, you may find HTML syntax is clearer. For example, both of the following would work:

```
<ol reversed>
    <li>item 1</li>
    <li>item 2</li>
</ol>

<ol reversed="reversed">
    <li>item 1</li>
    <li>item 2</li>
</ol>
```

Next, the **start** attribute allows authors to start the numbering of an ordered list at a number other than 1, which is useful if you need to interrupt an ordered list, such as in the case of a list of search results split over several pages. Interestingly, this attribute was deprecated in HTML 4.01 but is back to good standing in HTML5.

Finally, the **type** attribute can be used to change the marker at the beginning of the list from a decimal number (the default) to an alphabetical listing or roman numerals. However, it is strongly recommended to use the CSS **list-style-type** property instead, which offers far more options and also moves this presentational change to the CSS instead of the HTML.

The **li** element, when part of an unordered list, has only the global attributes but gains one more when inside an ordered list: **value**. This attribute allows authors to give a specific list item an out-of-sequence number.

With the attributes out of the way, let's move on to an example of implementing a list. Thankfully, though the markup may not be exciting, it is at least flexible, and with CSS you can display a list in a wide variety of ways: horizontally, vertically, expanding/collapsing, and so on. For instance, take the following navigation menu:

```
<ul>
        <li><a href="/">Home</a></li>
        <li><a href="/about/">About</a></li>
        <li><a href="/archive/">Archive</a></li>
        <li><a href="/contact/">Contact</a></li>
</ul>
```

We can turn this into a horizontal menu very easily using the following CSS rule:

```
li {
        float: left;
}
```

Simple! But it's clearly quite ugly and a bit unusable at this stage, so let's tidy things up a little:

```
li {
        border: 1px solid; float: left; list-style-type: none; padding: 0.2em 1em;
}
```

By adding a border, removing the list bullet, and adding a touch of padding, we get the list shown in Figure 2-3.

| Home | About | Archive | Contact |

Figure 2-3. *An unordered list with the list items floated left, bordered, and padded*

As you can see, we already have a very serviceable horizontal menu. We could jazz this up even more with some styling of the anchor tags, giving them a **background-color**, using **display:block** to allow them to fill the whole list item area, changing their background with the pseudoclass **:hover**, and so on.

■ **Note** Russ Weakley, a co-chair of the Web Standards Group, has created a huge collection of different list styles (more than 70 at the current count) available at **http://css.maxdesign.com.au**. To help take some of the pain out of creating lists of links, it's also worth trying Accessify's List-O-Matic (**http://accessify.com/tools-and-wizards/developer-tools/list-o-matic**), an online list-builder that lets you select from a variety of prebuilt styles.

So, already you can see that a simple list can be displayed in a different way from its default style. It's possible to use CSS to create quite dynamic behavior with lists. For example, as documented by Eric Meyer (**http://meyerweb.com/eric/css/edge/menus/demo.html**), the **:hover** pseudoclass can be used to display nested lists as pop-out menus. The CSS to accomplish this is very simple:

```
li ul {display: none;}
li:hover > ul {display: block;}
```

This means any **ul** that is a descendent element of an **li**—that is, a nested list—should not be displayed. The second line says that any **ul** that is a child element of an **li** that is being hovered over should display as normal. In compliant browsers, the end result (with a few more presentational styles added) looks like Figure 2-4.

css/edge		
complexspiral	...devolved	
Pure CSS popups	...distorted	
curvelicious		
slantastic		
ragged float		
boxpunch		

Figure 2-4. A pure CSS nested menu

All very neat. Patrick Griffiths' Suckerfish Dropdowns script (**www.htmldog.com/articles/suckerfish/dropdowns**) provides both a CSS solution and a JavaScript solution that are pretty robust (multiple nested menus are catered for) and very easy to implement, requiring only the inclusion of a small script and the addition of a class selector to your CSS file.

Description lists: dl, dt, and dd

The description list consists of an opening **dl**, followed by a term (**dt**), and then any number of descriptions (**dd**). A typical description list looks like this:

```
<dl>
        <dt>Bottle</dt>
        <dd>A receptacle having a narrow neck, usually no handles, and a mouth that can be
        plugged, corked, or capped.</dd>
        <dd>To hold in; restrain: "bottled up my emotions."</dd>
        <dt>Rocket</dt>
        <dd>A vehicle or device propelled by one or more rocket engines, especially such a
        vehicle designed to travel through space.</dd>
</dl>
```

Most browsers would display the preceding code in a similar way to that shown in Figure 2-5.

> Bottle
>   A receptacle having a narrow neck, usually no handles, and a mouth that can be plugged, corked, or capped.
>   To hold in; restrain: "bottled up my emotions."
> Rocket
>   A vehicle or device propelled by one or more rocket engines, especially such a vehicle designed to travel through space.

Figure 2-5. A description list, with the terms on the left and the descriptions indented

Description lists are, as noted, fairly flexible. As long as there is a direct relationship between the term and the description(s), many constructs can be represented using this list. For instance, a photograph as the term could have descriptions including information about both the photographer and the camera. In addition, a description list could be used to display a schedule for a series of presentations at a conference, with the title of the presentation as the term and the descriptions including details of the presenting author and the date and time. A description list could also be used in an online shopping application to describe product details, and so forth.

Although description lists are flexible in use, you should bear the following caveat in mind: a definition term can only contain phrasing content, not flow content, so no paragraphs, headers, or lists—which means that terms cannot be given differing levels of importance in the same way that headings can (**h1**, **h2**, and so on). A description element (**dd**) in the list, however, can contain any flow element or series of elements, so long as they're well-formed.

Diagrams, photos, illustrations: figure and figcaption

The idea behind the **figure** element is to provide diagrams, images, code, and so on, optionally with a caption or legend (**figcaption** element) as a self-contained unit that is relevant to the main content of the document. The figure should be able to be moved or removed without destroying the overall layout of the document.

For example, the following shows two images side by side, with a caption below (see Figure 2-6):

```
<figure>
        <img src="earth.jpg" title="View of Earth" alt="Photograph of the Earth from space.">
        <img src="mars.jpg" title="View of Mars" alt="Photograph of Mars from space.">
        <figcaption>The Earth and Mars shown side-by-side.</figcaption>
</figure>
```

The Earth and Mars shown side-by-side.

Figure 2-6. Example output from the figure and figcaption elements

Creating divisions: div

A **div** (short for "division") is used for marking out a block of content. It adds no special meaning to the content it surrounds but is simply used for being able to add additional CSS styles or JavaScript. The **div** has traditionally been a frequently used element to aid with layout of a page but has been superseded in many situations with more semantically specific elements (covered in more depth in Chapter 3).

Text-level semantic elements

We're down to the finest-grained control now: text-level elements that imbibe individual words and sentences with meaning. There are nuances of the correct semantic use of these elements that are best discussed together with the document sectioning elements in the next chapter, so for the time being familiarize yourself with the sizable number of these elements in Table 2-9, and we'll discuss them further in Chapter 3. Most have been around for a while, but several such as **i** and **b** have a changed meaning in HTML5.

Table 2-9. *Content model categories for text-level semantic elements*

NEW in HTML5 ▪	Element	Description	Major Content Model Categories						
			Metadata	Sectioning	Heading	Flow	Phrasing	Embedded	Interactive
	a	Hyperlink anchor				●	●[9]		
	em	Denotes emphasis				●	●		
	strong	Denotes importance				●	●		
	small	Side comment				●	●		

[9] Only if it contains exclusively phrasing content.

	s	Inaccurate text				●	●		
	cite	Title of a work				●	●		
	q	Inline quotation				●	●		
	dfn	Definition of a term				●	●		
	abbr	Abbreviation or acronym				●	●		
■	time	Date/time				●	●		
	code	Computer code				●	●		
	var	A variable in a mathematical or programming context				●	●		

	samp	Computer output				●	●		
	kbd	User input				●	●		
	sub	Subscript text				●	●		
	sup	Superscript text				●	●		
	i	Text in an alternative voice or mood				●	●		
	b	Separated text				●	●		
■	mark	Highlighted or otherwise marked text for reference purposes				●	●		
■	ruby	Ruby annotations				●	●		

■	rt	Ruby annotation text							
■	rp	Ruby annotation parentheses							
■	bdi	Text that ignores the text directionality of its surrounding text				●	●		
	bdo	Bidirectional override; allows text direction to be explicitly set, overriding any other direction currently specified				●	●		
	span	Generic container for phrasing content				●	●		
	br	A line break				●	●		
	wbr	Designates where the line could break, if needed				●	●		

`ins`	Content that has been inserted into the document					●	●[10]		
`del`	Content that has been deleted from the document					●	●		

Tabular data elements

Several years ago it was quite common practice to use tables to generate pixel-precise website layouts. At the time, this use of tables provided, to the untrained eye, a leap forward in web design, because designs could be created in Adobe Photoshop, sliced into a grid of pieces, and reassembled inside a table to create the original design in a web page. However, the inflexibility and accessibility concerns of this method of design soon saw it scorned in favor of CSS, when the touted "tableless layout" became a catchphrase to mean a pixel-perfect layout created *without* a table. Ouch. Where did tables go wrong? In the standards world, they went wrong when they were used for a purpose they weren't intended for—presentation. The table is for displaying data, à la spreadsheets and nothing more.

As Table 2-10 shows, the table element is a single unit that fits into the flow content model category. All other table-related elements work within a **table** element to define its structure, so they do not fit any of the major categories. Like with the **body** element, a large number of attributes that were presentational in nature have been thrown into the obsolete bin; for example, in **tr** all the attributes except for the global attributes have been stripped away.

---

[10] May be placed in phrasing content, if it contains only phrasing content.

Table 2-10. Content model categories for tabular data elements

NEW in HTML5	Element	Description	Major Content Model Categories						
			Metadata	Sectioning	Heading	Flow	Phrasing	Embedded	Interactive
	table	A table for spreadsheet-style data				●			
	caption	Caption for **table** element							
	colgroup	Group of columns in a **table**							
	col	Column in a **colgroup** element							
	tbody	Group of rows in a **table** element							

thead	Group of heading rows in a **table** element								
tfoot	Group of footer rows in a **table** element								
tr	Row in a **table** element								
td	Cell (table data) in a **table** element								
th	Header cell in a **table** element								

Table basics

It is reasonably straightforward to create a simple table when hand-coding markup. The bare essentials of a single table include an opening **table** tag, followed by at least one table row (a **tr**), followed by at least one table cell (a **td**, meaning "table data"). Here's an example:

```
<table>
        <tr>
                <td>Some data</td>
        </tr>
</table>
```

That's about as minimalist as you can get when it comes to creating tables, but you're unlikely to create a table with only one item of data, so let's make things a touch more interesting. The following markup is for a two-column table with two rows of data (the embedded style is to provide a **border** to act as a visual aid to better distinguish the layout of the table; ideally, its effect should be placed in an external CSS file in a production environment):

```
<style type="text/css">
```

```
    td { border: 1px solid #ff0000; }
</style>
<table>
    <tr>
        <td>Name</td>
        <td>Place of residence</td>
    </tr>
    <tr>
        <td>Anselm Bradford</td>
        <td>Auckland</td>
    </tr>
    <tr>
        <td>Paul Haine</td>
        <td>Oxford</td>
    </tr>
</table>
```

This will create a basic table, but let's take it a little further with table headers.

Adding table headers

You can make this table a bit clearer and easier to read by marking headers at the top of the table to indicate columns. Although you can do this by adding a class name to each table cell and then styling it with CSS, a far better way is to turn those uppermost table cells into bona fide table headers with the **th** element used in place of **td**.

```
<table>
    <tr>
        <th>Name</th>
        <th>Place of residence</th>
        </tr>

    ...

</table>
```

The preceding markup renders as shown in Figure 2-7.

Name	Place of residence
Anselm Bradford	Auckland
Paul Haine	Oxford

*Figure 2-7. A basic table using **th** for header cells*

This approach has several benefits. To begin with, it's a great aid to accessibility. While a screen-reading device may, in the hands of a competent user, read the first table example as "Name, Place of residence, Anselm Bradford, Auckland, Paul Haine, Oxford," with table headers available it can understand how the headers relate to the data and read it as "Name, Anselm Bradford, Place of residence, Auckland, Name, Paul Haine, Place of residence, Oxford…"[11] Of course, in this simple example, it would be easy enough to infer the table structure. It's not hard to work out that "Name, Place of residence, Anselm Bradford, Auckland, Paul Haine, Oxford" is a person's name followed by a place name, but when tables get more complex (by having more rows and columns), this becomes much more of an issue.

■ **Note** You can also use the `speak-header` CSS property to control whether table header cells are read out **once** or **always**, in an aural style sheet.

Besides making the table more accessible to users of screen readers, using proper table headers also provides sighted users with a useful visual cue as to the structure of the table and makes life marginally easier for the web author, who doesn't have to include an extra class name for every header. In addition, this gives the designer an extra hook for CSS and scripting.

Adding legends: caption

Now that you've headed up the table, you can make things even better by including a table caption, in the form of the **caption** element. This element needs to be placed directly after the opening **table** tag:

```
<table>
        <caption>Personal details</caption>
        <tr>
                <th>Name</th>
                <th>Place of residence</th>
        </tr>
        …
</table>
```

Most user agents will render the caption as shown in Figure 2-8.

Personal details	
Name	**Place of residence**
Anselm Bradford	Auckland
Paul Haine	Oxford

Figure 2-8. A basic table using a caption

---

[11] The W3C provides a tool to help understand how your tables could be read by assistive devices at `www.w3.org/WAI/References/Tablin`.

Adding structure: thead, tfoot, and tbody

If your table looks like it's getting a bit long and unwieldy, you can add some further structure with **thead**, **tfoot**, and **tbody** to help your browser make sense of things. These elements allow you to group rows into a header section, a footer section, and a body section. Much like the **th** elements, if needed, these three elements give you another hook for CSS and scripting without having to add extra classes or IDs. Like **caption**, these elements must be placed within the table markup in a very specific order and location. First, if you include any of the three, you must include **thead**. This element can go anywhere you like, but it's good practice to place it directly under the opening **table** tag—unless you've included a **caption**, in which case the **thead** element must go directly underneath that. You can place it underneath your **tfoot** and **tbody** if you like, and it would still be valid markup, but do this only if you want a bit of a brain ache when you come back to your markup a few months down the line and wonder what on earth you were thinking.

The **tfoot** element, however, *must* come before the **tbody** element. Why does the footer come before the body? It's so that a user agent can render the top and bottom of the table before starting on the middle, which is useful if you plan to have your table body scroll and you have many rows.

Finally, you add the **tbody** element. This tag is actually implicit in your table regardless. For example, try adding **tbody {font-style: italic}** to your CSS and apply it to a basic table, and you'll see that it styles the text in your table in an italic font. Even though its existence is implied, you *must* explicitly include the **tbody** tag if you're using **thead** and **tfoot**. So, once these elements are added, your markup should look a little like this:

```
<table>
	<thead>
		<tr>
			<th>Name</th>
			<th>Place of residence</th>
		</tr>
	</thead>
	<tfoot>
		<tr>
			<th>Name</th>
			<th>Place of residence</th>
		</tr>
	</tfoot>
	<tbody>
		<tr>
			<td>Anselm Bradford</td>
			<td>Auckland</td>
		</tr>
		<tr>
			<td>Paul Haine</td>
			<td>Oxford</td>
		</tr>
	</tbody>
</table>
```

With the exception of the headers now repeated at the foot of the table, there's no visual difference between a table that has these elements and one that doesn't, but it's good to include them because they provide extra, useful information about the structure of your table that can be exploited when printing or when viewing on-screen.

Be careful when using the **tfoot** element. Because this element may repeat itself over several pages, it's best used as a duplication of the **thead** element's content (as in the preceding example), rather than the literal conclusion of a long table, such as a final total beneath a column of prices (which would make little sense if it appeared before the table had been completed).

Adding even more structure: colgroup and col

If you need a table cell to span more than one row or column, you can achieve this effect with the **rowspan** and **colspan** attributes, each of which takes a numerical value indicating how many cells a particular cell should stretch across. This is all quite straightforward. For example, let's imagine that in addition to residing in Auckland, New Zealand, I have a second residence in Vermont. Adding this data to the table requires an additional row, but rather than leaving an empty table cell next to the new place of residence, I'll insert a **rowspan** attribute so that the cell containing my name pairs up with both places of residence:

```
...
<tr>
        <td rowspan="2">Anselm Bradford</td>
        <td>Auckland</td>
</tr>
<tr>
        <td>Vermont</td>
</tr>
<tr>
        <td>Paul Haine</td>
...
```

The table now renders as shown in Figure 2-9.

Name	Place of residence
Anselm Bradford	Auckland
	Vermont
Paul Haine	Oxford
Name	Place of residence

Figure 2-9. *A basic table using the* rowspan *attribute*

A table cell can span both rows and columns if necessary. You just need make sure your cells and spans add up. For instance, if your table has two rows, one containing five **td** elements, then the second row can span only up to five cells—any more than that and the table will not be valid and will render unpredictably, and any fewer than that and the slack must be taken up by remaining cells.

I've heard it suggested in the past that **rowspan** and **colspan** are presentational and should be avoided, but this is incorrect; you're using the attributes to define structure, not presentation, so you should keep that information in the markup.

As you may have noticed by now, most of the table markup presented so far relates only to rows and individual cells within those rows—there is no **tc** element. Instead, we have two elements that can define columns and groups of columns, and both are optional: **col** and **colgroup**.

The **colgroup** element allows you to specify how many groups of columns will exist in the table (so one **colgroup** per group of columns, and a group can contain just one column) and how many columns are contained within each group with the use of a **span** attribute and a numerical value. This element is placed directly after the opening **table** tag, and it does not contain any markup other than optional **col** tags, described shortly.

Consider, for example, the table shown in Figure 2-10.

Personal details		Date of birth		
Name	Place of residence	D	M	Y
Anselm Bradford	Auckland	14	11	1979
Paul Haine	Oxford	14	6	1978

Figure 2-10. *A table with multiple columns: there are three column groups here, headed by "Name,"* *"Place of residence," and "Date of birth"*

Reading along the uppermost headers, you can see that this table has three groups of columns, with the final column spanning the width of three cells. Using **colgroup**, you can define that structure at the start of the table like so:

```
<table>
    <colgroup></colgroup> <colgroup></colgroup> <colgroup span="3"></colgroup>
    <tr>
    ...
```

With this markup, you're saying that this table contains three groups of columns, the first two of which contain a single column (a single column is implied; you don't need to add a **span="1"** attribute in this case), and the third group contains three columns.

As shown in Table 2-10, there exists a **col** element, a self-closing element that also has a **span** attribute and that's used for specifying the existence of columns within a **colgroup**. Functionally and semantically, it's practically the same as **colgroup**, but unfortunately the HTML specification does not allow for nested **colgroup** elements, so you must use **col** instead. Using the preceding example, you can specify the final set of three columns in two different ways, either with one **col** per column, like this:

```
<table>
    <colgroup></colgroup> <colgroup></colgroup> <colgroup> <col /> <col /> <col />
    </colgroup>
    <tr>
    ...
```

or with a single **col** and a **span** attribute, like this:

```
<table>
    <colgroup></colgroup> <colgroup></colgroup> <colgroup><col span="3"></colgroup>
    <tr>
    ...
```

This is starting to look like a lot of work—why would anybody bother with this at all? It's true that at first glance it might appear that you're supplying redundant information, but this markup does have its uses. There are some side benefits, but the main reason for the existence of **colgroup** and **col** is to allow browsers to render the table even if all the table row data has yet to arrive. Without the information provided by these two tags, a browser must first parse the entire table to find the row with the largest number of cells in it. Next, the browser must calculate the width of that row, and only then will it know the width of the table and allow it to be rendered. When you let the browser know up front about the column structure of the table, the browser can render the data as it arrives.

Form elements

By their very nature web forms are a large topic—even larger so in HTML5 with the addition of many new elements. The form elements can often require careful coding of attributes to get groups of elements to work together properly and to have the form successfully submit its data to the server. Forms will be covered in depth in Chapter 4, but as a taste we will look at a basic example here:

```
<form action="handle_form.php">
    <label for="feedback">Please provide feedback on our form!</label>
    <br />
    <textarea id="feedback" rows="5" cols="50" placeholder="Enter your comments
    here..."></textarea>
    <br />
    <input type="submit" value="Submit!" />
</form>
```

When rendered in a web browser, this will look like Figure 2-11.

Please provide feedback on our form!

Enter your comments here...

Submit!

Figure 2-11. The appearance of a simple web form

This is just a simple example that shows the form structure. Forms generally follow the following format:

- Enclose form components within a form element that defines the file that will handle the form data when it is submitted.

- Define a number of controls for gathering input, such as text fields, drop-down lists, radio buttons, and so on.

- Provide a button for submitting the form so that the entered data can be retrieved and processed.

If you are at all familiar with forms, you may notice an unfamiliar attribute in the previous example—**placeholder**, which adds grayed-out text in the **textarea** element that provides a tip on what should be entered. The **placeholder** attribute is one new attribute in HTML5, but it is barely the tip of the iceberg! There have been enormous changes to web forms in the latest specification. In addition to the new and updated elements listed in Table 2-11, a large number of new input types can be created using the **input** element, such as much-needed form inputs for e-mail addresses, phone numbers, dates and times, and more! You will have to wait until Chapter 4 where these will be covered in more depth. In the meantime, familiarize yourself with the basic form-related elements and then let's move on for the moment to an overview of embedded content elements.

Table 2-11. Content model categories for form elements

NEW in HTML5 ■	Element	Description	Major Content Model Categories						
			Metadata	Sectioning	Heading	Flow	Phrasing	Embedded	Interactive
	form	User-submittable form				●			
	fieldset	Group of form controls				●			
	legend	Caption for fieldset							
	label	Caption for a form control				●	●		●
	input	Form control				●	●		●[12]

---

[12] Fits in the interactive category if the type attribute is not set to hidden.

	button	Button control				●	●		●
	select	Menu control				●	●		●
	datalist	List of data for other form controls				●	●		
	optgroup	Group of options in a **select**							
	option	Option in a **select** or **datalist**							
	textarea	Multiline text field				●	●		●
■	**keygen**	Cryptographic key-pair generator form control				●	●		●
■	**output**	Output from the result of a calculation				●	●		

■	progress	Progress bar					●	●	
■	meter	Measurement gauge					●	●	

Embedded content elements

For years HTML was rather bad at doing anything other than formatting documents. Still images were the epitome of complex content that could be embedded in a page, and animated GIFs were the *crème de la crème* of animation. These shortcomings were instrumental in spreading technologies such as Adobe Flash Player, which addressed the lack of developed solutions for animation, interactivity, video, and audio on web pages. With HTML5, the language has made a serious shift toward being a platform for developing web applications, as opposed to purely formatting web documents. Perhaps more so than any other element, the new **video** element exemplified what HTML5 may hope to represent—a rich multimedia experience using open standards of HTML/CSS/JavaScript. Before the **video** element was introduced, video without Adobe Flash seemed impossible. Certainly, other solutions exist such as the Apple QuickTime plug-in, but for years Flash video has dominated on popular video-sharing websites such as YouTube.com.

In the spring of 2010, Apple Inc.'s Steve Jobs released an open letter slamming Adobe Flash as a buggy, antiquated technology that would fall to the wayside as HTML5 video spread. HTML5 was thrust into the public consciousness as the future of the Web. For the time being, that future is still ahead; Flash video still enjoys widespread use, and HTML5 video has suffered from disagreements over which video format should be used. But slowly the family of HTML5 technologies is making healthy progress toward standardizing functionality previously possible only with Adobe Flash and other third-party plug-ins— and not just in video. The new **canvas** element provides a bitmap drawing surface, which can be manipulated using JavaScript to create complex renderings and experiences[13] analogous to the rich multimedia experiences previously produced with Adobe Flash.

The embedded content elements are such a rich and diverse set of elements that we will explore them in depth in Chapter 5. As with other sets of elements covered in this chapter, Table 2-12 shows the new and updated elements as well as the content model categories to which they belong. Familiarize yourself with these, and we'll get back to them in a few chapters. Now, onward!

---

[13] See Project Rome at http://ro.me for a glimpse at the capabilities of the embedded elements.

Table 2-12. *Content model categories for embedded content elements*

| NEW in HTML5 ■ | Element | Description | Major Content Model Categories | | | | | | |
			Metadata	Sectioning	Heading	Flow	Phrasing	Embedded	Interactive
	img	Embedded image				●	●	●	●[14]
	iframe	Nested web document				●	●	●	●
■	embed	An external plug-in software component, such as the Adobe Flash Player				●	●	●	●
	object	Image, nested web page, or external plug-in software component				●	●	●	●[15]

---

[14] May be placed in interactive category if the usemap attribute is set.
[15] Like img element, may be placed in interactive category if the usemap attribute is set.

	Tag	Description							
	`param`	Parameter for `object`							
■	`video`	Video player				●	●	●	●
■	`audio`	Audio player				●	●	●	●
■	`source`	Media source for `video` or `audio`							
■	`track`	Timed text track for `video` or `audio`							
■	`canvas`	Scriptable bitmap drawing surface				●	●	●	
	`map`	Image map				●	●[16]		

[16] May be placed in phrasing content, if it contains only phrasing content.

			Metadata	Flow	Sectioning	Heading	Phrasing	Embedded	Interactive
	area	A defined area (most likely a hyperlink) on map				●	●		

Interactive elements

This last group of elements are a small set that covers elements that are intended to be interacted with, typically with a click, without additional scripting or other mechanisms of creating interactivity. Three of the four elements in this group, details, summary, and command, are new, while menu has been redefined in HTML5 after being depreciated in HTML 4.01. See Table 2-13 for the usual summary of these elements.

Table 2-13. Content model categories for interactive elements

NEW in HTML5	Element	Description	Major Content Model Categories						
			Metadata	Flow	Sectioning	Heading	Phrasing	Embedded	Interactive
■	details	Disclosure control for hiding details		●					●
■	summary	Caption for details							
■	command	Command for menu	●	●			●		

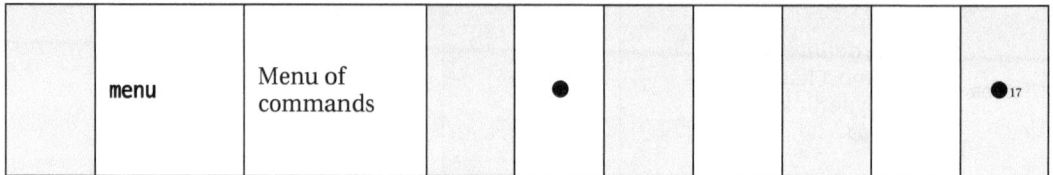

menu	Menu of commands		●					●17

Showing more info: summary and details

The **summary** and **details** elements work together to provide a "widget" that can show and hide additional text without the use of JavaScript or CSS. The **summary** element acts as a header (or summary, as the element name suggests) that provides a toggle that may be clicked to show and hide the text between the **details** tags. By default, the text inside **details** will be hidden until the toggle is clicked; however, a Boolean attribute, **open**, may be added to the **details** element in order to show the text by default.

Unfortunately, the **details** and **summary** elements are not well supported at the time of this writing, with only Google's Chrome browser, supporting this feature.[18] If the browser you are using does not support these elements, all content within the details area will be shown, and there won't be a toggle of any sort.

A basic example might look like this:

```
<details>
        <summary>Legal Notice</summary>
        <small>All content copyright 2011 Anselm Bradford</small>
</details>
```

This will show a toggle and the text "Legal Notice," which can be clicked to show and hide the copyright statement. The **details** element can contain any flow elements, which means the details could take on considerable complexity. For instance, this next example presents some HTML that might appear on a theater's website. This example uses the **summary** and **details** elements to show and hide additional information about the theater's currently performing play:

```
<details>
    <summary>A Midsummer Night's Dream</summary>
    <p>Duration: 1hr 42m</p>
    <p>Showtimes: </p>
    <ul>
        <li>Tuesday, 8pm</li>
        <li>Wednesday, 8pm</li>
        <li>Thursday, 8pm</li>
        <li>Friday, 6pm and 8pm</li>
    </ul>
</details>
```

---

[17] Fits in interactive category if type attribute is set to toolbar.

[18] Visit the website http://caniuse.com and type *details* in the search field to see the current state of browser support.

Unlike the previous example, which toggled only one line of text, this example shows and hides two paragraphs and an unordered list.

Interacting with the elements will look something like Figure 2-12.

```
▶  A Midsummer Night's Dream


▼  A Midsummer Night's Dream

Duration: 1hr 42m

Showtimes:

   •  Tuesday, 8pm
   •  Wednesday, 8pm
   •  Thursday, 8pm
   •  Friday, 6pm and 8pm
```

Figure 2-12. A details element showing the hidden and shown state after clicking the summary toggle

■ **Note** The `summary` element is optional; if it is omitted, the browser will create its own label for the `details` element, such as the text "Details."

Using JavaScript, the **details** element could be used to set up a user preferences panel in a web application, for example. In this example, the summary is a nickname for the user, which they can then toggle open and change. Saving their changes updates the value in the **summary** element, which will change the appearance of the label for the details.

```
<script type="text/javascript">
    function update() {
        var nick = document.getElementById("nickname");
        var input = document.getElementById("input");
        nick.innerHTML = input.value;
    }
</script>
<details>
    <summary id="nickname">Mac</summary>
    <p><label for="input">Nickname: <input type="text" id="input" value="Mac" /></label></p>
    <p><button onclick="update();">Save...</button></p>
</details>
```

Figure 2-13 shows the process to open the details, change the name, and hit Save…, which (using JavaScript) then updates the summary text. Obviously, this would need to permanently save the changes to be really useful, either in a back-end database or possibly in a client-side storage (so-called web storage is available in an associated API, discussed in Appendix A).

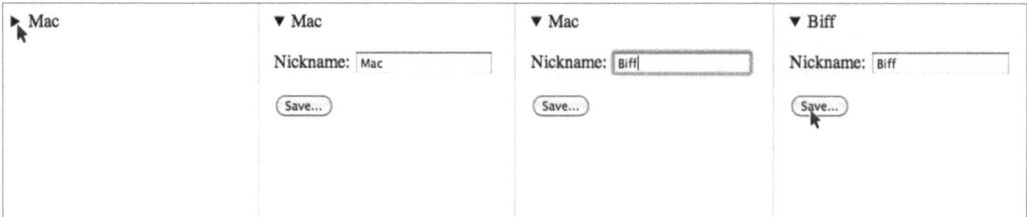

Figure 2-13. A details element using JavaScript to update the details summary dynamically

Providing toolbars: menu and command

Individual **command** elements placed inside a **menu** element can be used to create a menu bar like those found in desktop applications. Not only that, but it can be used to create a contextual menu or other interactive listing of menu options. Remember the **contextmenu** global attribute, which used these two elements? Unfortunately, like the **contextmenu** attribute, the **command** attribute has not been implemented in any major browser yet, so these menus remain in the theoretical space of the HTML5 specification.

Summary

Congratulations! This has been a very dense chapter, filled with lots of information, but I hope you have walked away with knowledge of what new elements exist in HTML5 and perhaps a refresher on other elements that have been there all along. Now it is time to turn to the specifics we glossed over in this chapter and look at how to practically use these rich new HTML elements.

CHAPTER 3

Recognizing Semantics

OK, OK, we've drudged through the available elements, and that is all well and good, but you may be wondering how you go from knowing the HTML elements to *mastering* the HTML elements. Well, after knowing what elements exist, the next step is knowing when to use one over another. This chapter will guide you on that path, focusing on the elements that define the structure and semantics of your web page. We'll code a simple web page outline to learn about structural semantics and then delve into a case study to explore the nuances of text-level semantic elements.

What are semantics and why should I care?

"Elements, attributes, and attribute values in HTML are defined (by this specification) to have certain meanings (semantics). For example, the ol element represents an ordered list, and the lang attribute represents the language of the content.

Authors must not use elements, attributes, or attribute values for purposes other than their appropriate intended semantic purpose."

WHATWG HTML SPECIFICATION

The word *semantic* can often be heard in the web development communities in such phrases as the *Semantic Web, good semantics, semantically rich HTML,* and so on, but it can feel a bit like a catchphrase being tossed about to make the speaker seem hip to contemporary web development. What exactly does it mean? That very question is what semantics seek to answer. **Semantics** is the meaning of something, especially in regard to the components of a language. Semantic HTML is about HTML elements that describe the type of content they contain. It is concerned with what is meant by enclosing content in one HTML element versus another. It is also about using appropriate elements for particular pieces of content, as per the guidelines in the HTML specification.

Sometimes it is quite clear what kind of content an element will contain. For instance, seeing time will likely key you in quickly to this element's contents. On the other hand, seeing s may necessitate a careful review of the relevant passages in the HTML specification. But let's look at the time element again. Is it as clear what it will contain as it first seems? For instance, could I write the following:

```
<p>Innovations of the <time>21st century</time>.</p>
```

Or the following:

```
<p>The machine ran <time>infinitely</time>.</p>
```

Well, no; every element has constraints it's put under, and while both of those pieces of content are related to time (a time period and a property of time), they are not the type of time-related content the `time` element was meant to describe. We'll talk about `time` more later, but in short, the specification tells us that it is a precise *date* in the Gregorian calendar, optionally with a *time*. So, it's not as clear as we first thought! Why is the element not called `date` or `datetime` instead? Well, element names aside, the point is there are subtle nuances to each, regardless of how clear the name makes its purpose seem. Mastering these nuances will go a long way toward creating pages that are logically structured, easier to maintain, and more friendly to data-mining services (for example, search engines). So, leave your assumptions at the door, and let's dive into the nuances of HTML's elements! We'll begin with structural elements.

Thinking in outlines

See whether you can relate to this scenario. You have a new website project to undertake. After mulling over the general concept of the site, you boot up your favorite graphics editor and begin shuffling blocks of color around and fiddling with textures and lines. You throw in a title and logo and shuffle the header around until it looks right. Does this strike a chord? When tackling a new website project, it is tempting to immediately dive in and start designing the appearance of the site, but if you find yourself doing this, it's worth pausing and looking at the big picture. Ultimately, a well-designed website is one that provides efficient delivery and access to its content. Your design should aim to create a hierarchy of information—parts of the page should pull viewers' attention first, then second, and so on. If you don't have all the content organized into a hierarchy beforehand, you may find yourself scrapping your design over and over as you discover this or that piece needs more or less prominence on the page.

So, pause, leave the design alone for a moment, get some paper and a pen, and write down the major pieces of content on your site. Think of a label for each piece and where it stands in relation to the rest of the page's content. Forget about the details for the moment, and focus instead on creating labels that could sit above major sections of content. For instance, you might come up with something like Figure 3-1 for a simple homepage.

```
1. Site Title
      1. Main Navigation
      2. Featured Content
            1. An Article
                  1. Article Synopsis
      3. Other News
            1. Another Article
```

Figure 3-1. A simple homepage outline

Think of this list as the table of contents or site map for your website's content, what comes before what, and what is a subsection of a larger section. In this example, the website's title (perhaps a company name) is the piece of information all other content falls under. Below that is the main navigation to other pages (remember this is the big picture, so individual links aren't shown in this example), and next comes the featured content on the homepage, which includes a featured article with a brief summary of the article's contents. Lastly, the other articles on the homepage are placed in an "Other News" section.

Developing a list like this can help you organize and visualize the hierarchy of information on your site, but this isn't just a lofty exercise that may or may not help when developing your website—the HTML5 specification actually provides a concrete algorithm for building a website structure based on an outline such as the one in Figure 3-1. Not only that, but the algorithm is a great guide for learning how to properly structure your web pages.

HTML5 outline algorithm

Known as the HTML5 **outline algorithm**, this part of the HTML5 specification provides rules for breaking content into a nested list of sections, each with a heading. Providing a standard algorithm for understanding and parsing the structure of a web page means every properly structured web page automatically gets a "table of contents" that may be used by, for example, screen readers (for vision-impaired users) or used in syndicating sections of content.

■ **Note** A *section*[1] is just a grouping of content—think of it as a box around some content on the page—while a *heading* is like the label slapped on the box, saying what it contains.

To simplify a bit, the outline algorithm parses a document using the following rules:

1. Assign the body element as the root section under which all other page sections are grouped.

2. Assign the first heading content element found to be the heading for the body.

3. For each subsequent sectioning content element found, define and add new sections and subsections to the outline.

4. Assign the first heading content element found in each subsequent section to be the heading for that section.

In the preceding steps, notice the two content model categories mentioned, heading content and sectioning content. Elements in these two categories were under the section "Semantic sectioning elements" that appeared in Chapter 2. Both contain a small group of elements; heading content encompasses the h1, h2, h3, h4, h5, h6, and hgroup elements, while the article, aside, nav, and section elements fall under sectioning content.[2]

---

[1] There is a section element in HTML, but in this context "section" is used as a general term that covers the HTML elements present in the sectioning content model category.
[2] Note that (perhaps surprisingly) div is not included in sectioning content.

Implicitly creating an outline using heading content

The previous website outline (Figure 3-1) could be created using h1, h2, h3, and h4 elements to establish the order and hierarchy, like so:

```
<!DOCTYPE html>
<html>
        <head>
                <meta charset="utf-8" />
                <title>HTML5 Outline Algorithm</title>
        </head>
        <body>
                <h1>Site Title</h1>
                <h2>Main Navigation</h2>
                <h2>Featured Content</h2>
                <h3>An Article</h3>
                <h4>Article Synopsis</h4>
                <h2>Other News</h2>
                <h3>Another Article</h3>
        </body>
</html>
```

Hold on! If you read the outline algorithm parsing rules closely, you might notice a problem here. The h1 through h4 elements are *heading content* elements, not *sectioning content* elements, so would this page have any sections other than the root section created by the body? The answer is yes. Sections may implicitly be created if the algorithm encounters a situation where they would be expected.

The h1 through h6 heading elements are said to have a **rank**, which is the number given in their names (for example, h1 has a rank of 1, h2 a rank of 2, and so forth). A lower-ranked heading element, when placed below higher-ranked elements, will be nested within the section of the higher-ranking heading element. If, however, the heading element has the same or higher rank as its predecessor, it will implicitly create a new section, if one is not already defined (Figure 3-2). Note that no elements are being added here; this is just how the HTML5 outline algorithm interprets how the content on the page is grouped together.

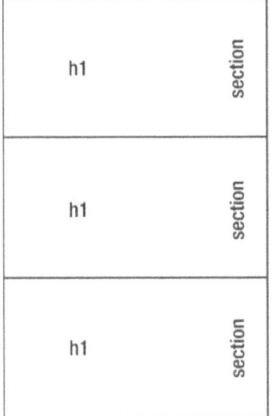 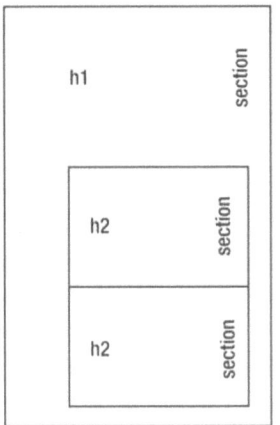 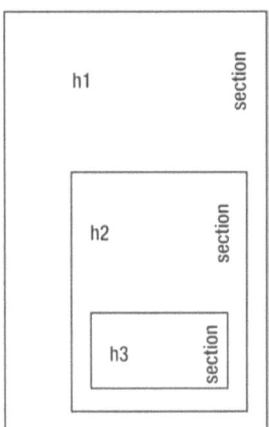

Figure 3-2. Implicit section creation of adjacent heading elements. Adjacent heading elements with the same rank will implicitly create new sections, while those with a lower rank will implicitly create nested sections.

In earlier times, it was a common practice to use the h1 through h6 elements inside div elements to structure the sections of a page. The problem with this is that the div element is not part of the sectioning content group of elements, so it won't break the page into sections according to the HTML5 outline algorithm. Implicitly creating sections provides some backward compatibility with this older coding style, because sections can be created automatically based on the heading elements used inside the div elements. However, this isn't the preferred means of structuring the sections in the page. Instead, explicitly including sectioning content elements will make the nesting structure more apparent when viewing the source code, which is what we'll do next.

Creating an outline using sectioning content

Of the four sectioning content elements, the section element[3] is the most generic, providing a grouping of content that is (ideally) thematically related. By adding section elements to the code, we can explicitly show where the sections will show up, which may make it easier to see how the page is organized (refer to Figure 3-2 if the nesting of elements in the following example does not make sense):

```
...
<body>
        <h1>Site Title</h1>
        <section><h2>Main Navigation</h2></section>
        <section><h2>Featured Content</h2>
                <section><h3>An Article</h3>
                        <section><h4>Article Synopsis</h4></section>
                </section>
        </section>
```

---

[3] The others are article, aside, and nav.

```
            <section><h2>Other News</h2>
                    <section><h3>Another Article</h3></section>
            </section>
</body>
…
```

> ■ **Note** The first h1 does not need a section, because the body element serves this role. You may have noticed, however, that the body element is not included in the sectioning content category. The body belongs to a special category of elements called **sectioning roots**, which are elements that may have an outline defined inside them, but it is hidden if they are included in another outline. For example, the blockquote element is a member of the sectioning root category and can contain sectioning elements forming an outline, but this in not visible in the page's outline, because it is encapsulated in the blockquote. Other members of this category are the details, fieldset, figure, and td elements.

By including sectioning elements, the different ranking of the heading elements is actually no longer needed. On this matter, the specification states the following:

> *"…authors are strongly encouraged to either use only h1 elements, or to use elements of the appropriate rank for the section's nesting level."*

So, it may be wise to convert all the heading elements in the code to h1 elements; otherwise, the page becomes less flexible to changes in structure. For example, if the nesting structure was changed, the heading ranks would need to be updated to reflect any nesting depth changes (not doing this wouldn't break anything but would be a semantic no-no).

> ■ **Note** That said, there are currently search engine optimization (SEO) concerns with using only h1 elements for headings. For instance, Microsoft's Bing search engine publishes a Webmaster FAQ (www.bing.com/toolbox/webmaster/) that states a page should not have more than one h1 element per page. This instruction heralds from earlier days of the Web, so ideally going forward this will eventually be removed, but in the meantime, if SEO is critical to your web projects, perform due diligence on whether the search engines you are targeting will have issues with multiple h1 elements, or rigorously use heading ranks appropriate to their nesting level.

Note that converting all heading elements to h1 means the headings on the page may have the same size on the page by default, regardless of how the sections are nested. For example, as of the time of writing, the latest versions of Google Chrome and Firefox are smart enough to reduce the size of heading elements that are nested within other sections, while Safari and Opera are not. Whether the latter two implement this behavior is a moot point, however, because all presentational qualities of the page (heading size included) should be handled using CSS, not HTML.

Improving outline semantics

Sections are a great general-purpose grouping element, but much of the content on this page could be better defined using more specific sectioning elements. Let's look at the three remaining elements in the sectioning content group and see which would be a better fit than the section element. Using the flowchart in Figure 3-3, we will work our way through the content.

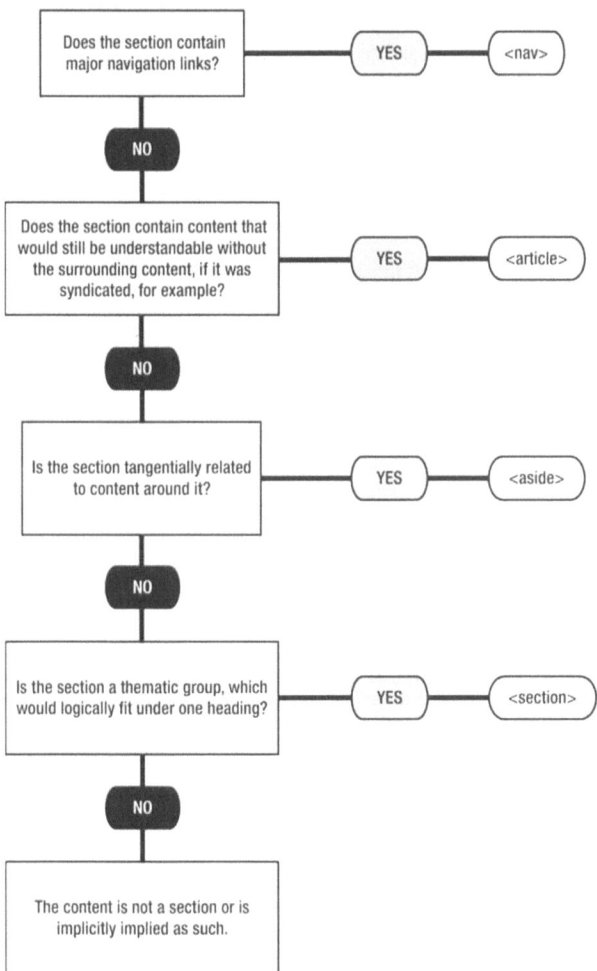

Figure 3-3. Flowchart for choosing a particular sectioning content element

First, the navigation can be wrapped in nav, because this section will define the main navigational links for the web page (for this simplified example, the links have been omitted, but they normally would not be). Next is the "Featured Content" area. Hmm, this is an interesting one because it contains content (an article) that could be understandable on its own if it were separated from the rest of the website. It therefore could be wrapped in an article. But wait a moment; is that really the most appropriate option? To tailor your markup to be semantically correct, you have to focus on the purpose of a piece of content on the page; what does a particular section of content contain, and what will it foreseeably contain in the future? The article element is made for content that is completely self-contained and could be syndicated in an RSS feed, for instance. In this example, the featured content area is for content that has been separated from the rest of the content for the purposes of being prominently displayed on the site. It therefore is arguably not self-contained, because it contains content that is emphasized within a larger set of content on the site. Therefore, the designation of "Featured Content" is rather meaningless without the surrounding content. Additionally, the featured content area could conceivably contain more than one article or other piece of content, which may not be related at all. The area is for featured content, not necessarily related content. If there were more content in this area, would it still make sense to bundle all that content (related and unrelated) together and syndicate it? I think not. So, this leaves us with a group of content that thematically fits together (in that it is all being featured) but is not self-contained enough to be considered an article. This content is therefore best left as being contained in a section.

■ **Note** The HTML5 specification aims to articulate the semantic uses of the elements as best as possible, but there is still a world of content out there with varying meanings and interpretations. While a flowchart such as Figure 3-3 helps narrow down when one element will be more appropriate than another, you may well run into circumstances where the answer to the question of which element to use becomes ambiguous. In these cases, it is best to err on the side of a more generic element that will definitely fit a given piece of content than to apply a more specific element that may or may not be appropriate.

Next, the "Other News" section can be treated like "Featured Content." It thematically groups content together (all content that is not featured) but is not self-contained enough to warrant the use of an article, so it gets a section as well. The two articles shown are self-contained and would make sense on their own, so they are wrapped in article elements.

Next, the "Article Synopsis" would not make sense on its own and is related to the article it's nested inside, so it is best wrapped inside an aside. Lastly, despite the concerns about using multiple h1 tags, we'll convert all headings to h1 so you can see what that looks like.

The end result looks like this:

```
...
<body>
        <h1>Site Title</h1>
        <nav><h1>Main Navigation</h1></nav>
        <section><h1>Featured Content</h1>
                <article><h1>An Article</h1>
                        <aside><h1>Article Synopsis</h1></aside>
                </article>
```

```
            </section>
            <section><h1>Other News</h1>
                    <article><h1>Another Article</h1></article>
            </section>
</body>
...
```

Much better! This markup is now much less generic. The navigation can be easily identified; we see there is a featured article on the page, a brief synopsis on the side, and another article in another section of the page. At the moment, there is no content (paragraphs, figures, and so on) other than the headings in the separate sections, but there easily could be! This is just establishing the outline of the document.

■ **Note** In this example, the `aside` has been nested inside an `article`, which is further nested inside a `section`. If the aside had instead been directly in the `body` element, it would be expected to be related to content on the whole page, not just one part. For a web page with minimal content, that may be OK, but on a web page filled with content, grouping and/or nesting `aside`s together with their related content will most likely be necessary.

Headers and footers

Every section may optionally have a `header` and a `footer` element. A header[4] is used for grouping together introductory content or navigational aids[5] for a section, so it will likely contain the heading element for the section as well as other introductory content (a table of contents, relevant logos, and so on). A `footer` contains content related to the section or page as a whole, such as who the author is, copyright information, contact address, and other (generally) small snippets of information. Sometimes related links or duplicate links to the page's main navigational menu may be found in the footer, but in general they do not need to be put into a `nav` element if they are extraneous or redundant links and are not critical to the main navigation of the site.

■ **Note** It's important to note that the whole page can have a header and a footer as well as sections on the page, so a single page could easily have multiple headers and footers.

Should we add a `header` to the existing code? Sure, but it actually isn't necessary at the moment. A header is for grouping introductory content together. Currently we have a single heading element for each section, so there is nothing to group together. Or is there? The main navigation is a navigational aid, so that could be grouped under the header for the page. Also, let's add a subtitle under "Site Title"

---

[4] Not to be confused with "heading," which refers to the h1 through h6 elements. The header element is not even a part of the heading content category!
[5] A navigational aid could be, for example, a main menu or a search field, as often can be found in the upper-right of many websites.

named "Site Slogan!"—now we have three introductory elements to group! Wrapping these in a header gives us the following:

```
...
<body>
        <header>
                <h1>Site Title</h1>
                <p>Site Slogan!</p>
                <nav><h1>Main Navigation</h1></nav>
        </header>
        <section><h1>Featured Content</h1>
...
```

Notice that the "Site Slogan" is in a paragraph element. If a heading element had been used, the title and slogan would be implicitly broken into two sections, which doesn't seem right. However, a paragraph doesn't seem right either. An h1 for the title and an h2 for the slogan seems more appropriate, because there is a clear hierarchy of importance between the two, yet they are part of the same introductory text. Here's where the last element in the heading content category comes in handy: enter hgroup!

Using hgroup

The hgroup element allows a group of heading elements to be placed together and have only the highest ranked one among them be exposed to the HTML5 outline algorithm, which is useful for situations where you may want to have two headings in one section, such as a single article that has a title and subtitle. By wrapping the title in an h1 and the subtitle in an h2 and then grouping them together with an hgroup, the h2 will not create a new section, because it won't be seen by the outline algorithm. Another advantage of this is the order in which the heading elements appear can be changed, since the lower-ranked headings are effectively ignored for structural purposes. For the example code we have been working with, we could move the slogan above the title with no structural repercussions, giving us the following code appearance:

```
...
<body>
        <header>
                <hgroup>
                        <h2>Site Slogan!</h2>
                        <h1>Site Title</h1>
                </hgroup>
                <nav><h1>Main Navigation</h1></nav>
        </header>
        <section><h1>Featured Content</h1>
...
```

Formatting a footer with an address

A common element to include inside a footer is a way to contact the author of an article or owner of a site. A typical element to find in the footer for this purpose is the address element. This element is not for a P.O. box or similar address that would not be the most direct means of contacting the author (though that information may appear in the footer as well). It is instead for providing direct contact information (e-mail address, phone number, and so on) for the nearest article or the page as a whole.

■ **Note** It is not appropriate to use the `address` element inside a sectioning element other than `article` or the body of the document. So, a `section` element may have a footer, but it would not have an `address` element included. If an `address` element were included in this situation, the address would semantically apply to the first article encountered that contained the section or to the body, whichever was encountered first.

Let's add a footer to the existing code, which provides an e-mail address contact for the whole page:

```
...
<body>
        <header>
                <hgroup>
                        <h2>Site Slogan!</h2>
                        <h1>Site Title</h1>
                </hgroup>
                <nav><h1>Main Navigation</h1></nav>
        </header>
        <section><h1>Featured Content</h1>
                <article><h1>An Article</h1>
                        <aside><h1>Article Synopsis</h1></aside>
                </article>
        </section>
        <section><h1>Other News</h1>
                <article><h1>Another Article</h1></article>
        </section>
        <footer>
                <address>Contact: <a href="mailto:wm@example.com">Webmaster</a></address>
        </footer>
</body>
...
```

Determining header and footer contents

Refer to Figure 3-4 for a flowchart that summarizes the process of determining header and footer contents.

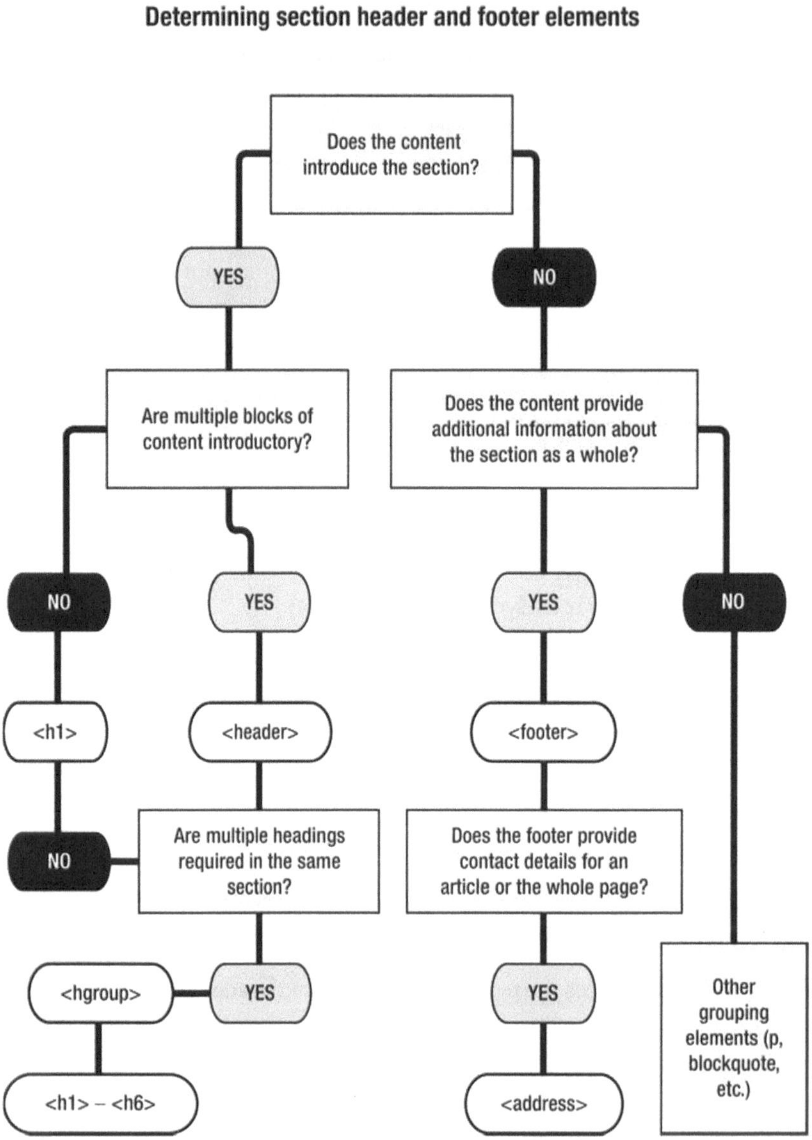

Determining section header and footer elements

Figure 3-4. Flowchart for determining the section header and footer elements

Viewing HTML5 outlines

Now that we have a skeleton of a simple site, let's view the outline! There is a great tool built by Geoffrey Sneddon (http://gsnedders.com) for parsing HTML5 markup and returning an outline. Head over to http://gsnedders.html5.org/outliner/ where you can upload HTML, enter a URL to parse, or enter the

HTML directly into a web form. After hitting the "Outline this!" button, you'll be presented with an outline of the sections in the HTML document you supplied. Try entering the code we've been building. You should see an outline like Figure 3-5. Experimenting with this tool is a great way to learn the nesting structure of sectioning content.

If you'd prefer to have a tool built into the browser, there is a Google Chrome extension available from the Chrome Web Store. Go to https://chrome.google.com/extensions/ and search for *HTML5 Outliner*. The extension installs in the address bar. When visiting an HTML5 web page, the extension can be clicked to show the page's outline (Figure 3-6). Unfortunately, this does not work for web pages you are viewing locally.

Opera has an equivalent extension at https://addons.opera.com/addons/extensions/details/html5-outliner/.

Additionally, if you visit the HTML5 Outliner project at http://code.google.com/p/h5o/, you will find an experimental add-on for Firefox and a bookmarklet that has been tested in Firefox and Opera (there is a link to the Chrome extension there as well, as this is the project that developed that extension).

1. **Site Title**
   1. **Main Navigation**
   2. **Featured Content**
      1. **An Article**
         1. **Article Synopsis**
   3. **Other News**
      1. **Another Article**

Figure 3-5. Example output from the HTML5 Outliner by Geoffrey Sneddon

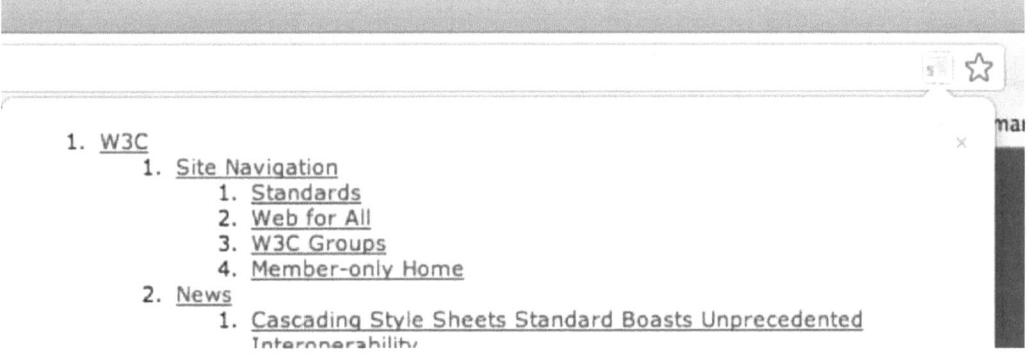

Figure 3-6. The Chrome HTML5 Outliner extension appears on the right side of the address bar. The image shows part of the outline of the http://w3.org site.

Are divs (and spans) obsolete?

All this discussion about sectioning content on a page and barely a mention of divs! How times have changed. Before HTML5, divs were found all over web pages; they were the unavoidable scaffolding used to created headers, footers, columns, and all the other sections of a page. With all the new sectioning elements, has the div gone the way of blink? No, divs are still very much present; they have been augmented and supplanted in some cases with more semantically defined elements, but they are still a valid element and have their place. Since div elements do not have any semantics of their own, they can appropriately be used to, for instance, group related content, unrelated content, the whole page, or a sentence.[6] These are all equal from a semantic perspective, and the div is not adding further meaning to these groupings. Their versatility is in their lack of extra semantic baggage. Therefore, they continue to be useful for applying CSS rules or accessing a piece of content from JavaScript. When no other element will fit, a div is a great catchall element!

Likewise, the span is still very much present in HTML5. It holds an analogous place to div; where div is used for flow content, span could be used for phrasing content.

If you have a piece of content that does not appear to fit under another element, the following are two good rules of thumb to determine whether you should use a div (or span, if you're dealing with text-level phrasing content):

- Are you using the markup purely as a hook to apply CSS styles or to access the content from JavaScript?

- Can the meaning of the content be described only with a class or id attribute? The div and span elements don't introduce any semantics of their own, but you may add meaning through class and id attributes if no other element is appropriate.

Case study: the City Press

Now that you feel comfortable organizing the structure of a web page using HTML5 sectioning elements, we're going to turn our attention to the details, the text-level semantics of a page. These are the elements that enclose phrasing content—the text inside paragraphs and so on. We'll use the homepage of the *City Press* (Figure 3-7), a fictitious newspaper, as an example around which to explore these elements. The *City Press* page has been coded with a large number of different elements for demonstration purposes.

---

[6] However, it is important to note that divs are not in the sectioning content category, a div used in place of a section will not add a new section to the document outline.

YOUR LOCAL INDEPENDENT DAILY NEWSPAPER

THE CITY PRESS

— ONLINE —

MAIN MENU

Home | Special Issues | Send a Letter | Comics | About

Today: Monday, October 10th, 2011

Oh là là!

Unusually warm weather brought many outside to soak up the sunshine this past weekend. As this couple found, secluded beach spots such as *Lover's Rock* proved to be the perfect place to while away the afternoon.

Chris Elhorn | The City Press

More sunshine forecast, drought feared

by Ellen Deling

Meteorologists predict more sunshine and scorching temperatures for the upcoming week, prompting area farmers to install irrigation systems.

With little rain in the past month, the threat of drought looms for area farmers, with anticipated crop loses as high as $1 million, estimated George Granger, spokesman for the NFA (National Farm Association). "We're all hoping it rains soon, some farmers have installed irrigation systems, at *considerable* expense," Granger said.

Last Friday, *IrrigationDirect*, a supplier of irrigation equipment, offered farmers who were members of the NFA discounts in an effort to help eliviate the financial burden facing area farmers.

While the sunshine will likely continue through the week, the good news, say area weather forecasters, is that the dome of hot air causing the high temperatures would eventually pass, allowing temperatures to return to normal.

Ellen Deling is a staff writer for The City Press, comments may be emailed to her directly.
Posted October 10, 2011

Weather

Sunny

High: 82°F 96°F
Low: 70°F 79°F

City Voice

"We're all hoping it rains soon, some farmers have installed irrigation systems, at *considerable* expense"

George Granger, NFA spokesman.

The City Press
123 General Street
Springfield, OH 45501

Copyright 2011 The City Press

News Tip Line: 800.123.4567

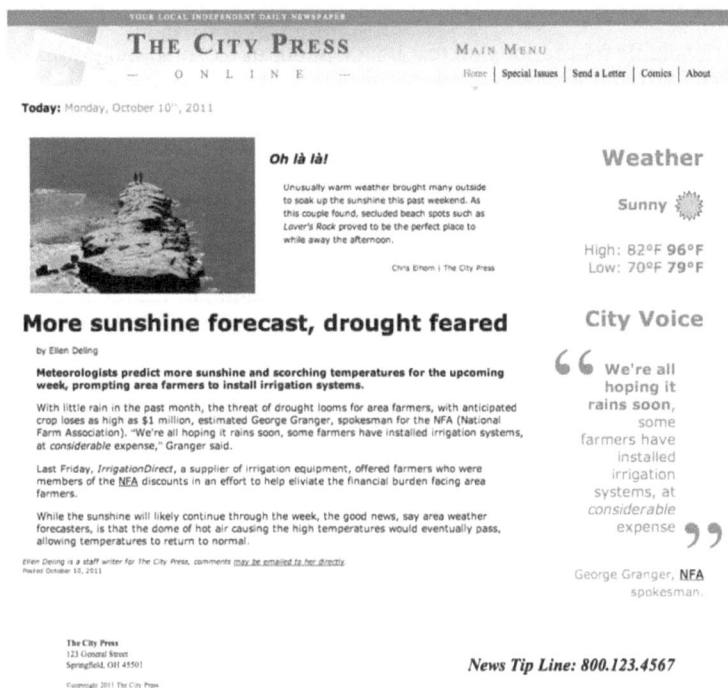

Figure 3-7. *The fictitious newspaper homepage used as a case study into the use of semantically rich HTML elements*

Before we dive into the text-level semantics, let's take a look at the outline of this page to see how it is structured (Figure 3-8).

1. The City Press
   1. Main Menu
   2. Today: Monday, October 10th, 2011
      1. More sunshine forecast, drought feared
      2. Weather
      3. City Voice

Figure 3-8. *The outline of the City Press web page*

Looking at the outline, you can see that the text "The City Press" is the heading for the body, which contains two nested sections, "Main Menu" (nav element) and "Today: Monday, October 10th, 2011" (`section` element). Inside the "Today" section, there is an `article` element ("More sunshine forecast…") and two `aside` elements, one for the weather and one for the "City Voice," which contains a blockquote from the article story.

Adding text-level semantics

A great number of elements are available for marking up text inside paragraphs and other groups of content. These elements are used for defining which words precisely are hyperlinks and what should be emphasized, labeled important, set apart from the rest of the text, and so forth. We'll dive into each of these elements individually.

Hyperlinks: a

Links are most likely up there alongside paragraphs as among the first pieces of HTML you ever learned, but we can still plumb the depths of obscurity and poke around at a few potentially useful behaviors. Strictly speaking, the a element is not a link; it's a **hypertext anchor**, which can either link to a new file, point to any element via its id attribute, or, if it lacks the href attribute, act as a placeholder for where a link might otherwise have been placed.

An exciting new change in the a element from prior iterations of HTML is that there is much more flexibility in what can be placed as content inside the link. Any flow content can be nested inside, as long as it isn't from the interactive content category (buttons, links, and so on), so where in the past a link may have looked like this:

```
<a href="newpage.html">link text that appears on web page</a>
```

it now can look like this:

```
<a href="newpage.html">
        <section>
                <h1>Wow an entire section in a link!</h1>
        </section>
</a>
```

As a quick refresher, the href attribute is what determines where the link goes, while the text between the tags is what becomes interactive when viewed in a web page. When the text is clicked, it will connect to whatever is specified in the href attribute, which usually is a file (a web page most often). However, it may connect to what's known as a **fragment identifier**, which is the value in the id attribute of an element in the linked document. If the href attribute contains a fragment identifier, the user not only is directed to the linked document but is also taken to whatever element has the same ID as the fragment identifier.

To link to a fragment identifier, a hash sign and value are added at the end of the URL, like so:

```
<a href="newpage.html#parttwo">link</a>
```

If you want to link to a fragment identifier element on the same page, there is no need to include the document filename:

```
<a href="#parttwo">link</a>
```

This would link to the element with the id of "parttwo," which may look like this:

```
<h3 id="parttwo">Part Two</h3>
```

Linking to an identified element on the same page can have multiple uses, such as for a table of contents for a lengthy document and sometimes a "back to the top of the page" link:

```
<a href="#top">back to top</a>7
```

■ **Note** Another common use is to create **skip links**, which are links that allow people to skip past long blocks of navigation links to get at the content. Skip links are usually included for users who navigate with a keyboard or a mobile or screen-reading device, but sometimes they also present visually for users who are zooming in and may not enjoy scrolling around. A useful article that summarizes a good use of skip links is Jim Thatcher's "Skip Navigation" (www.jimthatcher.com/skipnav.htm).

It's perfectly acceptable to have an anchor element that does not include an href attribute. For example, the menu on the *City Press* web page includes a link around "Home" that does not link anywhere:

```
<nav>
        <h1>Main Menu</h1>
        <ul>
                <li><a class="current" title="Home">Home</a></li>
                <li><a href="special.htm" title="Special Projects">Special
                Issues</a></li>
                <li><a href="contact.htm" title="Send a Letter">Send a Letter</a></li>
                <li><a href="comics.htm" title="Comics">Comics</a></li>
                <li><a href="about.htm" title="About">About</a></li>
        </ul>
</nav>
```

It doesn't make sense to have a hyperlink that links to the page the user is currently on, but at the same time, for semantic or styling purposes it may not make sense to remove the anchor element from the menu item in question. In the case of the *City Press* web page, the href attribute is removed, and class="current" is added dynamically on the server side, which provides a CSS "hook" that can easily style the home link differently from the rest of the menu (Figure 3-9).

---

[7] It's a good idea to explicitly include an anchor or identified element with an ID of "top"—some browsers will infer such location.

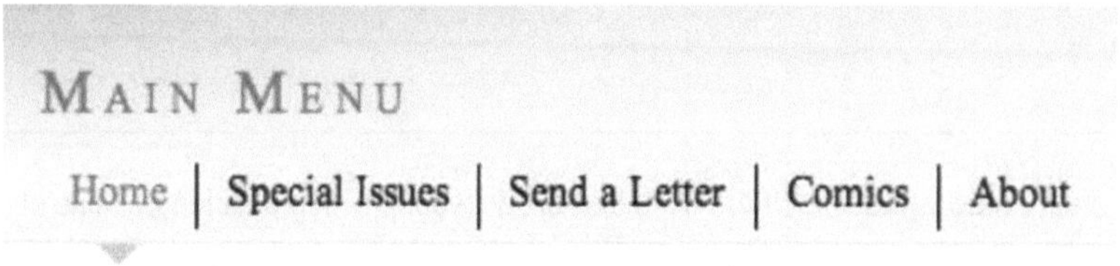

MAIN MENU

Home | Special Issues | Send a Letter | Comics | About

Figure 3-9. The City Press menu, with the disabled Home link showing separate styling being applied through a class

HTML5 has added three new attributes to the a element, media, type, and download, which specify, respectively, whether the link is optimized for display on a particular media/device; the MIME type of the linked resource (image/jpeg, text/html, and so on); and, finally, whether the link specifies a resource that is meant to be downloaded. If the resource is meant to be downloaded, the value in the download attribute is the default filename that is given to downloaded file. As of the time of this writing, this attribute had only just appeared in the latest build of Google Chrome.

The remaining attributes on the anchor element are target, hreflang, and rel. The target attribute, which defines where the link will open, will be discussed further in Chapters 4 and 5, but it generally has one of the following values: _blank, _self, _parent, or _top, which determine whether the link opens in a new window, the current window, the containing window (if inline frames are used, for instance), or the topmost containing window (if multiple frames are nested together). The hreflang attribute defines the language of the linked resource; however, it is purely advisory and actually does not have any power to set the language of a linked page (which may have a lang attribute set on its html element anyway). Lastly, the rel attribute defines the type of link. It has many possible values, as shown in Table 3-1.

■ **Note** The area element (discussed in Chapter 5) uses the same values shown in Table 3-1 for its rel attribute. Also, many of these values are also used in the link element (see the overlaps with Table 2-5 in Chapter 2).

---

*Table 3-1. The a element rel attribute values and descriptions. The * indicates values that are not found on the link element.*

rel value	Description
alternative	Links to an alternative form of the current document, such as a translation.
author	Links to a document that provides further information about the author of the nearest article or the whole document.
bookmark*	Links to a permalink URL for the nearest article or the whole document (such as the URLs used in a blog to link directly to a particular post).

external*	Links to a document that is not part of the current website.
help	Links to a help document that provides further information that is relevant to the context of where the link is placed.
license	Links to a copyright license that covers the current document.
next	Indicates the current document is part of a collection and that the link points to the next document in the series.
nofollow*	Indicates that the link is not endorsed by the user, meaning services such as search engines should not factor in the link in any ranking of the page based on a link analysis of the page.
noreferrer*	Indicates that the user agent should not notify the host of the linked document where the link came from.
prefetch	Identifies the linked resource as one that should be preemptively cached.
prev	Indicates the current document is part of a collection and that the links points to the previous document in the series.
search	Links to a resource that can be used to search through the current document and its related pages.
sidebar	Links to a document that is intended to be shown in the browser's sidebar (if it has one). Practically what this means is the link will be added as a bookmark in Firefox and Opera, while other browsers will treat it like a regular link.
tag	Indicates that tag-aware services and aggregators can determine that the link belongs in a certain category (as determined by the href attribute URL) and that the resource indicated can be considered as a part of a collection of related articles.

■ **Note** The WHATWG HTML specification defines a ping attribute for links (a elements and area elements— covered in Chapter 5) for defining URLs that should be notified when a link is visited. However, there is controversy over its inclusion (over concern it could be abused), and the W3C version of the HTML5 specification does not include this attribute. Until this is sorted out, you're best leaving this attribute alone for the time being.

Emphasis and importance: em and strong

While web browsers will usually display an em and strong with italic and bold text, respectively, these elements should not be viewed as a means to bold or italicize text, because that presentational function should be left to CSS style sheets; rather, the em element should be used to indicate *emphasis*, while the strong element should be used to indicate importance. Nesting either of these elements conveys more and more emphasis and/or importance on the enclosed content, for example:

```
<strong>CAUTION</strong>
<strong><strong>WARNING</strong></strong>
<strong><strong><strong>DANGER</strong></strong></strong>

<p>I am <em>worried!</em></p>
<p>I am <em><em>very</em> worried!</em></p>
```

You may not want your emphasis displayed in such a way. Remember that you can always restyle em and strong elements to display however you like, while still retaining their meaning. For instance, if the text of your document was in Japanese ideographic text, then you would be unlikely to need an italic version for emphasis. A change in background color would likely be more appropriate.

■ **Note** This preceding issue of internationalization is discussed in more detail in Molly E. Holzschlag's article "World Grows Small: Open Standards for the Global Web" (www.alistapart.com/articles/worldgrowssmall).

For the *City Press* web page, strong is used in the weather forecast to give the forecast values importance over the surrounding labels (for example, "High" and "Low"):

```
<aside>
        <h1>Weather</h1>
        <p><strong>Sunny</strong></p>
        <ul>
                <li>High: <strong>82°F</strong></li>
                <li>Low: <strong>70°F</strong></li>
        </ul>
</aside>
```

From a semantic point of view, the actual weather content is what is most important in this section, so the strong element is appropriately applied to the weather values and not to the surrounding labels.

■ **Note** The stricken-out temperatures shown in the *City Press* screenshot in Figure 3-7 will be added later in the "Inaccurate text" section.

Text set apart: i and b

The i and b elements historically are for the presentation of bold and italicized text and in practice will, without additional styling, appear visually indistinquishable from the em and strong elements in a web browser. So, why in HTML5 have they not been thrown into the obsolete bin? Each actually differs in subtle, semantic (meaning) ways that have been codified in HTML5. Although the em element is for emphasis, the i element is for offsetting text from other text so that when read, it may appear as being in a different voice or mood. What does that mean? Well, take the following text excerpt:

> *Simon smirked, "Yes, I'm happy to take the garbage out." "Ugh, I really don't want to!" he thought as he picked up the garbage bag.*

The second piece of speech is Simon's internal dialog, so it would be read in a different voice than what was actually spoken. The HTML for this text might look like:

```
<p>Simon smirked, "Yes, I'm happy to take the garbage out." "<i>Ugh, I <em>really</em> don't want to!</i>," he thought as he picked up the garbage bag.</p>
```

Notice an em has been thrown in there so you can see the difference in meaning between the two elements.

The i element may also be used when the content is a technical term or taxonomic designation or is a phrase in a foreign language. The *City Press* web page includes the French phrase "Oh là là," a good candidate for the i element! The HTML looks like this:

```
<i lang="fr">Oh là là!</i>
```

Note the use of the lang attribute to specify that this text is in the French language. Using the lang attribute has implications on how the browser handles text, because different languages can use different glyphs for quoted text, for instance.

The b element is for separating text without conveying any extra importance (in contrast to the strong element) or alternative voice or mood (in contrast to the i element). For example, product names in a product review might be set apart from the accompanying text using b. Or it could be used for ingredients in a recipe:

```
<p>After bringing <b>water</b> to a boil, add <b>potatoes</b> and <b>carrots</b></p>
```

Another use is in the lede (pronounced "lead") of an article or story. This is the first paragraph, which draws the reader in. It's not more important than the rest of the text, but it should stand out so as to grab attention. The *City Press* web page includes the following:

```
<p><b class="lede">Meteorologists predict more sunshine and scorching temperatures for the upcoming week, prompting area farmers to install irrigation systems.</b></p>
```

In this case, the purpose of the b element is specifically defined using a class attribute.

Side comments: small

Like i and b, small was traditionally used as a presentational element. It made text—you guessed it— smaller! This is a task that is much better suited to the CSS font-size property. In HTML5, small gains real semantic meaning. It now means the small print, fine print, side comments, all places that might hold legal disclaimers, license agreements, copyrights, and the like. It may also be used to indicate attribution of a piece of work, such as text or images. The reporter names in the *City Press* are placed in the small element. For example, at the end of the main photo's caption, the HTML reads as follows:

```
<small>Chris Elhorn | The City Press</small>
```

Inaccurate text: s

Yet another element that has changed meaning in HTML5, the s element historically meant strikethrough text and, being presentational in nature, was slated for the obsolete bin. However, in HTML5, s has been redefined as text that is no longer accurate or relevant. For example, the *City Press* web page shows temperatures in the weather sidebar. The values have been recently updated, so the old values are labeled inaccurate using the s element, while the new values are given importance using the strong element (as shown earlier in the "Emphasis and importance" section):

```
<ul>
        <li>High: <s>82°F</s> <strong>96°F</strong></li>
        <li>Low: <s>70°F</s> <strong>79°F</strong></li>
</ul>
```

■ **Note** In some cases, it may be necessary to mark text as having been deleted, such as when viewing page changes in a wiki (the more generic term for user-edited sites like Wikipedia). Although it may be tempting to use the s element for text that has been labeled deleted, there is the del element for that.

Highlighting text: mark

mark is a new element that can be used for highlighting some text for reference purposes. Think of it as a highlighter marking some text in a book. It also may be used to emphasize part of a quotation that was not emphasized in the original quote. In the *City Press* web page, the mark element is used in the blockquote in the lower right to add bold to the beginning text (by default most browsers would render content in mark as having a yellow background, but you can use CSS to change this):

```
<blockquote cite="#article1">
        <p><mark>We're all hoping it rains soon</mark>, some farmers have installed
        irrigation systems, at <em>considerable</em> expense</p>
</blockquote>
```

■ **Note** Notice that a fragment identifier is used in the cite attribute of the blockquote. This links it back to the original source article on the page, which has the attribute id="article1".

Inline quote: q

The q element is for adding inline quotes to a block of text. It is to phrasing content what blockquote is to flow content. This element has been around for a while but has in the past suffered from inconsistent browser support, so its use was not recommended. Things have gotten better, however, and the q element is finding wider support in modern web browsers. The browser is supposed to automatically include typographically correct quotation marks at the beginning and end of the quote, meaning that you, the author, should *not* include them. Furthermore, with judicious use of the lang attribute, those quotes should be displayed in the style appropriate to the specified language (for example, some European languages will use chevrons or *guillemets*: « and », instead of " and "). If that doesn't happen because of poor browser support, CSS can be used to append the appropriate quotes using ASCII codes and the quotes property. For instance, to append the proper quotes to a <q lang="fr"> element, use this:

```
q:lang(fr){ quotes: "\AB" "\BB" "\2018" "\2019"; }
```

However, this is not supported in Safari.

Also, browsers should display an awareness of nested quotes (in English, if a quote begins with the double-quote character, then quotes within that quote should use the single-quote character, and vice versa). So, for example, the following fragment of HTML:

```
<p><q>This is a quote that has a <q>nested quote</q> as part of it.</q></p>
```

should display as follows:

```
"This is a quote that has a 'nested quote' as part of it."
```

While this may all sound very exciting, the reality is more humdrum. For instance, Safari does not support this either, but the majority of other browsers do. While support has gotten better, you may still find q is best left out of your toolkit for the time being, even if it does provide a unique bit of semantics.

Handling terms: dfn and abbr

The dfn (definition) element is useful in marking the defining instance of a term that will be used repeatedly throughout a document. It is often used in combination with the abbr (abbreviation) element to define the first occurrence of an abbreviation or acronym for later reference. After using the dfn element, a definition for the term needs to appear within the same paragraph, description list (dl element), or section as the dfn element. Usually, this equates to having the text following the closing dfn tag define the term in question. In the *City Press* web page, a fictitious organization, the National Farm Association (NFA), is wrapped in an abbr element and, on its first occurrence in the text, a dfn element:

```
<dfn id="nfa"><abbr title="National Farm Association">NFA</abbr></dfn> (National Farm
Association)
```

It is highly recommended that you use the title attribute with the abbr element to provide a full-text expansion of the abbreviation when hovering over the element. Also, the dfn element is given an id attribute that can be used to link future occurrences of the abbreviation back to its defining instance:

```
<a href="#nfa"><abbr title="National Farm Association">NFA</abbr></a>
```

The link targets the earlier dfn element using a fragment identifier, so the user can jump back to where the meaning of "NFA" was defined in the text (in the parentheses that followed dfn) (Figure 3-10).

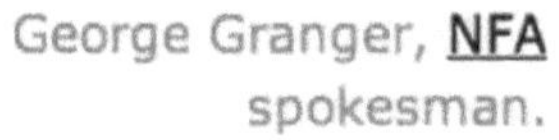

George Granger, <u>NFA</u>
    spokesman.

Figure 3-10. Abbreviations can be linked back to the first instance of where they were defined using the dfn element.

Subscript and superscript: sub and sup

There is a joke in science circles where two people are in a restaurant and the waitress asks what they would like to drink. The first replies "H_2O." The waitress then looks at the second patron, who thinks for a moment and says, "I'll have H_2O too!"

A short while later the waitress returns with their drinks. The first person takes a gulp from theirs. The second person gulps from theirs and falls to floor foaming at the mouth. "Idiot," the first exclaims.

The joke is that the second person—instead of appearing brainy like the first—inadvertently ordered "H_2O_2" (hydrogen peroxide) instead of H_2O (water).

While sup and sub (superscript and subscript) appear presentational in nature, as this joke demonstrates, they convey important meaning about the text they surround.

Consider the two following equations:

- $e=mc^2$

- e=mc2

Although they look alike, only one of the preceding equations is Einstein's; spelled out, the former equation is "e equals m times c squared," while the latter is "e equals m times c times 2."

■ **Note** For equations more complex than this, you should use Mathematical Markup Language (MathML), which is defined in a separate specification from that which describes HTML but may be embedded in an HTML document.

Or how about this:

- H_2O

- H2O

The first is chemical equation for water—two hydrogen atoms and one oxygen atom—and the second is simply the letter *H* followed by the number 2 and then the letter *O* and is meaningless. So, the placing and styling of the 2 is therefore important, and if you removed its styling and positioning and placed it in a style sheet, some browsers could lose the meaning.

The W3C also notes that some languages (other than English) require the use of subscripted and superscripted text. Here's an example in French: M[lle] Dupont.

Stylistically, superscripts and subscripts also appear in English. You'll most likely have seen them in dates or to indicate the presence of footnotes/endnotes:

- The 14th of September

- The committee report stated that the minister had acted in good faith[ii].

In the *City Press* example, a superscript appears in the date at the top of the page, inside a time element, which is discussed next:

```
<time datetime="2011-10-10">Monday, October 10<sup>th</sup>, 2011</time>
```

A specific date: time

The time element is an excellent addition to the HTML palette, especially for syndicated content. As mentioned at the beginning of the chapter, it defines a specific date in the Gregorian calendar. It may include a time and a time zone offset, but it doesn't need to do so. It's best to use the datetime attribute to specify the date/time exactly, because the actual contents can be fairly loose, for instance:

```
<time datetime="2011-05-08">Mother's Day</time>
```

The datetime attribute follows the format *YYYY-MM-DDThh:mm:ssTZD* (that is, 2011-10-23T10:23:44+05:00). The time and time zone portion are optional.

The only other attribute is a Boolean attribute, pubdate, which indicates the date/time is the publication date of the nearest article element or, if no articles are found, the document as a whole. The *City Press* web page uses this in the footer of its main article (where the publication date would usually be found):

```
<small>Posted <time datetime="2011-10-10T12:16:20Z" pubdate>October 10, 2011</time></small>
```

■ **Note** The Z in the time zone offset represents Universal Coordinated Time (UTC), which is the same as +00:00.

Breaking lines: br and wbr

The line break element, br (rendered as `<br>` or `<br />`, because it's self-closing) is typically used in content where a new line is an expected part of the content format, such as is the case with a postal address or poem. The *City Press* uses this in the footer section for the postal address:

```
<p>
<b>The City Press</b><br />
123 General Street<br />
Springfield, OH 45501
</p>
```

The other line breaking element, wbr (or `<wbr />`), is new in HTML5. It defines where in a word it would be OK to break to a new line if space didn't permit the whole word. In the *City Press* web page, a company named *IrrigationDirect* (all one word) is mentioned. This is a perfect candidate for the wbr element, because the HTML can instruct the browser to break the name in the middle if need be, and the name will still make sense. Here's the code:

```
<i>Irrigation<wbr />Direct</i>
```

Other text-level elements

This section covers a few stragglers that didn't get used in the *City Press* web page—let's briefly run through them anyway!

Title of a work: cite

The cite element represents the title of a work such as a book, song, film, TV show, a painting, and so on. We've already encountered the cite attribute, used within the blockquote element to attribute a source to the quote, but there is also a cite element to contain stand-alone references not associated with any particular element or citations of other material. Most user agents will display a citation in italic font, a typographic convention you'll often see in the print world as well.

Formatting computer I/O: code, var, samp, kbd

The code, var, samp, and kbd elements are all unchanged from the prior HTML specification. They define a fragment of computer code, a variable, sample output from a computing system, and user input, respectively. Since there is nothing new to report here, we will move along.

Marking text edits: ins and del

Sometimes it is useful to be able to indicate the edits that have occurred in a document, for instance, indicating what content has been added and what content has been deleted. For example, the administration area on a blog will have an area to create and edit posts. It can be useful to mark up and view the revisions to a blog post indicating what has changed from the original. HTML5 has just the elements for this purpose! The ins element is for marking the insertion of a piece of text, while the del element is used to mark a deletion. The important point here is that it is marking the content as edited, but the content would be expected to still be present (in the case of content marked removed with del).

JavaScript guru John Resig has an example script that uses ins and del to show the changes to an edited piece of text. You may view the example at http://ejohn.org/projects/javascript-diff-algorithm/.

■ **Note** Without further styling, the default appearance of ins text is usually underlined, while del is displayed with a strike-through. This means del will look like s by default; however, they certainly are not interchangeable. s is for marking inaccurate content, whereas del is for marking deleted content, regardless of whether it is accurate.

---

ins and del have two attributes, cite and datetime. The cite attribute is for specifying the web address of a document that explains the edit, while the datetime attribute is used to indicate the date and optionally the time the edit occurred. Refer to the time element earlier in this chapter for the formatting of this value, but it would look similar to this:

```
<p>
<ins datetime="2011-10-26T12:00Z" cite="edit10262011.html">new text</ins> is added, while
```

```
<del datetime="2011-10-27T12:30Z" cite="edit10272011.html">old text</del> is removed.
</p>
```

Handling foreign scripts

Several elements exist for the purpose of displaying the different formatting requirements and semantics of written scripts from around the world. While the Latin alphabet (used in English) has had a predominant presence on the Web for many years, as a global phenomenon the Web needs to be able to handle different alphabets correctly. The elements that follow will help format ruby notation and bidirectional text.

Ruby notation: ruby, rt, and rp

Ruby refers to a fragment of text that has an association with another fragment of text, known as the **base text**—it is most often used to provide a short annotation of the base text, or a pronunciation guide, and is used in East Asian typography. Typically it is presented with the ruby text appearing above the base text, but browser support varies, as shown in Figure 3-11.

This is ruby text This is ruby base	This is ruby text This is ruby base	This is ruby base (This is ruby text)

Figure 3-11. Ruby text rendered in (l to r), Safari, Chrome, Firefox

The text in Figure 3-11 has the following HTML source:

```
<ruby>
This is ruby base <rp>(</rp><rt>This is ruby text</rt><rp>)</rp>
</ruby>
```

As you can see, the top text is specified in the rt element. The rp element is for defining backup content for browsers that don't support ruby. In this case, they're used for setting up parentheses that show up on Firefox (Figure 3-11).

■ **Note** For more information on ruby notation, refer to the W3C Ruby Notation specification at www.w3.org/TR/ruby/.

Text direction: bdo and bdi

If you are marking up text in a foreign language, then you may find use for the bdo element (that's "bidirectional override") and the dir attribute (which is required for this element). bdo controls the direction of a text fragment and a block of text, respectively, and is best used when marking up Arabic and other languages that are written from right-to-left instead of left-to-right. Use bdo when the directionality of a word or phrase differs from the directionality set in the containing element. By default, the directionality of the containing element is left-to-right. Let's look at an example using English (even though this is all a left-to-right language, you'll be able to see the effect of the bdo element):

```
<p>When rendered by a browser, <bdo dir="rtl">these words</bdo> will appear as 'sdrow
eseht'</p>
```

This markup renders as shown in Figure 3-12.

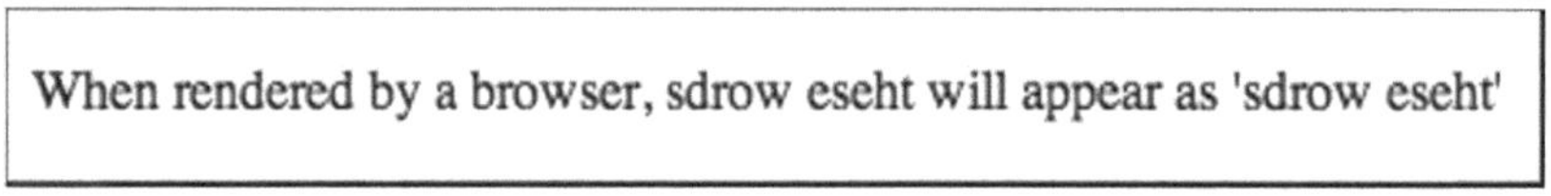

When rendered by a browser, sdrow eseht will appear as 'sdrow eseht'

Figure 3-12. The words "these words" have been reversed by the bdo element.

For a detailed overview of how to create pages that use right-to-left scripts, refer to the following W3C internationalization tutorial: www.w3.org/International/tutorials/bidi-xhtml/.

■ **Note** There is a new element called bdi that is meant for isolating a piece of text so that it can be formatted to flow left or right completely independent of the directionality of its surroundings. This element has yet to be implemented in any major browser, so you'll have to wait to use it, but the idea is that it might be used when the directionality of a particular piece of text is unknown. For example, multilingual comments left by visitors to a blog might include text written in left-to-right and right-to-left languages, but you wouldn't know beforehand which direction the text went in. Normally a block of text will inherit a left-to-right or right-to-left directionality from its parent element, but text appearing in bdi will ignore any inherited directionality settings and will set its dir attribute to auto by default, which seeks to detect the directionality of the text automatically based on its character set.

Summary

The goal with structured markup is to use the available elements as appropriately as possible. Sometimes the chosen elements will more closely describe their contents than other times. Sometimes the appropriate element to use will be ambiguous—in which case close study of the specification and a careful judgement call is warranted—but HTML5 provides a greater selection and better rules to follow than prior iterations of the language. The key is to stop thinking *visually*. If you are working from a design in Adobe Photoshop or Fireworks, then when it comes to building the site, you may find that it helps to begin by just forgetting about the style and typing in all your content—or placeholder text if you don't have all of your content at the time (http://lipsum.com is a good source of filler text)—straight into your document. By "content," I mean *everything*—not just body text but also any navigation, headers, footers, and so on. If something may end up as an image in the end (for example, a corporate logo), then don't worry about it at this stage. Just include some text in its place; you can always replace it with an inline image later if required.

As you do this, think about the content you're typing, think about how you would describe it to someone else, and think about what elements are available that fit your description. Forget about how things are going to look for now—don't think of an h1 as being "large, ugly, and bold" because that's just how it appears by default. Think about it as the heading—a bullet point—in the outline of your web page's content. As far as appearance goes, well, everything can be restyled using CSS.

CHAPTER 4

Form Mastery

In Chapter 2 we took a glance at what is new in web forms. Now it is time to turn our attention to them in more depth. Well, let's be honest, if that was said with excitement in many circles, even web-related ones, it may well be met with chuckles over the absurdity of getting excited over web forms. In the past, forms have been relegated to a unpleasant corner of web development, the domain of those interested in the finicky nit-picking of radio button groups, text input widths, and option-laden drop-down menus. Where's the sexy design and rich interactivity? But perhaps more importantly, where are all the form input types that should be there that instead needed to be hacked together using JavaScript? Form markup has been with us for many years, appearing at least as early as the HTML 2 specification, and has not changed in any remarkable way since then. It will be a relief to know then that in HTML5 the light has been cast on them, and they have grown into a capable set of input-handling HTML. Added are a capable new set of form input types, form elements, and attributes, as well as new methods for interfacing with JavaScript and CSS. With HTML5 a lot of functionality that had to be built in other ways is now given for free. Now that is exciting!

I begin this chapter by working through the available form markup, examining new features added to forms in HTML5 (and there are a lot), how best to use the different types of form controls, and how to enhance usability and accessibility with simple structural markup. We'll dissect a complete form and then finish off with some big-picture thoughts in regard to web form usability and related concerns.

Form markup refresher

In essence, forms are quite simple—they allow the user to input some data at one end and then send that data on to the other end to be dealt with by a form handler. A **form handler** typically means a script that processes the incoming form data, which is written in a server-side programming language or framework such as PHP, Python, or ASP.NET. Think of forms as the HTML equivalent of an intermediary for your data, located between you and the web page's server.

A form consists of a form element that establishes a container around any number of "form controls" (form HTML elements for gathering input) as well as any other body markup such as paragraphs and other flow content (however, having one form nested inside another is not allowed). Below all the input form controls will be a button of some sort for submitting the form—sending the entered data off to the server. Forms can send data using two different methods: GET and POST. The most obvious difference between these methods is that when using the GET method, the data from a form submission appears in the website's address URL. For example, the URL of a form submitted using the GET method might look like this:

```
handle_form.php?name=Anselm+Bradford&age=31.
```

which could have been the result of submitting the form in Figure 4-1.

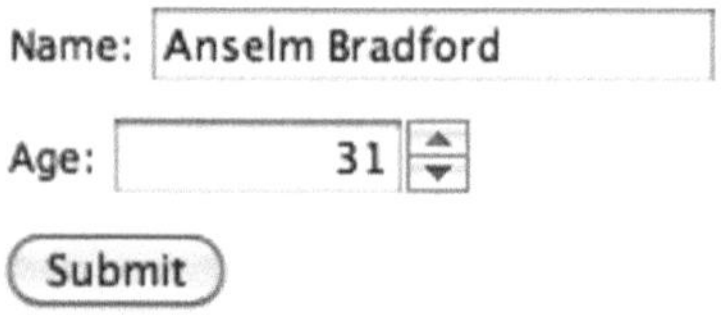

Name: Anselm Bradford

Age: 31

Submit

Figure 4-1. A simple web form for gathering user input

For this form, the HTML may look like this:

```
<form method="get" action="handle_form.php">
    <p><label>Name: <input name="name" /></label></p>
    <p><label>Age: <input type="number" name="age" /></label></p>
    <p><button type="submit">Submit</button></p>
</form>
```

This example uses a PHP script to process the form, but plenty of other server-side languages could be used such as ASP.NET, Python, or others. In the case of PHP, there are three "superglobal" variables that allow it to access the data submitted in a form. The variables $_GET and $_POST get access to form data submitted via the GET and POST methods, respectively, while $_REQUEST acts as a container for all data submitted, regardless of the method. For instance, to echo back (display in the web browser) the values submitted in the previous form, the following PHP code might be used:

```
<p>
<?php
if (isset($_REQUEST["name"]) && isset($_REQUEST["age"])){
    echo "Name: " . $_REQUEST["name"] . "<br />";
    echo "Age: " . $_REQUEST["age"];
}
?>
</p>
```

■ **Note** This is just a simple example used to display what was submitted; in a production environment, form input would need to be screened to ensure no malicious code was submitted as part of the form field data. For instance, for a form that updated a database, SQL commands could be entered into the form, and if the server-side script was not written to filter out commands of this sort, a malicious user could potentially delete data in the database or worse!

Dissecting the form element

Ignoring the other elements for the moment, the form element is quite simple, existing only as a container with a handful of attributes. In addition to the method and action attributes shown earlier, the form element has the following attributes (as well as the global attributes listed in Chapter 2): accept-charset, autocomplete, enctype, name, novalidate, and target. One attribute, accept, has been tossed to the obsolete bin in HTML5, while two attributes, autocomplete and novalidate, are new. Here's an example of a fully constructed form element:

```
<form action="handle_form.php" method="post" target="_blank" accept-charset="UTF-8"
enctype="multipart/form-data" autocomplete="off" novalidate>
```

While this uses all the attributes (excluding the global ones), it is not necessary to enter all or any attributes, because they are all optional. Typically, at very least the action and method (as in the earlier example) attributes will be specified. In the next section, we will discuss what each of these attributes do, so you can decide for yourself which you need.

Form element attributes

The following sections describe each of the form attributes in detail.

The action attribute

The action attribute tells the user agent (the web browser) what it's supposed to do with the contents of the form when the form is submitted (with a submit button, which is a form control element we'll discuss later). As in the earlier example, a server-side script can be specified to handle the submitted form data. If it is omitted, the form will redirect to the same URL it is submitted from.

The method attribute

The method attribute is where the form is set to use GET (the default) or POST. The general rule of thumb is that if the form submission is actively modifying data (such as updating a server-side database in some way) or includes sensitive information (such as a password), your form should use **POST**. On the other hand, if the form submission is passive, such as a database query for a search engine, then use **GET**. Why? Having the data visible in the page's URL (using GET) will allow the page to be bookmarked, which is useful for a search query, while not having it in the URL (using POST) offers better security for sensitive data. Also, GET is better suited to short amounts of data since it has size limitations because the URL can only be so long (the actual length varies by web browser).

The accept-charset attribute

The accept-charset attribute allows you to specify which character encodings the server can handle in the submitted form data. If not specified (the usual scenario), the character set of the page is used (as should be set in the head section using the meta element and/or sent in the server's HTTP response header). This attribute can be a space-separated list of values if several character sets are acceptable; however, to avoid issues of characters displaying incorrectly, always use UTF-8 when dealing with encoding. UTF-8 supports all the world's major languages.

The enctype attribute

The enctype attribute is used to specify how to encode the form data when it is sent. It takes three possible values: application/x-www-form-urlencoded, multipart/form-data, and text/plain. In most cases, it can be omitted, because it will default to the first value mentioned, which will encode the data in a URL-safe manner. This is typically needed to differentiate ambiguous form data from other information. For instance, if some form data had a forward slash (a solidus) in it, this would cause problems if it were placed in the URL of the web page in an unencoded state, since forward slashes mean to move to a new directory on the web server. Instead, a forward slash would be sent as %2F, which is the hexadecimal value assigned to a forward slash in the UTF-8 character set. Even if the POST method is used to send the data, this format will help pick out the form data from other information sent to the web server.

The time to change this attribute is when using a file input element (for uploading files, which is described later), in which case this attribute should contain a value of `multipart/form-data`, which allows the form to cope with binary data. The last value, `text/plain`, sends the form data unencoded. This value generally should not be used because it makes it difficult to pick out the form data. It is available mostly for historical reasons.

The target attribute

The `target` attribute works like the `target` attribute found on links (the a element) and tells the browser where to open the URL specified in the `action` attribute. The value `_blank` will open the form submittal result in a new window, `_self` will open it in the same window, and `_parent` will open it in the parent browsing context. For instance, an `iframe` element could be used to embed an HTML page with a form inside another HTML page, which would be considered the nested HTML page's parent browsing context. Lastly, the value of `_top` would load the page in the topmost page, if the form were nested several pages deep (using multiple `iframe`s, for example).

The name attribute

The next attribute, `name`, is used to identify the form to scripts. It's essentially a unique ID given to a form to identify it among all forms used on a page. In JavaScript, forms can be accessed through the `document.forms` property, which contains a reference to all forms on the page. For instance, for a form that has the attribute `name="contactform"`, the JavaScript `document.forms.contactform` could be used to access it. If you are not very familiar with JavaScript, just know that you could use the `id` (or even `class`) attribute to access a form as well, and that may well be a better route to take toward interacting with a form from JavaScript.

The autocomplete and novalidate attributes

Finally, the last two attributes, `autocomplete` and `novalidate`, will be discussed more later, but in brief they tell the browser whether to automatically fill in remembered values in the form and whether to validate the form's input, respectively.

Gathering input

The `form` element is just a container for data-gathering elements, called **form controls**, which are the `input`, `select`, and `textarea` elements. The specifics of how each of these work will be addressed in due course, but first it is important to make note of an attribute they all use: the name attribute. Unlike the name attribute that appears on the `form` element, this attribute has more of a critical role in this context. All form controls that are passing data to the form handler must have a name attribute; otherwise, they will not pass their values on when the form is submitted. Except for cases where form controls are being grouped together, such as is the case for radio buttons, the name attribute value should be unique so that a particular form input value can be picked out from the rest. For example, the following form snippet shows two input fields:

```
...
    <input name="firstname" type="text" value="Anselm" />
    <input name="lastname" type="text" value="Bradford" />
...
```

The name/value pair here is *firstname/Anselm* and *lastname/Bradford* (these values are the default set using the `value` attribute but could be changed via data input by the user). As discussed earlier, if the form were submitted using the GET method (and the web page filename was `handle_form.php`), then the URL of the page would look like this:

`handle_form.php?firstname=Anselm&lastname=Bradford`

This shows the `name` attributes and their associated values in the URL.

Generally, the real heart of a form will be found in the shape-shifting `input` element. I call it shape-shifting because the `input` element is rather unique among the HTML elements in that it can take on many different appearances and behaviors, depending on the value in its type attribute. The type attribute takes one of a set of keywords as its value. For example, the preceding example sets the input type to be a text input for both form controls with `type="text"`. The list of available types has been substantially increased in HTML5, as shown in Table 4-1. The appearance of each input type will be determined by the web browser (and will likely vary between browsers) but can be styled with CSS.

■ **Note** If no `type` attribute is specified on the `input` element or if a type is used that is not yet supported in your preferred web browser, the input type will become a one-line text input field.

Table 4-1. *Form input types*

■ NEW in HTML5	Attribute	Description
	button	A clickable button
	checkbox	A clickable check box
■	color	A color picker
■	date	A date picker
■	datetime	A date and time picker (UTC time zone)
■	datetime-local	A date and time picker (local time zone)
■	email	A text field for e-mail addresses
	file	A file upload button

	hidden	Arbitrary value used for sending additional metadata with the form submission
	image	An image used as a form submission button
■	month	A date picker with a year and month
■	number	A numerical input
	password	An obscured text field
	radio	A radio button
■	range	A slider for a range of values
	reset	A button for resetting the form values
■	search	A search field
	submit	A button for submitting the form
■	tel	A text field for a telephone number
	text	A generic single-line text field
■	time	A time picker
■	url	A text field for a URL
■	week	A date picker with a year and a week

Original input types

Traditionally input had a small set of possible types: text, password, file, checkbox, radio, hidden, button, reset, submit, and image. To acquaint you with the different types, we'll briefly run through the original ones and then introduce the new ones in more depth.

■ **Note** As I cover the input types in the sections that follow, I provide screenshots for many of the form input fields. Don't be surprised if what you see here doesn't exactly match up to what appears in your own preferred web browser. Some fields may look different, some may function slightly different, or some may not be supported at all. There is a rapidly improving landscape of browser support for the new form elements and other features codified in the HTML5 specification. However, the goal here is not to show you exactly which browser to use to find a particular form input field; rather, it is to show you what is possible in the most up-to-date web browsers and what to expect, we hope, in the coming iterations of browsers that are still catching up. It is the road ahead, whether that is demonstrated by Safari, Chrome, Opera, Firefox, or Internet Explorer.

Text input

A text input is used, unsurprisingly, for gathering typed text input. This is the default type the input uses, and it is likely the most common input you have encountered. It is a single-line control and normally appears in the form of a rectangular box with an inset border, as shown in Figure 4-2.

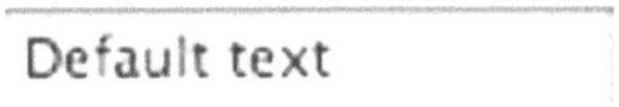

Default text

Figure 4-2. A text input showing some content entered into the input

The allowed length of the input string can be specified with the addition of a maxlength attribute, which takes a numerical value equating to the maximum number of allowed characters. There is not a direct feedback mechanism provided in the event that the user tries to insert more than the allowed number of characters—the form control just ceases to accept extra characters and will truncate an overlong string if such a string is pasted into the control. If you want to alert users that they've run out of room, you'll need to use JavaScript.

Note The maxlength attribute isn't foolproof; longer lengths of text can be added to a text input via JavaScript, for instance, and this text would be submitted to the server without being truncated. To limit the length of text submitted with complete certitude, the length would need to checked on the server as well.

You can also include a value attribute that presets the content of the text control:

```
<input type="text" name="data" value="Default text" />
```

The text entered into the value attribute will appear inside the text field when the page loads, as shown in Figure 4-2.

Note Using the value attribute is a way to include default data that gets submitted if the user doesn't update the input's value before submitting the form. The value attribute has also traditionally been the way to prompt the user on what to type into a text field. This is such a common need in fact that HTML5 has added an attribute for such "placeholder" text. But don't worry about this feature for now because it will be covered later in this chapter!

Password input

A `password` input is almost identical to a text input; functionally the only difference is that character input is masked upon entry, usually by a series of dots, as shown in Figure 4-3. It shares the same possible attributes as a text input; the only difference is that the type attribute is set to `type="password"`.

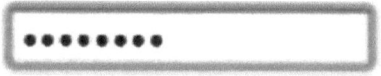

Figure 4-3. A password input showing text being entered

This type of input is not very secure—the form data will still be transmitted as plain text and will be visible in the URL if your form uses the `GET` method. This visual masking is really only to hinder anybody peering over your shoulder from seeing the input (for example, when you're in a public place and you're logging into your bank's website).

File input

A `file` input usually takes the form of a browse button of some sort and an area displaying information about the file that has been selected, if any. The appearance varies significantly between browsers, more so than with other common input types, as shown in Figure 4-4.

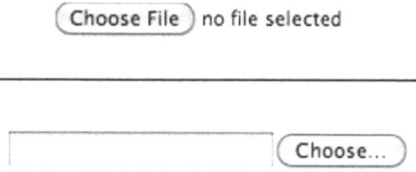

Figure 4-4. The appearance of the file input control in two different web browsers, Google Chrome (top) and Opera (bottom)

The file input control allows you to browse for a file on your local network for the purposes of uploading it to a website. Once you have selected the file, the file is displayed in some way, depending on the web browser, as shown in Figure 4-5.

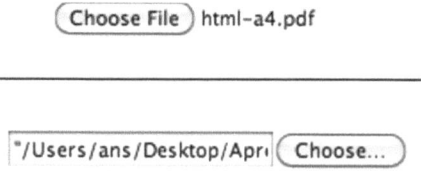

Figure 4-5. The appearance of the file input control in two different web browsers: Google Chrome (top) shows the filename while Opera (bottom) displays the path to the file.

As mentioned earlier, for a form to successfully send binary data, such as is the case when uploading a file, set the enctype attribute on the associated form to `enctype="multipart/form-data"`. This will properly format the form data so that the file is available to a server-side script to process.

114

■ **Note** In PHP, there is a global variable called `$_FILES` that can be used to get access to the uploaded file(s). You can find information on handling uploaded files in PHP at `http://php.net/manual/en/features.file-upload.php`.

By default only one file can be uploaded at a time; however, by adding the Boolean `multiple` attribute to the file input control, multiple files can be selected for uploading:

```
<input type="file" name="filedata" multiple />
```

Without this attribute, only one file at a time can be selected in the operating system's file browser; however, with this attribute included, the Command key (Mac) or Control key (Windows) can be held down to select multiple files. Again, the appearance of the file input control will vary by browser, but it may look like Figure 4-6.

Figure 4-6. The appearance of the file input control in Safari after multiple files have been selected

---

■ **Note** As is unfortunately all too commonly the case for contemporary HTML features, don't expect Internet Explorer support for the `multiple` attribute for the foreseeable future. However, it does work on Windows if another major web browser is used.

The `file` input includes an `accept` attribute, which can in theory be used to restrict the types of files uploaded; however, in practice it is purely advisory and likely will be ignored. It accepts a comma-separated list of MIME types pertaining to acceptable file types, which, for example could look like `accept="image/gif,image/jpeg,image/jpg"`. This would advise the browser that the server accepts only GIF and JPEG images. Even if the browser heeds this attribute, in a production environment you will need to use a server-side filter to check that the files submitted are in fact the correct types, since client-side checks of this sort are easily circumvented.

Check boxes

This is the old check box we know and love for gathering input that is either true or false. Along with text inputs, this is one of the most common input types you are likely to run into. A `checkbox` input usually takes the form of a square box that can be checked or unchecked, but using JavaScript, a third "indeterminate" state can be set that gives the appearance of neither being in a true or false condition, as shown in Figure 4-7.

Figure 4-7. Three check boxes: one unchecked and one not, and one in an indeterminate state

The indeterminate state is set through the Boolean indeterminate property on the checkbox element, like so:

```
function init() {
        document.getElementById("option3").indeterminate = true;
}
window.onload = init;
```

This code would be placed in a script (either in a script element on the page or, preferably, in an external file) and would affect the following HTML snippet:

```
<input type="checkbox" name="option3" id="option3" />
```

To set a check box to the checked state, a Boolean checked attribute is added. Only check boxes that are checked will have their data submitted with the form. The value attribute can be used to set the value sent when the form is submitted, but it may be omitted, in which case the default value will be the text "on." The check boxes in Figure 4-7 might look like this:

```
<input type="checkbox" name="option1" id="option1" />
<input type="checkbox" name="option2" id="option2" checked />
<input type="checkbox" name="option3" id="option3" />
```

When these are submitted as part of a form, the web page's URL will be appended with the querystring ?option2=on (if using the GET method).

Radio buttons

Like check boxes, radio buttons are probably something you have run into before. They are perhaps a little less common but still widely prevalent on the Web. A radio input has two states, either selected or not, as shown in Figure 4-8.

Figure 4-8. Two radio buttons, one selected and one not

You use radio buttons to indicate that only one choice out of several—a **radio group**—can be selected.

To indicate to the user agent that a radio button is part of a group, you give each radio input element an identical value for their name attribute. When the form is rendered, the user agent will not allow more than one radio input to be selected if that input shares a name value with another. Here's the markup for the preceding example:

```
<input type="radio" name="example" value="first" />
<input type="radio" name="example" value="second" checked />
```

As you can see in the previous code, the state of a radio button can, like a check box, be preset with the checked attribute.

■ **Note** A real-world form would also include form labels, but we'll get to those in the section "Adding structure with fieldsets and labels."

Adding hidden input

A hidden input type is used to include extra data within a form that is not visible to the user but is submitted along with the rest of the form data. Here is an example:

```
<input type="hidden" name="hiddenValue" value="42" />
```

When the form that contained this input is submitted, the value hiddenValue=42 would appear in the URL (if using the GET method) and would be passed to the server side along with the other data in the form.

■ **Note** A hidden input is sometimes used with the file input type to tell the server the maximum file size that is acceptable to upload. For instance, a form might include the following input to tell the server script that a file upload should be limited to a maximum 20 kilobytes (approximately) in file size:

```
<input type="hidden" name="MAX_FILE_SIZE" value="20000" />.
```

Button, submit, reset, and image inputs

The button input type has a lot of overlaps with the button element (discussed later in this chapter), and between the two, the button element is probably the better choice to use. Both create a clickable button with a text label, but the essential difference is that the button element can use HTML elements in its label, whereas the button input type can use only plain text (see the "Submitting forms using buttons and images" section later in this chapter for an example), making it less flexible. The submit and reset types create buttons as well, with the additional ability to submit the form (send the data to the server) and reset the form values to their default values when clicked. As with the button input, button can be used for these tasks as well. In short, if it looks like a button, use the button element!

The last type, image, is for using an image in place of a submit button; it will be discussed later in the "Submitting forms using buttons and images" section.

New input types

As you saw in Table 4-1, there is a great variety of new types for the input element. Some are more general, such as the input for numbers, while others are very specific, such as creating a color picker.

■ **Note** Many of the form elements are not yet implemented in modern web browsers. Opera and Google Chrome seem to be leading the pack, but for those that do not support the new types, the input fields will fall back to the default—the basic text input. As with other HTML5 features, you can use Modernizr (http://www.modernizr.com) to detect support for the new input types. To add support for features missing in older web browsers, you can use a script such as html5Widgets, which is a JavaScript polyfill—meaning it fills in missing form features using

---

JavaScript in browsers that do not support them natively. Download the html5Widgets script and find implementation details at `https://github.com/zoltan-dulac/html5Widgets`.

Color picker

The `color` input type creates a **color picker** (also known as a **color well**) that can be used to choose colors, as shown in Figure 4-9. The color values are sent as URL-encoded[1] hexadecimal values on form submission. For instance, black (the default) will be sent as %23000000, where "%23" is the URL-encoding for the hash symbol (#), which means %23000000 is the color value #000000 (which is the more usual way of encountering colors in, for example, CSS code).

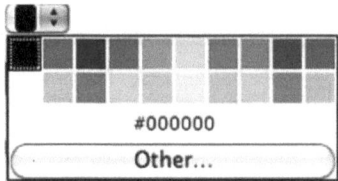

Figure 4-9. Pop-up color picker created with the color input type, as shown in the Opera web browser

This particular input may seem rather esoteric, and you may even go so far as to ask yourself when you would actually need it. Here's an example to get your gears turning on how it could be used: a search engine that includes a "search-by-color" feature, perhaps as part of a search form for a car dealership that allowed the user to include a preferred color in their search for a new car:

```
<p><label>Preferred color: <input type="color" name="carcolor" /></label></p>
```
[2]

While you might not find yourself using this input very often, when you need it, it's certainly invaluable to have. And at the end of the day, how cool is it to be able add some color to a form, literally, when so often forms are a sea of bland text input fields?

Date and time input

Date/time controls are a common requirement for websites that need to gather input for a specific date and time, such as airline booking sites or hotel accommodation booking systems. To address this need, HTML5 has added quite a few inputs related to selecting particular date and time values and ranges. The `date`, `time`, `datetime`, `datetime-local`, `month`, and `week` input types create finer- or coarser-grained methods of gathering time and date information. These form controls typically feature a numerical stepper and/or what looks like a standard drop-down list (Figure 4-10). The most sophisticated implementation at the moment, in Opera, produces a pop-up calendar control when clicked for selecting the desired date (Figure 4-11).

---

[1] URL-encoded means special characters are converted to a code that is safe to transmit via a website URL address.
[2] As mentioned in an earlier example, we'll get to the `label` element later.

2011-10-31

01:38

2011-10-3   04:38   UTC

2011-10-3   01:38

2011-1(

2011-W4‹

Figure 4-10. All the different date- and time-related inputs as shown in the Opera web browser. From top to bottom: date, time, datetime, datetime-local, month, week.

2011-W4‹							
◀		October		▶	2011		
Week	Mon	Tue	Wed	Thu	Fri	Sat	Sun
39	26	27	28	29	30	1	2
40	3	4	5	6	7	8	9
41	10	11	12	13	14	15	16
42	17	18	19	20	21	22	23
43	24	25	26	27	28	29	30
44	31	1	2	3	4	5	6
				Today			

Figure 4-11. A pop-up for a date/time control showing the calendar control available natively in Opera

Perhaps more than any other control, these input types show how much potentially comes for free with the new additions to web forms. The calendar control in Figure 4-11 is provided natively by the web browser with one line of HTML, which would normally require a significant amount of JavaScript, CSS, and HTML to create. As of the time of writing, Opera is the only browser providing a calendar control natively, so a JavaScript/CSS/HTML solution is still the route that is needed for the majority of contemporary web browsers. Unfortunate as this is, utilizing what the browser provides natively, where possible, will prepare your pages to transition to a natively provided interface once wider support is gained for these input types. We can only hope that other web browsers will catch up shortly, but in the meantime, a project such as jQueryUI (http://jqueryui.com) can be used in conjunction with Modernizr (http://modernizr.com) to provide a fallback for when the date/time inputs are not supported. jQueryUI includes a calendar control called datepicker (http://jqueryui.com/demos/datepicker/) that produces a calendar control very much like that in Figure 4-11, but since it is not a native control, circumstances where JavaScript is disabled would need to be handled if the control were a critical part of the form input.

To preset the input with a date/time, the value attribute can be supplied with a string of text that sets the initial value. Table 4-2 shows the format of this text string for each date/time input type.

Table 4-2. How to format the value attribute for different date/time input types

Input type	Value text string	Example
date	YYYY-MM-DD	2011-10-31
time	hh:mm:ss.s	12:39:20.5
datetime	YYYY-MM-DDThh:mm:ss.sZ	2011-11-14T07:14:02.25Z
datetime-local	YYYY-MM-DDThh:mm:ss.s	2011-12-25T22:45:12.02
month	YYYY-MM	2011-10
week	YYYY-Wnn	2011-W44

YYYY = Year

MM = Month

DD = Day

hh = Hour

mm = Minute

ss = Second

s = Decimal fraction of a second, such as .75 for three quarters of a second

T = *T* is used as a separator between date and time values

Z = Time zone for Zulu time, otherwise known as Coordinated Universal Time (UTC)

Wnn = Week number, starting at 1 for the first week in January and ending at 52 for the last week in December

Note the difference between datetime and datetime-local in Table 4-2. The *Z* in datetime means the entered date and time are sent to the server with the expectation that they are in the UTC time zone (in England, for example). This gives the time a common time zone, which may be easier to work with, but it means the server, the client, or the user would need to offset this time zone to get to their own. The other type, datetime-local, does not include a time zone value, so the data is expected to be in the time zone of wherever the visitor is located when they submit the form.

This same text string formats in Table 4-2 can also be used with the min and max attributes, which can be used to create a date range with a minimum and/or maximum allowed date/time value. Also, the attribute step can be added to set the amount a date/time field can be moved by. For instance, for the input types involving time (time, datetime, and datetime-local), there is a default step of 60 seconds—meaning each click of the control to advance the value will move it 1 minute forward (or backward). For the input types that include time, the step attribute is expressed in seconds, so by adding step="120", the default value would be changed to 2 minutes (60 seconds multiplied by two) instead of 1 minute. The date, week, and month input types have larger units of measurement and have default step values of 1 day, 1 week, and 1 month, respectively. For example, the following code snippet would provide a control that would allow the selection of every other week (by setting the step to 2 weeks) and would be limited to dates during the (northern hemisphere) summer:

```
<input type="week" name="event" step="2" min="2011-W25" max="2011-W38" />
```

Numerical inputs: number and range

The number input type does what you'd expect—it handles numerical input. In supporting browsers, the appearance is a stepper control like that of the time input type (Figure 4-12). As with the date/time controls, the min and max attributes can be used to confine the range of possible numbers within a range. Also, the step attribute can be used to increment or decrement the value by a certain amount (the default is 1). Fractional values can be used if the min and/or step attributes are set to a decimal value.

Figure 4-12. A number input type with a value being entered

In situations where displaying the actual value of the number isn't of utmost importance, there is the range input type (Figure 4-13), which displays a draggable slider between a minimum and maximum value (0 and 100 by default). The min, max, and step attributes can be set on this type as well.

Figure 4-13. By default the range does not show the value it is currently at.

Search input

The search input type is the simplest of the new types added in HTML5. Depending on the browser, it may be indistinguishable from a regular text input type control. So, why is it there? This is an addition added primarily for semantic reasons. Setting a form input type to search separates that field from other text fields on the page. In the future, this may be used to apply functionality or behavior expected of a search field. For instance, Safari currently adds an x button to the right of the search field that clears any text typed in the field (Figure 4-14). This is consistent with how the built-in web search field in the toolbar behaves.

Figure 4-14. Safari provides a button for clearing the search by default on search input types.

Personal details: e-mail, phone, and website URL inputs

Like the search input type, the last three input types—email, tel, and url—are just text fields with additional semantic meaning attached. They even look like regular generic text input fields (Figure 4-2), but under the surface, they have a special quality that will save you a lot of time fiddling with scripts on your page. They are great examples for showcasing a new feature in HTML5—built-in form validation! Let's get to that next.

Validating and submitting forms

I mentioned in passing when discussing the form element that there is an attribute called novalidate that can be added to a form to bypass a number of validation rules that would otherwise be checked on the input. It's like dialing back the form to the old days. I merely mention its existence should you want to do that, but let's look at what these validation rules are about instead.

Take the email input type; it provides the semantic meaning that whatever text is entered into it will be in the form of a valid e-mail address. This is something that the web browser can check when the form is submitted. If the entered value is not a properly formed e-mail address, the browser can throw up an error message to tell the user to enter a correct value (Figure 4-15).

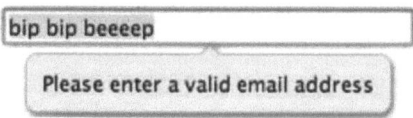

Figure 4-15. Invalid text entered into an email *input type field produces a validation error when the form is submitted.*

For browsers that don't support the new HTML5 client-side validation, a JavaScript by Weston Ruter called webforms2.js can be included to provide support. This script can be downloaded at https://github.com/westonruter/webforms2.

■ **Note** It's a good rule of thumb to double-check the input received from a form on the server side as well. The client-side validation behavior shown here is primarily to increase the usability of your forms. They provide the user with some immediate feedback that they entered the wrong type of information, without necessitating you create that functionality yourself using JavaScript or other means. When it comes to processing the data on the server side, you will want to check it again to make sure the correct type of information was submitted. Who knows, maybe the user visited your form from some obscure web browser that doesn't support client-side validation and slipped through all your browser-sniffing checks and managed to mangle their e-mail address when entering it into the form. These things happen, so double-check the submitted data on the server.

By default the email input type supports only one e-mail address being entered and will fail validation if more than one is added to the field. This can be changed, however, if the Boolean attribute multiple is added the input field. It will then tolerate a comma-separated list of e-mail addresses entered into a single field.

The url input type will also complain if the wrong kind of information is entered into the field. Any malformed URL address entered will throw a validation error similar to Figure 4-15. Additionally, it will add http:// when needed to complete a full URL address.

The tel input type is a bit looser in that it is not looking for a particular format but will complain if non-numerical characters are entered. It can't be strict on the format of the numbers since telephone number formats differ around the world. To refine this input type so that it *does* validate a particular telephone number format, there is attribute just for that purpose. Called the `pattern` attribute, this attribute takes a **regular expression (regex)**[3] as a value and validates input into the field based on whether it matches the regex. Regex is a topic that is beyond the scope of this book, but as a quick example, the following code snippet would limit input into the telephone field only to the format NNN-NNN-NNNN, where the first digit would be a number between 2 and 9 and the rest would be between 0 and 9[4]:

```
<input type="tel" name="usphone" pattern="^[2-9]\d{2}-\d{3}-\d{4}$" />
```

It is cryptic looking for sure! If you want to discover how regex works, do a quick web search for *regex*, and you will find loads of resources. For some handy, prebuilt regex patterns to match everything from credit card numbers to latitude and longitude, check out `http://html5pattern.com`, which also includes a test bed where you can develop and test your own patterns.

■ **Note** The `pattern` attribute isn't just found on the telephone input type; it's found on all the text-based input types. Those are `text`, `search`, `url`, `tel`, `email`, and `password`.

Making input required

A simpler form (pun unintended) of validation is requiring that certain fields and form controls be given at least some kind of value before the form is submitted. This is where the Boolean `required` attribute can be utilized. By adding this attribute to a form control:

```
<p><input type="text" name="example" required /></p>
```

an error pop-up will appear if nothing is entered into the field (Figure 4-16).

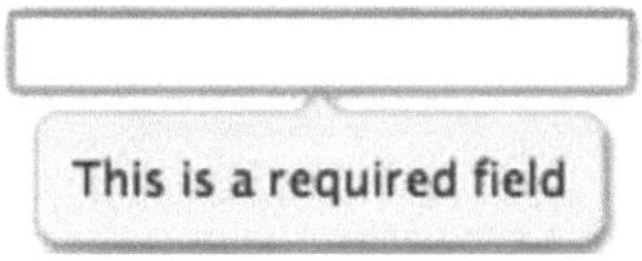

Figure 4-16. A validation error showing that a required field was not filled in

Submitting forms using buttons and images

A submit button is used to submit all the form data to the file indicated in the form's `action` attribute (or to itself, if no `action` attribute is specified). As mentioned earlier in the chapter, the `button` element is a

---

[3] A regex is a very compact syntax for matching text that fits a particular pattern.
[4] Ideally, a regex should be built with flexibility in mind in certain respects but strict where it needs to be. This simple example is not wholly ideal, because it requires dashes between the numbers. Better would be a regex that handled any combination of dashes or no dashes as long as the appropriate sequence of digits was there.

more flexible option than the input element for creating buttons. For instance, compare the two lines of code in the following HTML snippet, which produces the buttons in Figure 4-17:

```
<p><input type="submit"/></p>
<p><button type="submit"><img src="star.png" alt=""
/><strong><em>Submit!</em></strong></button></p>
```

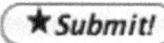

Figure 4-17. Two submit buttons, one created with the input element (top) and the other created with the button element (bottom)

Since the button element is not a self-closing element, it allows HTML to be enclosed within the text that creates its label, which provides the possibility of greater styling of the label.

If the type attribute is set to type="reset", a reset button is created. A reset button input resets all form controls within the same form to their initial values. Including a reset button used to be a common practice, but it's since become unfashionable because of the high risk of users accidentally resetting their form instead of submitting it. Without any undo function, reset buttons are of little use and should be used with caution, if at all.

■ **Note** Come on, we've all done it: reached the end of a form, tabbed to what we thought was the submit button, pressed Enter, and watched in despair as all our form data promptly vanished. If you're ever thinking of including a reset button on a form, just try to remember how many times in the past you have filled in a form, reached the end, and thought, "Actually, I think I'll just delete all of that and not bother." Exactly.

One use case where the button element's submission type does not overlap with the input element is if you want to use an image as a submit button, in which case an input with a type attribute of image and an additional src attribute need to be used. While an image can be used inside a button (like in Figure 4-17), using an image input control makes the entire image the button, without any additional UI elements added by the browser. The src attribute points to where the image file resides on the server, just like an img. Also like an img, remember to include an alt attribute that describes the purpose of the image, for accessibility reasons.

Using an image for a submit button will also send x and y coordinates along as values (the x and y coordinates of the location in the image you clicked); this is for when image submits are being used in conjunction with a server-side image map. And if your image has a name attribute, that will also get sent along with those coordinates. For instance, if your form uses the GET method, an image submit button like this:

```
<input type="image" name="imagesubmit"/>
```

will pass values like this:

```
handle_form.php?imagesubmit.x=10&imagesubmit.y=20
```

If you aren't doing anything with these values, don't worry about them. They don't do any harm when they're submitted along with the rest of the form data. If you really want to prevent them from showing up in the URL, then you can change the method attribute of the form from GET to POST, which will hide all values from the user.

Other common input element attributes

While not central to the functionality of the form controls, several attributes are worth noting. To begin with, there are a number of attributes that can be used to override a form's behavior on specific elements. Table 4-3 lists these attributes, which you can see by their names will override specific values set in the attributes for the parent form element (refer to the discussion of the attributes on the form element if need be).

Table 4-3. Form input controls' form overriding attributes

Attribute	Description	Applies to
formaction	Overrides form's action attribute	button or input elements where type is set to submit or reset
formenctype	Overrides form's enctype attribute	
formmethod	Overrides form's method attribute	
formtarget	Overrides form's target attribute	
formnovalidate	Overrides form's novalidate attribute	button or input elements

Each form control element (button, input, and so on) also has an attribute called form, which can be used to associate a form control element with a form that is different from the one it is contained in within the HTML structure. This is perhaps clearer if viewed through some example code:

```
<form id="form1">
    <p><button type="submit">Submit!</button></p>
</form>
<form id="form2">
    <p><input name="example" form="form1 form2" /></p>
    <p><button type="submit">Submit!</button></p>
</form>
```

In this case, the input element with the name example has its form attribute set to the value form1 form2, which means it is treated as if its containing forms were form1 and form2. When either form is submitted, the example input control will be submitted as well. In this way, the form attribute can be used to simulate a nested form, even though that structure is not allowed in HTML. The form attribute can also be set on submit buttons so that one submit button can submit another form. This feature could be used if, for example, you had a search field in the header and footer of your page and you wanted both search inputs to be submitted to the same form. Instead of putting the whole page content inside the form (which would prevent creating additional forms on the page), the header and footer submit controls can be associated with the same form.

■ **Note** Like with other contemporary form features, Opera is ahead of the pack on this one. Be sure to test this feature in your preferred browser, but don't be surprised if it isn't implemented yet!

Providing placeholder text

There are little things that can be done to a form that help so much to make it more polished and usable. This is one such thing. Instead of having blank text fields on a form, you can add text to the fields to hint at what they are for (address, telephone number, and so on). Traditionally this was done by setting the value attribute on the input element. The problem with this approach is that the text added initially could be erased, which didn't make sense for something that really was just a hint and not meant to be an editable feature. This problem has been solved in HTML5 with the placeholder attribute. Text added to this attribute will appear in a text field when it is empty. Figure 4-18 shows what this looks like.

Figure 4-18. *Four different text-based input fields (search, email, tel, and url) with placeholder text added*

Making input read-only

The readonly attribute is available for preventing the content in an input control from being modified from its initial value. This can be useful if a form field value is updated via JavaScript without allowing the user to change the value, as may be done if the value was the result of a calculation in some way. This is a Boolean attribute, so you can simply add it to the element:

```
<input type="text" value="You can't delete this" readonly />
```

Autocomplete and autofocus

Autocomplete is a feature web browsers have for helping fill out the details on a form automatically. If someone is filling in their name, address, phone number, etc., repeatedly on different forms (when creating accounts on e-commerce sites, for instance), the autocomplete feature can store these values and then fill them into similar forms that are filled out in the future. This is a preference set in the web browser application. In coordination with this feature comes the autocomplete attribute, which allows the browser's autocomplete feature to be turned off for individual elements in a form or for the form as a whole. This might be done for fields that are receiving sensitive data or that will never be needed for another form. The attribute has a value of either on or off, as follows:

```
<form method="post" autocomplete="off">
```

This will turn autocomplete off for all the form controls in this example form.

The autofocus attribute is straightforward enough; it is a Boolean attribute, which when added to a form control makes the focus jump to the specified element immediately when the page loads. This means the user can start typing immediately without the need to click the first (or whichever) element beforehand. It is supported on button, input, keygen, select, and textarea. Adding this attribute is only really a good idea to do if there is no other input on the page that the user may want to click first.

Using data lists

The majority of the input types include an attribute called list[5] that works with a new element—the datalist. This element defines a list of options that are available when entering data into a form control input. The datalist element itself is not shown on the web page but instead provides data to the list attribute of other elements in the form. As an example, let's take a snippet from a form for an online job application. There might be a text input field that requests the desired salary range, like so:

```
<p><input type="text" name="salary" placeholder="Enter desired salary" /></p>
```

The user could enter any amount, but it would help to provide a list of common values for the user to choose from. For example, the following values might be shown:

40,000+
60,000+
80,000+
100,000+
120,000+

These could be represented as a data list like so:

```
<datalist id="salaries">
    <option value="40,000+" />
    <option value="60,000+" />
    <option value="80,000+" />
    <option value="100,000+" />
    <option value="120,000+" />
</datalist>
```

The text input field then can make use of this list by setting its list attribute to the ID of the data list:

```
<p><input type="text" name="salary" placeholder="Enter desired salary" list="salaries" /></p>
```

The result is that when the user starts typing a value in the field, relevant matches in the data list will pop up, as shown in Figure 4-19.

---

[5] Excluded are password, checkbox, radio, file, hidden, image, button, submit, and reset.

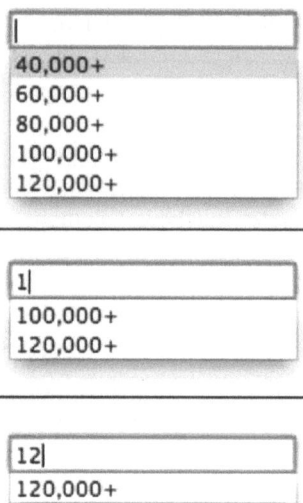

Figure 4-19. Three panels showing how a data list can be associated with a text input field. The associated data list appears when placing focus in the text input field, and the list is narrowed down to matching options as letters are typed.

Other form controls

The input element is undoubtedly a large and versatile element, but it isn't the only form control. We've talked about button, but there is also select (and option) and textarea. These aren't new to HTML5, however. What has been added has been datalist, which was covered in the prior section; progress; meter (otherwise known as a gauge); output; and keygen. Let's take a look at each of the controls that haven't been covered yet, from old to new.

Menus

The select element is a container element, allowing any number of option and optgroup elements. It normally displays as a drop-down list, as shown in Figure 4-20.

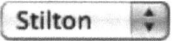

Figure 4-20. A select menu

This element has two specific attributes not covered elsewhere, disabled and size.[6] It also may use the multiple attribute (first brought up earlier in this chapter in the file input section). The Boolean disabled attribute can be added to disable (gray out) user interaction with the menu. The size and multiple attributes are related. If the Boolean multiple attribute is added, the select menu will normally

---

[6] It also has the global attributes covered in Chapter 2 and the name, required, autofocus, and form attributes covered earlier in this chapter.

display as a scrollable list box that permits multiple selections by the user, by holding down the Command key (Mac) or Control key (Windows) and clicking multiple items. The size attribute, which accepts a numerical value, determines how many rows of options are displayed. Figure 4-21 shows an example of a list menu.

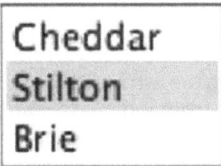

Figure 4-21. A list menu, created with a select element with a multiple attribute added

Each row within a select is contained within an option element, like so:

```
<select name="cheesemenu">
    <option>Cheddar</option>
    <option>Stilton</option>
    <option>Brie</option>
</select>
```

■ **Note** The datalist element shown earlier uses option elements, too, but formats them with self-closing tags and uses the value attribute for the list data.

The option element has four specific attributes: disabled, selected, value, and label. Like the disabled attribute on select, this is a Boolean attribute that prevents the user from selecting a particular item in the menu. The Boolean selected attribute is used to indicate to the user agent that a particular option should be selected initially; without it, the browser may display either nothing at all (just a blank select box) or the first option it encounters. For instance, to select the second option by default, selected is added like so:

```
<select name="cheesemenu">
    <option>Cheddar</option>
    <option selected>Stilton</option>
    <option>Brie</option>
</select>
```

Multiple option elements can have the selected attribute set, but only if the select has the multiple attribute added.

Adding different values

The value attribute is used to allow the submission of a value that differs from the content of a particular option. If the value attribute is omitted, then the content is used as the value. For example, given the following menu:

```
<select name="cheesemenu">
    <option value="ch01">Cheddar</option>
    <option value="ch02">Stilton</option>
    <option>Brie</option>
</select>
```

If the first or second option is selected, they will submit the values ch01 and ch02, respectively. If the third option is selected, it will use the content "Brie" for its value since there isn't a value attribute specified. This behavior is useful for situations where what you show the user differs from what you want to submit to the server. For example, if you were building a form for an e-commerce site, you might have a drop-down menu of products. You'd want to show the names of the products to the user, but a product number of some sort would be much easier for you to manage on the server side. So, along with adding each product name, you would add the product number as a value in each option in the list. The names would display to the user, but after selecting a product and submitting the form, the product number is what would be submitted to the server.

■ **Note** In practice, all the options should consistently use or not use the value attribute.

Adding shorthand labels

Finally, we come to the label attribute. This attribute is designed to accept a short value to use in lieu of displaying the content of an option. The label attribute can be used to provide an alternative display label, while still retaining the original content for the value passed to the server. The code for this looks like the following:

```
<select name="cheesemenu">
    <option>Cheddar</option>
    <option>Stilton</option>
    <option>Brie</option>
    <option label="All">All of the cheeses in all of the worlds</option>
</select>
```

Adding menu structure

To help provide structure to your menus, you can use the optgroup element to group similar option elements. So, instead of the following markup:

```
<select name="cheesemenu">
    <option>- - - English cheeses - - -</option>
    <option value="cheddar">Cheddar</option>
    <option value="stilton">Stilton</option>
    <option>- - -French cheeses- - -</option>
    <option value="brie">Brie</option>
</select>
```

you would use this:

```
<select name="cheesemenu">
    <optgroup label="English cheeses">
        <option value="cheddar">Cheddar</option>
        <option value="stilton">Stilton</option>
    </optgroup>
    <optgroup label="French cheeses">
        <option value="brie">Brie</option>
    </optgroup>
</select>
```

The preceding markup would render as shown in Figure 4-22.

Figure 4-22. *A select menu organized with multiple optgroup elements*

The optgroup element is a clear example of using the right tag for the right job. A benefit of using optgroup elements to divide your option elements is that the optgroup label cannot be selected, nor can its value be submitted as data, whereas in the former example the page author would either have to live with erroneous submissions or provide a client- or server-side validator to ensure such dividers had not been submitted. Additionally, the optgroup element has a Boolean disabled attribute, which can be used to disable whole groups of option elements, if required.

Text boxes

The textarea element is similar in some ways to the text input element, but it allows multiple lines of input rather than just one. It uses a pair of attributes, cols and rows, to control its size, and instead of using a value attribute to preset any textual content, it uses the content of the element itself. It's a container element, rather than a self-closing empty element.

The following code creates a textarea that is 20 columns wide and 5 rows high (a scrollbar will appear if the input exceeds the visible area).

```
<textarea cols="20" rows="5">Type your content here</textarea>
```

Even though the textarea element is a container for content, the previous code would be better formatted using the new placeholder attribute and leaving the content in the element empty, like so:

```
<textarea cols="20" rows="5" placeholder="Type your content here"></textarea>
```

Figure 4-23 shows the result.

```
Type your content here
```

Figure 4-23. *A textarea 20 columns wide and 5 rows high, with placeholder text added*

The textarea element includes an attribute not mentioned elsewhere: wrap. This attribute is used to indicate whether line breaks should be added to the submitted text area data at the points where the text wraps in the text box's available area. This attribute can have the value hard or soft. The first, hard, means that newline characters are added to the submitted form data at the points where the submitted text wrapped to a new line in the text area. After submitting the form in this state, you will see the URL-encoded newline character in the URL, which looks like %0D%0A (if using the GET method). On the other hand, a soft value means that while the text can wrap on-screen, the submitted data will be sent without any line breaks indicating where the text wrapped in the text area. This is the default behavior.

A text area control may also use the maxlength attribute to limit the amount of characters that can be input; this works like how the maxlength attribute works on a single-line text input control, and the same cautions apply (that is, double-check the length on the server-side if the data length is of critical importance).

Displaying progress

This is a new element in the HTML5 specification and it is pretty neat! Fundamentally, it's simple: show how far into a multistage process someone has gotten. For instance, a form might be spread over multiple pages, and this element is for indicating which page (out of the total number of pages) the user was on. What is this element called? progress! It works like this: there are two attributes, max and value. The max attribute is the maximum number of steps in a task, and value is the current step that the user is on.

Let's look at an example:

```
<progress max="3" value="1">Step 1 of 3</progress>
```

This defines being at the first of three steps. In a browser that supports this element, the display may look like Figure 4-24.

Figure 4-24. The progress element as rendered in a supporting web browser (Opera in this case)

■ **Note** For those browser's that don't support this element, it is important to put some meaningful text between the element's tags, since this will get displayed in cases where the progress element is not supported (Figure 4-25).

Page 1 of 3

Figure 4-25. In a web browser that does not support the progress element, the text content between the element's tags gets displayed instead

Displaying a gauge

The meter element (Figure 4-26) may look identical to the progress element (Figure 4-26), but there is an important schematic difference. The progress element is for the display of the progression through steps in a task, while the meter element is for the display of a gauge—that is, a specific value within a known range. It could be used to show how much hard drive space is remaining or how much inventory is left.

Figure 4-26. The meter element as it appears in Google Chrome

The min and max attributes set the minimum and maximum ends of the range, while the value attribute sets where in the range the gauge is. The element also has a good number of attributes that are used for schematic purposes to ascertain the meaning behind where a particular value is in a set range. The optimum, low, and high attributes allow segmenting of the range into regions. This can be used by the web browser to display the gauge differently depending on where the value is in the range, as is shown in Figure 4-27.

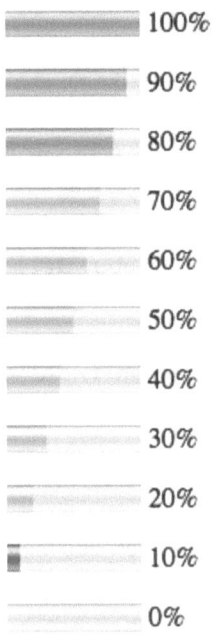

100%

90%

80%

70%

60%

50%

40%

30%

20%

10%

0%

Figure 4-27. A meter element reducing in value through the high and low ranges

The code for the preceding meters is as follows:

```
<p>
<meter min="0" low="20" high="80" optimum="90" max="100" value="100">Space left: </meter> 100%
</p>

<p>
<meter min="0" low="20" high="80" optimum="90" max="100" value="90">Space left: </meter> 90%
</p>

<p>
<meter min="0" low="20" high="80" optimum="90" max="100" value="80">Space left: </meter> 80%
```

```
</p>

<p>
<meter min="0" low="20" high="80" optimum="90" max="100" value="70">Space left: </meter> 70%
</p>

<p>
<meter min="0" low="20" high="80" optimum="90" max="100" value="60">Space left: </meter> 60%
</p>

<p>
<meter min="0" low="20" high="80" optimum="90" max="100" value="50">Space left: </meter> 50%
</p>

<p>
<meter min="0" low="20" high="80" optimum="90" max="100" value="40">Space left: </meter> 40%
</p>

<p>
<meter min="0" low="20" high="80" optimum="90" max="100" value="30">Space left: </meter> 30%
</p>

<p>
<meter min="0" low="20" high="80" optimum="90" max="100" value="20">Space left: </meter> 20%
</p>

<p>
<meter min="0" low="20" high="80" optimum="90" max="100" value="10">Space left: </meter> 10%
</p>

<p>
<meter min="0" low="20" high="80" optimum="90" max="100" value="0">Space left: </meter> 0%
</p>
```

Notice that, like with the progress element, some descriptive textual content is placed between the meter element's tags. This content will display in web browsers that don't support the element.

Displaying calculated output

The output element is for displaying the result of a calculation. It is very much a semantic element in that the output looks like plain text on the page.

In addition to the global attributes and form and name attributes (both discussed earlier), the output element has one other attribute: for. This attribute should contain a list of IDs of the elements that went into the calculation that this output element is displaying:

```
<input id="inputa" type="number"> +
<input id="inputb" type="number"> =
<output id="resultfld" name="result" for="inputa inputb"></output>
```

A typical use case would be the display of the result of a calculation generated by a script. The following script would update the value of the output element every time the two number inputs are changed:

```
var inputa;
var inputb;
var resultfld;
function init(){
     inputa = document.getElementById("inputa");
     inputb = document.getElementById("inputb");
     resultfld = document.getElementById("resultfld");
     inputa.oninput = updateResult;
     inputb.oninput = updateResult;
}
function updateResult(){
     resultfld.value = Number(inputa.value)+Number(inputb.value);
}
window.onload = init;
```

Cryptographic key generator

The keygen element is used to generate a private and public cryptographic key, the public side of which is sent to the server at form submittal. The element itself is rather cryptic-looking because it is by default a drop-down list of numbers and nothing more. These numbers are the bit size of the keys used in the encryption algorithm. Larger numbers will result in more difficult-to-crack keys. The expected use case for this element would be that the server would generate a certificate that is sent back to the client to establish a trusted secure communication between the two. Cryptography for encrypted communication between a web page and web server is beyond the scope of this book, and this element is not one you are going to use unless you know something about cryptography already.[7] Even if you do know something about cryptography, don't necessarily get too attached to this element in its current form. There is the distinct possibility that it will change course in the future (the HTML specification is still in draft status after all). For instance, representatives from Microsoft have stated they have no intention of supporting keygen (keygen was original developed by Internet Explorer competitor Netscape, so Microsoft approached implementing cryptography from a different direction). The current approach toward the element's standardization makes the actual algorithms used optional so that the element itself can be supported (for backward compatibility), but the cryptographic components may be omitted. Whether Microsoft implements the element under these terms is yet to be seen. Unless you have no other alternative, you're best to leave keygen alone for the moment until the dust settles.

■ **Note** This highlights an all too common problem with standardizing HTML, because each browser manufacturer may have a vested interest in one implementation over another, leading to either multiple implementations of the same functionality or functionality that is not standardized because an agreement can't be reached. This kind of disagreement is what led to video codecs not being standardized in the video element, which, as you'll see in Chapter 5, means more than one video file needs to be supplied to be compatible with all major browsers.

---

[7] IBM publishes a primer on public key encryption that you may want to take a look at to familiarize yourself with the concepts: www.ibm.com/developerworks/web/library/s-pki.html.

Adding structure with fieldsets and labels

The `fieldset` element allows web authors to divide form controls into thematically linked sections, making it easier for users to work through the form while also enhancing accessibility for assistive devices. Most browsers will display a `fieldset` with a simple border. For instance, the following markup displays the results shown in Figure 4-28:

```
<fieldset>
    <p>
    <select name="cheesemenu">
        <option>Cheddar</option>
        <option>Stilton</option>
        <option>Brie</option>
    </select>
    </p><p>
    <button type="submit">Submit!</button>
    </p>
</fieldset>
```

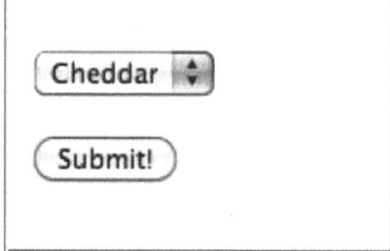

Figure 4-28. An example of the usual rendering of a `fieldset`

To identify each `fieldset`, you must use the `legend` element:

```
<fieldset>
    <legend>Cheeses of the world</legend>
    <p>
    <select name="cheesemenu">
        <option>Cheddar</option>
        <option>Stilton</option>
        <option>Brie</option>
    </select>
    </p><p>
    <button type="submit">Submit!</button>
    </p>
</fieldset>
```

The form will now look something like Figure 4-29.

Figure 4-29. A fieldset with a legend

The last form element to mention, label, also increases both usability and accessibility. This element is used to form an association between a textual label and a form control. When the label and form control are associated with each other, either can be clicked to interact with the control. For example, a label associated with a check box means that the label can be clicked, which will then select the box. There are two ways of creating clickable labels like this in the markup. The first—and preferable—way is by enclosing the form control within a label. Here is an example:

```
<label>Favorite cheese: <input type="text" name="ch" /></label>
```

In the preceding example, clicking the "Favorite cheese:" text in the label causes the nested input to gain focus, which in this case means the user could start typing in the text field. An alternative solution is to use the for attribute:

```
<label for="favcheese">Favorite cheese: </label> <input type="text" id="favcheese" name="ch" />
```

The advantage of using the for attribute is that the form control does not need to appear inside the label. The value in the for attribute is the ID of the associated form control, which means the two are associated, even if they are located in separate spots in the markup. This is potentially useful; however, because of this manual pairing of attributes, using the for attribute can be laborious. I don't recommend using it unless you absolutely must. A use case is in situations where a form appears inside a table and the labels appear in one column and the form controls in another column.

■ **Note** Remember that tables are used for arranging tabular data in rows and columns only and should not be used for layout; this includes using a table for the sole purpose of aesthetically laying out a form! Use CSS instead for this purpose.

Putting it all together

Remember the *City Press*? The fictional newspaper website from the previous chapter? Let's look at a form for the site for gathering news tips so we can see all these form controls coming together.

Page 1, gathering user details

The form is broken into two pages, the first for registering the tipster on the site and the second for recording the new tip they have. The form's first page looks like Figure 4-30.

Submit a Tip

Register as a Tipster

Progress: [_____]

┌─ Register New User ──┐
│ Username: enter a new username   │
│   │
│ Password: 6 digits or more   │
└───┘

┌─ Personal Details ───┐
│ Name: first and last name   │
│   │
│ Address: │
│   mailing address   │
│   │
│   │
│   │
│ City: mailing address city   │
│   │
│ State: two-letter abbreviation   │
│   │
│ Zip code: 00000 or 00000-0000   │
│   │
│ Email: you@example.com   │
│   │
│ Phone: 000-000-0000   │
│   │
│ Website: http://example.com   │
│   │
│ Age: [   ] [▲▼]   │
└───┘

Spam check. What color is snow? (choose a color) [■ ▼]

(Submit)

Figure 4-30. *The first form on the* City Press *"submit a tip" form*

To create this form, first we need a `form` element. We'll set two attributes: `action`, which will go to our second form page, and `method`. Which method do we need? GET or POST? Well, the users will be submitting data that will likely end up in a database, so it's a submission that will actively be modifying data. So, we use POST. Also, it should be a big hint to use POST if a password input field appears on the form, which it does. OK, this is our starting form:

```
<form action="form2.php" method="post">
</form>
```

Next, although the form is spread across two pages, there are three steps to progress through the form, since there will be a confirmation page after the data is submitted, so we should add a progress element to show that:

```
<form action="form2.php" method="post">
    <p>Progress: <progress value="0" max="2">1/3</progress></p>
</form>
```

Notice the value attribute is set to zero and the max is set to two, but the alternative content text is "1/3." This is because we will have three steps to complete: the first form, the second form, and a confirmation page after the second form is submitted. So the alternative text will go 1/3, 2/3, 3/3, while the value attribute will go 0, 1, 2.

Next we see that we need the user to create a username and password (presumably they would be able to log in elsewhere after going through this process), which we can separate into its own fieldset. A legend is used to add a title to the fieldset, and the text and password input fields are set to be required. Also, placeholder text is added to both. A regex pattern is added to the password field so that it will only accept passwords that are six characters or longer.

```
...
<fieldset>
    <legend>Register New User</legend>
    <p><label>Username: <input type="text" name="username" placeholder="enter a new username"
    required/></label></p>
    <p><label>Password: <input type="password" name="password" placeholder="6 digits or more"
    pattern="^.{6,}" required/></label></p>
</fieldset>
...
```

Below this we add another fieldset for the personal details area. The first field is a generic text input field for gathering the tipster's name. Placeholder text is added that hints as to the format of the information to enter:

```
...
<fieldset>
    <legend>Personal Details</legend>
    <p><label>Name: <input type="text" name="name" placeholder="first and last name"
    /></label></p>
...
```

Following the name input is a text area for gathering the tipster's mailing address followed by a single-line text input for gathering the city name. For the address input, we could use the label's for attribute in order to place a line break element between the label and the text area. The for attribute wouldn't be required in this circumstance, but you may find this to be a cleaner approach because it prevents including extra HTML elements inside the label's tags:

```
...
    <p><label for="address">Address:</label><br />
    <textarea id="address" name="address" cols="20" rows="5" placeholder="mailing
    address"></textarea></p>
    <p><label>City: <input type="text" name="city" placeholder="mailing address city"
    /></label></p>
```

...

Next is the state field. One option here is to create a drop-down list using the select element, with all 50 states filled in. This would likely be the best course to take when we were sure that only people in the United States would be filling out this form. But let's say we're not certain the users will necessarily be coming from the United States. In that case, an alternative is to have a regular text input field but set its list attribute to a data list containing the state names (or abbreviations). Just below the opening form element, a new datalist element is added for this purpose:

```
<form action="form2.php" method="post">
<datalist id="statelist">
     <option value="AL" />
     <option value="AK" />
     <option value="AZ" />
     <option value="AR" />
     <option value="CA" />
     <option value="CO" />
     <option value="DE" />
```

...

Then back in the personal details fieldset, the text input for state is added. Also added is the ZIP code input field:

...

```
<p><label>State: <input type="text" name="states" list="statelist" placeholder="two-letter abbreviation" /></label></p>
<p><label>Zip code: <input type="text" name="name" placeholder="00000 or 00000-0000" /></label></p>
```

...

Next is the only required field in this set, the e-mail address field. The user is reminded by the placeholder text to enter a valid e-mail address, but automatic validation of the form will pick up any inconsistencies as well:

...

```
<p><label>Email: <input type="email" name="name" placeholder="you@example.com" required/></label></p>
```

...

Next the optional telephone and website input fields are added:

...

```
<p><label>Phone: <input type="tel" placeholder="000-000-0000" /></label></p>
<p><label>Website: <input type="url" placeholder="http://example.com" /></label></p>
```

...

Last in this fieldset, the optional age field is added as a number input field. The min and max attributes are set to a realistic age range, with some padding on the upper end. The closing fieldset tag ends this group:

```
…
    <p><label>Age: <input type="number" name="age" min="0" max="150" /></label></p>
</fieldset>
```

Next, a required color picker input is used as a simple check against automated spam bots, which presumably wouldn't be able to pick the correct color for "snow." Sadly, the pattern attribute isn't available on the color input type, so this would need to be checked with JavaScript on the server side. We'll assume it's being checked on the server:

```
…
    <p><label>Spam check. What color is snow? (choose a color)
    <input type="color" name="captcha" required/></label></p>
…
```

Lastly, a submit button is added just before the closing form tag, which completes this form:

```
…
    <button type="submit" name="tipform1">Submit</button>
</form>
```

Page 2, gathering commentary

After filling in the form and clicking submit, the user ends up on page 2 with the second form, which looks like Figure 4-31.

Submit a Tip

Tip Details

Progress: ▭

```
┌─ Enter Tip Details ──────────────────────────────────────────────┐
│                                                                   │
│  Date/Time of incident: [          ▼]  :  [  ▲▼]                  │
│                                                                   │
│                         ┌──────────────┐                          │
│  Tip details:           └──────────────┘                          │
│  Attach supporting file: [              ]      ( Choose... )       │
│                                                                   │
│  Urgency: ●════════════○═══════════ 10 is most urgent             │
│                                                                   │
├─ Communication Preferences ──────────────────────────────────────┤
│                                                                   │
│  May we contact you about this tip? ☐                             │
│                                                                   │
│  ┌─ Preferred contact method: ────────────────────────────────┐  │
│  │  Phone:  ○                                                  │  │
│  │  Email:  ◉                                                  │  │
│  └─────────────────────────────────────────────────────────────┘  │
└───────────────────────────────────────────────────────────────────┘
```

Staff in the office ▭

(Submit)

Figure 4-31. The second form on the City Press "submit a tip" form

Like the first page, a form element is created with an action and method attribute. Also, because there is a file input field on the form, we set the enctype attribute to multipart/form-data so that binary data can be sent. Next, a progress element is added and incremented over the one that appeared on the first form:

```
<form action="complete.php" method="post" enctype="multipart/form-data">
    <p>Progress: <progress value="1" max="2">2/3</progress></p>
</form>
```

Next, a fieldset and legend is created for the tip details area. A date/time input field is added for the local date and time of the news incident. A textarea element is used for gathering the tip details, and a file input is used for allowing a supporting file to be attached, if necessary:

```
...
<fieldset>
    <legend>Enter Tip Details</legend>
```

```
<p><label>Date/Time of incident: <input type="datetime-local" /></label></p>
<p><label>Tip details: <textarea></textarea></label></p>
<p><label>Attach supporting file:  <input type="file" /></label></p>
...
```

Next, a range input type is added as an "importance" slider for the tip. The fieldset is then closed. Next to the slider is a read-only text input field that includes placeholder text to indicate that a higher value on the slider means "more urgent":

```
...
    <p><label>Urgency: <input type="range" name="range" id="range" min="1" max="10" /><input
id="rvalue" placeholder="more urgent" readonly /></label>
</fieldset>
...
```

Using JavaScript, we'll make the value in the read-only text input update dynamically when the slider is moved. We'll set the placeholder text to indicate that a high number on the slider means "most urgent" and update the text input to the value of the slider when the slider is moved. The JavaScript is added in a script element in the head of the document:

```
...
<script type="text/javascript">
    var range;
    var rvalue;

    function init(){
        range = document.getElementById("range");
        rvalue = document.getElementById("rvalue");
        rvalue.placeholder = "10 is most urgent";
        range.onchange = update;
    }

    function update(){
        rvalue.value = range.value;
    }

    window.onload = init;
</script>
...
```

▪ **Note** Remember that in a production environment you would want to move your script to an external file because this provides a better organizational separation of your markup and script.

A new fieldset is created for "Communication Preferences" regarding the tip. A check box is provided for indicating whether the user may be contacted. If so, then another fieldset is nested inside of the first, where two radio buttons allow the user to choose their preferred contact method. By default "Email" is selected (with the checked attribute):

```
...
```

```
<fieldset>
    <legend>Communication Preferences</legend>
    <p><label>May we contact you about this tip? <input type="checkbox" /></label></p>
    <fieldset>
        <legend>Preferred contact method:</legend>
        <p><label> Phone: <input type="radio" name="contactpref" /></label></p>
        <p><label> Email: <input type="radio" name="contactpref" checked /></label></p>
    </fieldset>
</fieldset>
…
```

Next, a meter gives some indication of how well the paper is staffed at the moment, with six out of ten staff in the office. We won't speculate how often this meter gets updated, but it is an appropriate element to use here as the number of staff is a known quantity.

Finally, like the last form, a submit button appears at the end, and the form is closed:

```
…
    <p><label>Staff in the office
    <meter min="0" value="6" low="2" optimal="9" high="8" max="10" >6/10</meter>
    </label></p>
    <button type="submit" name="tipform2">Submit</button>
</form>
```

Page 3, providing confirmation

Submitting the second form brings the user to the acknowledgment page, where the progress element is updated to its final position, and a short thank-you message is given:

```
<form>
    <p>Progress: <progress value="2" max="2">2/2</progress></p>
    <p>The tip was successfully received. Thank you!</p>
</form>
```

The resulting page looks like Figure 4-32.

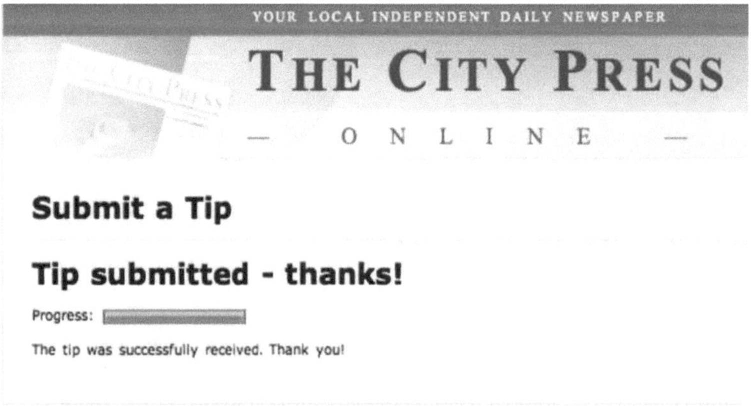

Figure 4-32. *The third and final acknowledgment page*

Form usability

It is easy to create a form, but it is much harder to create a really *good* form. The *City Press* tip form shows all the options and input variables that can be taken into account when creating even a simple form. Forms really do become more of an application than a web page the more complex they get, so you need to consider usability *seriously*. Even in the *City Press* tip form, more could be added to make it even more usable. For instance, the `title` attribute could be added to all input fields to give a hint to what those fields are expecting when the user hovers their cursor over them (or uses a screen reader). It gets more serious than that, though; if your form is at the point at which the general public starts giving you money, you need to test your form rigorously, observe people using it and record their reactions (even if your audience is just a few colleagues from the other side of the office), and make sure it works as well as it possibly can.

Exhaustive coverage of the subject of form usability is well beyond the scope of this book, but the guidelines outlined in the following sections should be enough to help you avoid some common form usability problems. Beyond the information you'll find in this chapter, I recommend reading the classic *Don't Make Me Think: A Common Sense Approach to Web Usability* by Steve Krug (New Riders Press, 2000).

Use the right input for the right job

So, you know about every input type there is, but which one is appropriate to use in a given situation? Some of these are obvious—a `file` input has only one purpose, and no other type of input can be used in its place—but what about, for instance, check boxes vs. radio buttons? A good rule of thumb is that if you have a list of two or more options and the user *must* select one and *only* one of them, use radio buttons. Selecting one radio button should then deselect any other radio button that is part of the same named group. But if the list contains many options to select from, consider using a `select` menu instead. You'll retain the inability to select more than one option, and you'll save some space (at the expense of "discoverability").

Check boxes, on the other hand, are used when there are several choices to make, and users can leave them all blank or select as many as they like. Checking one check box does not deselect any others within the group. The menu equivalent of a series of check boxes is a `select` menu with the `multiple` attribute present, but check boxes are generally easier to use because they do not require the user to understand what keyboard/mouse combination to use to select/deselect the options, so you may want to avoid multiple-select lists where possible.

You should also use a check box when there is a single option that users can switch on or off, such as for agreeing to sign up for a newsletter. You would not use a radio button here because a radio button can only be deselected by selecting another.

Remember also to use labels, fieldsets, and legends to aid in both usability and accessibility.

Keep it short and simple

Collect only the information you need and no more than that. Do you really need to know if I'm a Mr. or a Ms.? Do you really need my fax number? My occupation? My annual salary? Question the presence of every field you have in your form, and if it's a compulsory field, question again whether it needs to be. Your marketers may relish the opportunity to collect reams of personal data about your site visitors, but the longer your form is and the more irrelevant users start perceiving it to be, the higher the risk that they'll abandon it.

Don't make me think, don't make me work, and don't try to trick me

Make your form as easy to complete as possible. If at any point a user has to pause for a few seconds to try to work out what's gone wrong or what you mean, then that's a few more seconds when he might just think "Oh, forget it" and go off to make a sandwich. So, for instance, if your form contains compulsory fields, consider styling these fields more prominently (and, of course, add the `required` attribute so form validation will kick in). Make it clear from the beginning the fields that *must* be filled in. If this is the majority of the fields, consider adding the text "Optional" next to the optional fields.

If you need data in a certain format, don't rely on users entering it in that format—this is what your form handler on the server is supposed to deal with. For instance, if a user needs to enter a credit card number, let her fill it in as 1234 5678 9012 3456 if she wants (that's how it's formatted on her credit card), 1234567890123456, or 1234-5678-9012-3456—whatever works for the user, within reason. Deft use of the `pattern` attribute can allow flexibility in form input but still validate critical information and essentially formatting (such as checking that the correct number of digits was entered). Remember, computers are supposed to save *the user* time. Provide a guide to a preferred format if you like, but allow for the possibility of alternate entries.

If the user *has* made an error that can't be solved by server-side code, then let him know with a clear, meaningful, and appropriate error message—the sooner, the better. Use built-in form validation and provide JavaScript and/or server-generated validation and error messages as a backup. The more complex your form, the more things that can go wrong, so test, test, test, and make sure there are no meaningless error messages.

Remember that the Internet is global

If your form is not specific to any one country, try not to fill it with references to "states" and "ZIP codes," and certainly don't make those fields compulsory if you do include them. Also relating to the previous point, don't try to restrict the format of the user's data unless you are absolutely certain of its format.

▪ **Note** An upcoming attribute that is relevant to the internationalization of your form is the `dirname` attribute, which is specified on the `textarea`, `text` input, and `search` input elements. Remember how form data is submitted as key/value pairs? This attribute creates a key that is sent to the server, which has the directionality of the text entered into the form control as its value. This will appear as either `ltr` (left to right) or `rtl` (right to left). Don't expect this attribute to work today, though, because it has yet to be implemented by major browsers. More information about it and a code example is available at `http://dev.w3.org/html5/spec/common-input-element-attributes.html#attr-input-dirname`.

Provide a fallback when needed

A lot of material in this chapter is quite new and may not work in all browsers. Thankfully, input types will usually degrade to regular text fields when a particular input type is not supported. But this can still have serious consequences for the usability of your form if you designed it with all the rich controls that are in the HTML5 specification but didn't consider what it would look like in an older browser. Investigate projects like Modernizr (`http://modernizr.com`), jQueryUI (`http://jqueryui.com`), and webforms2 (`http://code.google.com/p/webforms2/`) because these projects will help you with implementing "polyfills" into your site, meaning they provide (through JavaScript) functionality that you would expect to be natively available in the browser.

Summary

It is fairly easy to create forms—just insert a couple of `input` tags, add a bit of text, slap a submit button on the end, and then you get to go home early—but it is a lot harder to create forms that are usable, accessible, and logical. Think about the meaning of your form content. What schematic elements make sense for use as input? These are not things that should be left to the last minute. Your form may be the most important part of your website, particularly if it's a form that allows people to enter their credit card details, so it should be a model of simplicity and ease of use. It should not upset people, anger them, or put them off—it seems odd to have to say that, but I've seen some terrible forms in my time that did just that. Lastly, be prepared for the reality that to create the ultimate usable form, you'll invariably have to turn to JavaScript or server-side code (or both) to help you provide users with the expected features of modern web forms.

CHAPTER 5

Multimedia: Video, Audio, and Embedded Media

Long gone are the days when websites were only lists of bulleted text, without any form of imagery. But if you think about it, HTML has never been really multimedia-savvy. Images appeared early on, and there were gimmicky elements like (the now defunct) bgsound, but the interactive experiences, the web applications, the video players—each has been provided by some form of plug-in for the most part that extended the capabilities of HTML. In this regard, enhanced multimedia capability in HTML5 is a very apparent coming of age for HTML to the end user. For instance, the video and audio elements offer a standardized way to handle video and audio media, respectively. That sounds like a huge advancement in web media, and it is, but it's not all smooth sailing. Although the elements are standardized as part of the HTML5 specification, the file formats used in these media elements are not, which leads to some verbose solutions for providing alternative content. But fear not, this by no means makes these implementations unusable, and in this chapter you will see that a consistent best-practice approach toward handling fallback content is possible.

I'll begin this chapter by running through some of the media elements in HTML and give you an overview of what has changed. This will cover topics such as images, image maps, generic embedded objects (the old-school way of handling video), and the state of frames. I'll then go into the new elements introduced into HTML for handling video and audio. Lastly, I'll briefly touch upon the canvas element, which is for defining an area where imagery can be dynamically rendered. Interacting with canvas will be covered in more depth in Chapter 7, but the foundations will be covered in this chapter.

Where it all began: img

Early in the evolution of HTML it became apparent that the platform needed to support some form of mixed media embedded into a page—at the very least images. Work toward implementing an HTML element that could be used for images and other media was occurring in early 1993 when 21-year-old Marc Andreessen proposed and later implemented the self-closing img element in the Mosaic web browser.[1] Mosaic is credited with being central in enabling the Internet boom of the 1990s by moving web browsers from text-based systems to graphics-enabled applications that more readily appealed to a nontechnical audience. Despite reservations about img's limitations (others wanted an element that could embed a greater variety of media than just images), the img element is still here today. Not much has changed in HTML5, other than the removal of the attributes align, border, hspace, and vspace, the functionality of which should be created through CSS.

---

[1] Marc Andreesen's original message proposing the img element is archived at http://1997.webhistory.org/www.lists/www-talk.1993q1/0182.html.

The img element generally requires two attributes: src and alt. The first, src, specifies the location of the actual image file. The location may be given as an absolute or relative URL, meaning it may be specified as an absolute address for the image, like src="http://example.com/images/pic.jpg", or an address relative to the current HTML page, such as src="images/pic.jpg". JPEG, GIF, and (relatively more recently) PNG images are popular image formats for the Web, but it is perhaps less well known that the img element is not limited to these formats and their variants. Depending on the web browser, TIFF, BMP, XBM, and even PDF[2] files may be displayed. This variety of support is because the HTML specification does not specify which image formats need to be supported by this element, only that the file to display is in fact an image.

WHEN TO USE ONE IMAGE FORMAT OVER ANOTHER

You can follow some general rules when deciding what image format to use for particular imagery on your website. For photographic content, where there are lots of tones of color, JPEG is the format to choose. If you have areas in your images that are solid continuous blocks of color, such as in a logo or illustration, choose between GIF or PNG. PNG offers more flexibility than GIF and was originally created to replace GIF because of a licensing issue with an algorithm in the GIF format. So, in general, go with PNG. However, GIF has more legacy support. PNGs that contained transparency would famously show up pink in Internet Explorer 6; however, it may well be time to drop support for browsers this far back in browser history and just go with PNG. PNG generally comes in two forms: PNG-8 and PNG-24. Use PNG-8 if the color palette in the image is quite small (256 or fewer individual colors) and if there aren't any gradated areas. If using transparency in the image, usually PNG-24 will provide a better result, because it will handle the transition between opaque and transparent areas of the image better.

■ **Note** Google recently introduced a new image format for the Web called WebP (pronounced "weppy") that is a competitor to the JPEG format. It's worth keeping your eye on, but currently browser support is too minimal (Google Chrome and Opera) to think about using it as your primary image format. You can find more information at http://code.google.com/speed/webp/.

The next attribute, alt, is for providing alternative content for the image if the image is not available or viewable. The text in the alt attribute should reasonably represent the image and not change the meaning of the content on the page if the image were removed. The alt attribute can be an empty string of text ("") if it is supplemental or redundant with other information on the page or if it is purely decorative, in which case CSS would likely be a better way to handle the image (see the "Is img obsolete? What about CSS?" sidebar). The alt attribute may also be omitted in cases where a textual representation of the image is not possible to provide, such as in a dynamically added image uploaded by a user, where the actual meaning of the image may not immediately be known. How to properly use the alt attribute in different contexts is a matter of surprising amounts of debate, but fundamentally it

---

[2] Where supported (for instance, in Safari), PDF documents will display only the first page, because img is not allowed to show paged content.

should be thought of as a replacement of the image, *not* a description of the image. A description is more correctly served by the title attribute. For instance, for an image showing a map of Andorra, it would be incorrect to provide alternative text that says "Map of Andorra" if the intent was to show Andorra's location in the world. A better alternative text would replicate the meaning conveyed by the image. In this case, it may be something like: "Andorra is a landlocked western European country bordered by Spain to the southwest and France to the northeast" (Figure 5-1).

Andorra is a landlocked western European country bordered by Spain to the southwest and France to the northeast

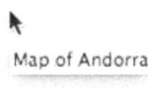

Map of Andorra

Figure 5-1. Alternative text displayed by the alt *attribute when an image is unavailable should reproduce the purpose of the image, not describe the image. A descriptive summary of the image is better provided by the* title *attribute, which appears when hovering over the image.*

While not required, it is a best practice to set the width and height attributes to the width and height in pixels of the source image. This will allow the browser to render the space an image will occupy before it has fully loaded. This also means the layout of a page won't change if an image is missing, since an empty box the dimensions of the width and height attributes will be rendered (Figure 5-1 shows such a box).

■ **Note** There is an issue in WebKit, the underlying layout engine of Google Chrome and Safari, which prevents alternative text from being displayed when an image is not found if the width and height are not large enough to fit all the alternative text on one line. If you do not see alternative text appearing in these browsers when an image is not available, the dimensions set is likely the reason.

IS IMG OBSOLETE? WHAT ABOUT CSS?

The img element is old—so old in fact that it predates Cascading Style Sheets (CSS). The presentation of content on the Web has developed a lot since the early 1990s, and compared to CSS, the img element is, in many respects, quite limited. Since CSS is concerned with the appearance of a page, which includes images, CSS offers capabilities for handling images that are often more flexible than those possible with the img element. Using CSS, images can be applied to the background of any element on the page (through the use of the background-image and related properties), and images can be tiled, offset, and more. The latest version of the CSS specification under development, CSS3, has added more image-handling capabilities such as the ability to layer multiple background images over each other.[3]

Additionally, the HTML5 specification specifically states that using the `img` element for layout purposes should be avoided. Examples of using images for layout include separating regions of content through the use of image-based backgrounds or borders or providing padding next to content on the page with the use of transparent images. These are tasks that are better suited to and commonly accomplished with CSS through the `background`, `border`, and `padding` properties.

Also, from a performance point of view, it is important to remember that the `img` element provides a placeholder within the HTML page to an external resource. Since a request must be made to the web server for each linked resource, a request is made for the HTML page, and additional requests are needed for each image on the page. Using CSS, a technique known as *CSS sprites*, may be used to consolidate a number of images together in one image for the purposes of reducing server requests. The images are laid out side-by-side and cropped to show different images from the one source image. Because this requires only one request as opposed to one for each image, there is a performance improvement to be gained.

So, why would you ever use the `img` element at all, when so much more flexibility can be provided by CSS? The answer lies in `img`'s `alt` attribute. Since this attribute is used to represent the image in textual form, it addresses accessibility concerns that are lost in CSS. The information in an HTML document should still be comprehensible even if its CSS styles are removed, so images that are critical to the presented information on the page, such as images or figures referred to elsewhere in the text of the document, should be presented in the `img` element.

The remaining attributes on the `img` element are `ismap` and `usemap`, which are both used for image maps, which we'll discuss next.

Image maps

Before the interactive animations and images built in Adobe Flash, which became all the rage in the late 1990s, the height of interactivity was clickable image maps, with their coded "hotspots" that linked a user to different pages based on where on the image the user clicked. There are two varieties of image maps: server-side and client-side. In a server-side image map, the pixel coordinates of the mouse click are sent to the server as an x, y coordinate pair. The server can then use that information to determine where on the image the user clicked and respond with a subsequent action. All that is required to enable this functionality is to add the Boolean `ismap` attribute to an `img` element that is enclosed in an anchor element (a):

```
<a href="process.php"><img ismap src="map.png" alt="" /></a>
```

After clicking the image, the coordinates of where the image was clicked (relative to the upper-left corner of the image) appear in the URL as a querystring, like `process.php?54,77`. (This example would

---

[3] As you will see in Chapter 6, CSS3 isn't one specification but several. However, like how "HTML5" is often used as an umbrella term to cover a family of related technologies, "CSS3" covers a number of different but related specifications. In the case of multiple backgrounds, the actual specification is "CSS Backgrounds and Borders Module Level 3."

mean the click occurred 54 pixels from the left edge and 77 pixels from the top edge of the image.) A server-side script could then access the coordinates and use them against a lookup table of coordinate areas to determine what action (if any) should happen.

A client-side image map works on the same principle as a server-side image map, but the hotspot areas are defined at the client (the web browser) instead of the server. This is a preferable method because the hotspot coordinates can be made accessible to people browsing that are unable to view the image, and they offer immediate feedback as to whether users are clicking an active region. However, compared to server-side image maps, the markup required is more involved. There are two distinct parts: the image element (img) and an associated map element, neither of which is nested within the other. The map element is a container element with a name attribute, which is referenced by the image element's usemap attribute to create an association between the image and the image map area coordinate data. The actual image map hotspot coordinates are defined inside the map element through any number of self-closing area elements. Here's an example:

```
<img src="banner.png" alt="" width="300" height="272" usemap="#bannermap" />
<map name="bannermap">
          <area shape="circle" coords="52,76,39" href="/about.html" alt="About" />•
          <area shape="rect" coords="120,56,187,102" href="/contact.html" alt="Contact" />
          <area shape="poly" coords="265,148,221,99,221,42,266,24" href="/portfolio.html"
          alt="Portfolio" />
          <area shape="default" href="/index.html" alt="Homepage" />
</map>
```

As you can see in the previous example, the area elements use a shape attribute to determine the shape of the hotspot area and a coords attribute to stake out the dimensions of the shape. The shape attribute may have the values circle, rect, poly, or default, which correspond to drawing a circle, a rectangle, a free-form shape with at least three points, or the whole image (in the default state no coordinates are given, since it covers the whole image). In most cases, the area will also contain an href attribute to determine where users should be taken to after they've clicked. Another attribute, nohref, is obsolete in HTML5 and is not to be used. This attribute had been used to specify that the area did not link anywhere, but it is sufficient to just leave off the href attribute to provide this functionality (or rather lack of functionality).

■ **Note** Why would you ever have an area in an image map that does not link anywhere? The reason may be to provide a tooltip over an image, but without the need to link anywhere. For example, consider a map of the 50 states of the U.S. If an image map was created that had an area defined for each state and had its title attribute set to the corresponding state name it was over—but the href attribute was not set—it would create a map of the United States that would show the state name the user was over when they hovered over the map, but the user would not link anywhere if they clicked. Additionally, creating an area without an href attribute allows areas to be "punched" out of other areas, so for example, a clickable donut shape could be defined by creating two overlapping circle areas, with only the larger circle having its href attribute set.

The meaning of the image map area coordinate points depends on the value of the shape attribute. Circles will have three values that correspond to the x and y coordinates of the center of the circular hotspot, with the last value determining the radius of the circle. For rectangular-shaped areas, there will be four values in the coords attribute, which correspond to the x, y coordinates of the upper-left and lower-right corners of the rectangle. Lastly, the poly area defines the x, y coordinates of each point in the shape, which could be quite a few! As you can imagine, hand-coding image maps is fairly laborious, but most WYSIWYG web-authoring software comes with the ability to create areas just by pointing, clicking, and dragging. Figure 5-2 shows an example of an image map created in Adobe Dreamweaver.

Figure 5-2. A complex image map area being drawn using Adobe Dreamweaver

Aside from defining shape coordinates for hotspots, the area element acts very much like the anchor element (a). If an href attribute is defined, the following additional attributes can be defined: target, rel, media, hreflang, and type, which work as they do on the anchor element (a) described in Chapter 3.

Additionally, the alt attribute should be set on the linked hotspots in the image map so that it gives a text representation of the link for scenarios where the image in the image map was not viewable.

Embedding other media

HTML5 includes two elements for embedding non-HTML content; that is, content that can't be handled by an existing HTML element and needs a third-party plug-in to display, such as Adobe Flash content, which requires the Adobe Flash Player. The two elements are embed and object. Generally, object would be used over embed because it is more flexible and can provide fallback content (content that displays in browsers that don't support the element), but we'll cover them both so you can see the differences.

The embed element

While the img element added richness to web pages, at the time it was introduced, it was apparent that support for only still images was not enough. The Web needed a way to handle a variety of embedded media. During the 1993 discussions about introducing the img element, another element was proposed by Tim Berners-Lee (widely credited as the inventor of the World Wide Web). He suggested adding an embed element in place of img that would address the latter's shortcomings, namely, that it only supported embedding images and not other media or data. Eventually both elements were implemented by web browser makers, img for images and embed for other media (video for instance), but an officially backed solution to support richer media would fragment in several directions for years to come.

embed was first implemented by Netscape, and while other browsers implemented it as well, it had quirks that prevented it from being standardized. Specifically, it can include arbitrary attributes (not just attribute values, but the attributes themselves), which can differ depending on the media being embedded. These additional attributes could be anything, because they will be passed as parameters to the plug-in used to handle the content, which may respond to them. This was a behavior that didn't rest easy with the W3C, particularly when the stricter syntax requirements of XHTML appeared to be the future direction of HTML. By the time the HTML 4.01 specification came about in 1999, embed was considered obsolete and was discouraged from being used. That could have been the end of the story for the embed element, but HTML5 has brought it back by officially standardizing it as part of the HTML specification, albeit in a stripped-down form. HTML5 aims to be backward-compatible and document what is in use—and despite its quirks, embed is still used today.

In addition to the global attributes, embed in HTML5 has a simple set of four attributes as opposed to fifteen, the number that previous implementations had attached to it. The four attributes are width, height, src, and type.

The width and height attributes specify the dimensions in pixels that the embedded media will occupy on the page, while the src attribute specifies the address of the source media file to embed. As stated earlier, additional attributes may be added to communicate settings to the plug-in set to handle a particular type of media. For instance, the following code snippet includes a loop attribute, which is passed on to Adobe Flash Player (the plug-in that will handle SWF content):

```
<embed src="game.swf" loop="true" />
```

The loop attribute isn't specified as an attribute on the embed element in the HTML5 specification, but the Flash Player will respond by looping the playback for this SWF file.

Notice in this example that the type attribute is not specified. When not specified, the browser will "content sniff" to determine which plug-in should handle the resource (specified in src). This may be as complex as looking for any metadata on the resource that indicates its type or as simple as looking for a plug-in that can handle a particular file extension. In this case, a resource with the .swf file extension will get handed off to the Flash Player. Of course, the type of file being embedded can be explicitly set by providing a suitable MIME type in the type attribute, like so:

```
<embed src="game.swf" type="application/x-shockwave-flash" loop="true" />
```

In addition to the ambiguity of attributes, there is another issue with embed. It is a self-closing element, like img, but it does not have an alt attribute. That means if the element was not supported, nothing would show up! To deal with this, browsers added a noembed element to provide content for situations where embed was unsupported. However, the noembed element has since been marked obsolete in HTML5 and must not be used.

All and all, despite its inclusion in the specification, embed is best avoided because of its limitations and quirks. A better alternative is the object element, which we'll look at next.

The object element

Because the issues with embed and the limitations of img, the object element was chosen by the W3C in 1996 as a replacement for both. Although it never superseded img, object did largely replace embed because it was more flexible (although Firefox lagged in support for awhile). For example, it has an opening and closing tag, so—unlike embed—fallback content can be provided in the content area of the element.

As with embed, object has been slimmed down in HTML5 and has had several attributes marked obsolete, but a few have been added as well. The attributes data, type, name, width, height, and usemap are the attributes retained from the previous specification, while the attributes form and typemustmatch have been added. As you can already see, object is a more sophisticated element compared to embed. object is not solely for plug-in media because it can also support images and nested web pages.

Let's get into object's attributes. The data attribute is like the src attribute on the img or embed element; it just specifies the location of the resource to load. The type attribute works like it does on the embed element; give it a valid MIME type for the resource being embedded. One or the other of the data or type attribute must be present, but they both don't need to be. If both are present, the Boolean typemustmatch attribute may be added, which adds a layer of security when loading the resource. For example, it's possible to use the object to embed media and other resources from third-party websites,[4] which presents a security issue if the third-party site says they are delivering a resource of one type, when in fact it is a malicious script, or similar, disguised as something harmless. The browser will content sniff the linked resource when the typemustmatch is set and won't embed the resource if its content type differs from the value set in the type attribute.

One aspect of the object element that may be a surprise is that object is meant to be able to take part in form submission and submit data along with a form. This isn't new in HTML5 either because it was included in the HTML 4.01 specification, which listed "object controls"[5] as one of the types of form controls. The new addition of the form attribute is just to make object consistent with other form controls. If you recall from the previous chapter, the various form controls (input, textarea, and so on) use the form attribute to associate themselves with one or more forms, even if they aren't nested inside the one they are referencing. This attribute works the same for object. The idea of including an object as part of a form addresses the need to have some plug-ins send data directly to a server. For example, a plug-in might be created that embedded a complex in-browser word processor of some sort, which had features that were beyond what was possible with HTML/CSS/JavaScript. The word processor could then be used in place of a plain old textarea, but at form submission time the word processor could submit data to the server directly from the plug-in (perhaps including all kinds of metadata about how the text was fancily formatted).

Typically when embedding a plug-in resource, the object element will need custom parameters to be sent to the plug-in; what these will be will differ from plug-in to plug-in. As mentioned earlier, the embed element addresses this with an unusual (and arguably messy!) solution of allowing any additional attributes added to the element, which then get handed off to the plug-in. object takes a different (and arguably cleaner) approach. Instead of allowing arbitrary additional attributes to be added, object utilizes another element, param, which is placed inside the opening and closing tags of object and can be used to pass values on to embedded plug-in. param has two attributes (in addition to the global attributes): name and value. When nested inside the object element, the value specified in the name and value attributes are passed on as a key/value pair to the plug-in in question. Earlier, in the embed element section, there was an example of using embed with a custom loop attribute to tell Flash Player to loop its playback. This example could be rewritten using the object and param elements like so:

```
<object data="game.swf" type="application/x-shockwave-flash">
        <param name="loop" value="true" />
</object>
```

---

[4] The object element was commonly used to embed YouTube videos, for instance (YouTube has since moved to using iframe for embedding video on other sites).
[5] See www.w3.org/TR/html4/interact/forms.html.

In this example, there are no custom attributes (unlike the analogous embed example); instead, the custom settings are communicated through the name/value attributes on param.

It's unlikely that you'll ever be hand-coding the parameters for embedded plug-ins (Adobe Flash, for instance, will generate the required param elements when you publish content out of the authoring environment), so I don't cover this sort of usage in great detail here. Simply be aware that when embedding plug-in-based media, the object element is what you usually need to use.

To wrap up this discussion on embedded media, it's important to mention a feature of the object element that came up earlier: the fallback content mechanism. How exactly is this done? Well, it's quite intuitive and easy to implement. You can nest object elements (or other elements), allowing the web browser to display alternative content if it cannot render the preferred choice. For instance, you can nest a video, an image, and finally some text like so:

```
<object data="video.mpg" type="application/mpeg">
        <object data="picture.jpg" type="image/jpg">
                Some descriptive text, and <a href="video.mpg">a download link</a>.
        </object>
</object>
```

The user agent should first try to display the video, but if it can't, it should then try to display the image, and if it can't do that, it displays the text—no need for alt attributes here! This concept of nesting alternative content within an element is particularly important to the elements to come later in this chapter, such as video, so keep it in mind.

■ **Note** Although object can theoretically be used to embed many types of media, the reality is that many new elements added in HTML5, as well as existing elements, have usurped object on several fronts. video and audio should be used in place of object for embedding those types of media, and img has long been the ubiquitous answer to embedded images, despite object's attempt to supersede it. Also, iframe (discussed in the next section) is a better alternative for nesting one web page inside another. The applet element for Java applets, however, is obsolete in HTML5, and for this type of content object should be used instead. It should also be used for plug-in-based media such as Adobe Flash content.

Embedding HTML: iframe

Netscape Navigator 2.0 introduced the ability to create frames, which seemed pretty innovative at the time. The ability to construct an HTML page out of numerous other pages meant, for instance, that in a page that had a frame for content and a frame for a navigation bar, the content of the page could be loaded without the need to reload the navigation bar. Also, the contents of the page could be scrolled while leaving the navigation bar stationary. Along with these advantages came a number of problems, however, which led to frames falling out of favor. Among these were difficulties search engines had navigating a frameset, leading to situations where a particular frame outside of its frameset context might turn up in search results. Since the days of Netscape Navigator, advances in web browser and web server technology have made frames obsolete (CSS, for instance, can fix the position of content so it does not scroll). In HTML5 the frame and frameset elements are obsolete and must not be used. What remains in HTML5 is the iframe element, known as an **inline frame**. This element allows an entire HTML page (or snippets of HTML code) to be embedded in another page. The ability to embed one page into another is useful for incorporating third-party HTML code into your own web page. For example, this element is often used to embed third-party ads (for instance, Google's AdSense ads). Other uses include Facebook's "Like" button and Twitter's "tweet" button, which are often seen embedded in blog posts or similar and are used to share the article on those social networks. An inline frame might also be used to embed more extensive third-party content on your site, such as a news feed or articles from another website.

Handling content in the iframe element

The iframe element creates a box with a set width and height into which the external document is loaded. It loads its content via a URL supplied to the src attribute. Like object, content can be added between the opening and closing tags as a fallback mechanism should the page be viewed by a browser that does not support inline frames. While all major browsers support the iframe element, from an accessibility perspective, it is a good practice to add fallback content anyway. If nothing else, it can be used like a comment to remind you what the linked resource is. Consider also including a link to the embedded document so that the user has access to the document even if the iframe is not supported. Here is an example:

```
<iframe src="embed.html" width="300" height="150">
        <a href="embed.html">View embedded web page.</a>
</iframe>
```

If the previous snippet were viewed in a browser that did not support iframe, the link would be displayed; otherwise, the contents of embed.html would be rendered within the boundaries of an inline frame, which is a 300 pixel wide by 150 pixel tall box (in this case, as set by the width and height attribute). Horizontal and vertical scrollbars appear as needed to fit the content, as shown in Figure 5-3.

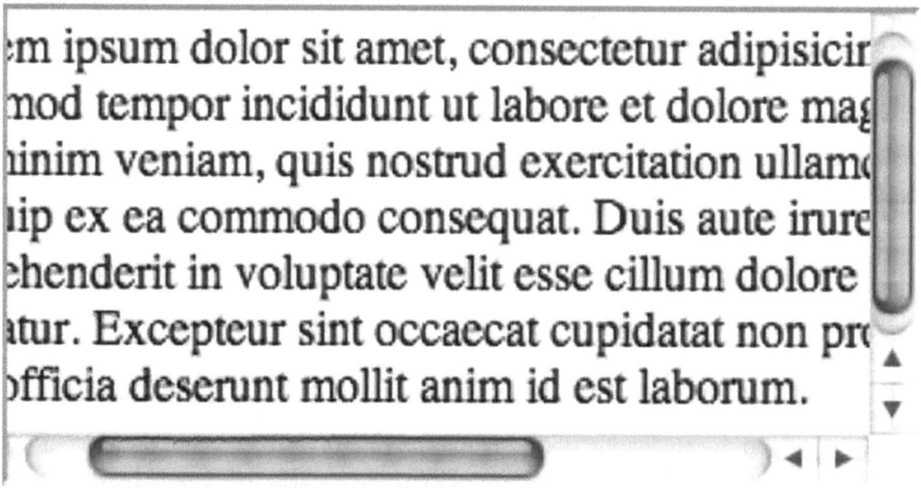

Figure 5-3. Appearance of an inline frame with scrollbars

Since it provides a fixed area to display the content within, an iframe can also be used to display a large amount of content (text generally) in a confined area on the page. For example, perhaps your website has a "terms and conditions" statement, which generally would be a long document filled with legalese text. The document is accessible through a link in the footer at the bottom of your pages, but you also want to embed this same document in a registration form for when a user registers on your site. Instead of having a duplicate of the terms and conditions page on your site—both linked in the footer and on a user registration form—you could embed the existing document into the registration page, such as shown in Figure 5-4.

Agree to Terms and Conditions ☑

Terms and Conditions of Use

The City Press and its associates provide their services to you subject to the following conditions. By registering you accept these conditions. Please read them carefully.

Figure 5-4. Example of using an inline frame to embed an existing text-heavy document in a small area

The source code for Figure 5-4 might look like this:

```
...
<p>
        <label>Agree to Terms and Conditions <input type="checkbox" title="Agree to Terms
        and Conditions" /></label>
</p>
<iframe src="tnc.html" width="500" height="100">
        <a href="tnc.html" target="_blank">View Terms and Conditions</a>
</iframe>
...
```

New iframe element attributes

As far as the attributes of iframe go, there has been the usual practice of presentational attributes being marked obsolete in HTML5. The following attributes should not be used: frameborder, marginheight, marginwidth, and scrolling. Additionally, the longdesc attribute has been dropped, which shouldn't be a loss, because it never had adequate browser support anyway.

HTML5 has added a small number of attributes related to the ability to embed HTML code snippets and pages that are **sandboxed**, meaning they are prevented from performing certain operations that could be used for nefarious purposes by third-party pieces of code. The idea is to use inline frames as a way to secure pieces of code added dynamically to a web page from a third-party source, as might be done as part of the commenting system on a blog or forum. The three attributes are srcdoc, seamless, and sandbox.

■ **Note** You may find that the new iframe attributes don't work in your preferred web browser, because they have yet to gain much support among major browsers. As of this writing, sandbox is the only one of the three new attributes to have support (in Safari and Google Chrome). We hope further support will be quick to arrive, but as with any new feature in HTML5, keep an eye out for changes to these attributes as the HTML5 specification is refined further in the months and years to come.

The srcdoc attribute allows snippets of HTML to be entered directly into the attribute's value, unlike src, which needs to be given a URL that points to another HTML file, so for example:

```
<iframe srcdoc="<p>This text is in an inline frame</p>"><p>This is regular text</p></iframe>
```

This code will create a snippet of HTML that will be inserted into an inline frame. If the srcdoc and src attributes are present, srcdoc will override src, but src can still be included and given a value so as to provide fallback content for when the srcdoc attribute is not supported (which currently is the case in all major browsers).

The seamless attribute, which is a Boolean attribute, makes the included content appear to be part of the containing document, meaning, for example, that links clicked in the inline frame will load in the parent document instead of loading inside the iframe by default.

The last attribute, sandbox, may be treated as a Boolean attribute but does not necessarily need to be (as you'll see momentarily). When treated as a Boolean attribute, it adds a number of security restrictions to the iframe's source content. These restrictions are as follows:

- **Restricted local access**: The content is treated as being from a different server, which prevents access to local server content such as cookies and other web storage options tied to the local server domain.

- **No form submission**: Form submission from the inline content is disabled.

- **No JavaScript**: Scripts in the inline content are disabled.

- **No external link targets**: Links in the inline content are prevented from targeting other browsing contexts, such as the containing document through the use of target="_parent", for example.

- **No plug-ins**: Inline content requiring plug-ins, such as for Adobe Flash content, are disabled.

As a Boolean attribute, sandbox just needs to be added to the iframe to enable these restrictions, like so:

```
<iframe src="external.html" sandbox><!-- Fallback content --></iframe>
```

If the sandbox attribute is not treated as a Boolean attribute, a number of text keywords values can be set that will negate almost all of the previous restrictions. Table 5-1 shows the available keywords. More than one keyword can be added to negate more than one restriction, with each separated by a space. Here's an example:

```
<iframe src="external.html" sandbox="allow-forms allow-top-navigation">
    <!-- Fallback content -->
</iframe>
```

The previous code would allow form submissions and external link targets in the embedded content but would have the other sandbox restrictions in effect.

Table 5-1. The sandbox attributes

Sandbox attribute value	Description
`allow-same-origin`	Allow content to be treated as if it is from the same origin as the local server's content
`allow-scripts`	Allow the execution of scripts
`allow-forms`	Allow form submissions
`allow-top-navigation`	Allow links to target other browsing contexts (such as the containing HTML page)

■ **Note** Notice that there is not a keyword to override disabling plug-ins. The reason for this is a plug-in could be built that circumvented some of the other restrictions, presenting a vulnerability to any selective restrictions in place. Therefore, plug-ins are always disabled as long as the `sandbox` attribute is present.

Targeting inline frames

The `iframe` has one last attribute—which isn't new—the `name` attribute, which can be used to identify a particular inline frame among other inline frames used on a page. Doing so means a particular inline frame can be used as a target for links when the `target` attribute is set to a particular inline frame's name. Here's an example:

```
<iframe name="terms" src="tnc.html">
        <a href="tnc.html" target="_blank">View Terms and Conditions</a>
</iframe>
<a href="page2.html" target="terms">Next page</a>
```

In this case, when the "Next page" hyperlink text is clicked, the `page2.html` page is loaded into the "terms" inline frame.

Video

More than any other element, the `video` element is what brought HTML5 into the public consciousness. To the wider public that just uses the Web, it became known that videos on YouTube could not be viewed on the iPhone/iPad because YouTube used Adobe Flash for displaying video.[6] However, there

---

[6] YouTube still predominantly uses Flash, but it has an HTML5 player at www.youtube.com/html5, and videos viewed with a device that does not support Flash will fall back to using this HTML5 video player.

existed a new solution called "HTML5" that could display video on the iPhone/iPad. Exactly what that meant was no doubt lost on the majority of users of the Web, but for you and others like you, it means there is a new element, video, that allows video files to be embedded into a web page without the use of any third-party plug-ins. It means native video playback in the browser. This differs from using object for video playback, because object just hands the video content off to a plug-in.

This is a huge addition to the HTML specification, because video can now be integrated anywhere other HTML elements can be used. For instance, CSS and JavaScript can interact with the video. However, implementing video has not been without its hurdles. Notably, a standard video format has not emerged, which leads to the need to encode video in different formats to handle all major web browsers. Let's begin our discussion there.

■ **Note** The video element has quite good support across major video browsers, but if you want to provide support for older browsers, consider a solution such as that found at http://html5media.info, which provides JavaScript code that emulates the video (and audio) element's functionality for older browsers.

Video formats

A video file is potentially a very large (in file size) piece of content to include on a web page. Outside of the Web, depending on the length and quality a video, a particular clip could easily stretch into gigabytes in size. Therefore, to display on the Web, a suitable form of compression needs to be applied to the video to reduce the size to make delivery over the Internet feasible. The form of compression applied to a video is referred to as a **codec**. Since video is a multimedia format, in that it can contain video *and* audio, the codec is only part of what makes up a video file. The video and audio are placed together in what is known as a *container* format, which is what the video file actually is. There are three major container formats for video on the Web: WebM, Ogg, and MPEG-4. The container format will contain a codec for video compression and a codec for audio compression, plus any metadata about the video, such as subtitles. The codecs used inside a particular container format can vary, but the commonly used ones on the Web are shown in Table 5-2, along with browser support for these formats.

Table 5-2. Major video formats used in HTML5 video

Container format	Video codec	Audio codec	Internet Explorer 9	Firefox 5	Google Chrome 13	Safari 5	Opera 11
WebM	VP8	Vorbis		■	■		■
OGG	Theora	Vorbis		■	■		■
MPEG-4	H.264 (also called MPEG-4 AVC)	AAC	■		□[7]	■	

As you can see in Table 5-2, currently there is not a single format that can be used across all major web browsers. It's a shame that Microsoft and Apple have not rallied behind WebM or Ogg,[8] but the reality of the current landscape of native browser video is such that web developers have to deal with delivering multiple formats for the same video file, if broad browser compatibility is a concern. We'll see how to do this after we've had a look at licensing issues.

The licensing issue

In addition to browser support issues, there is another issue to be aware of in regard to codecs. The codecs in MPEG-4, H.264, and ACC contain patented technology. This means certain uses of these formats are subject to royalty fees by the MPEG LA consortium, which holds the rights to these patents. You'll be fine streaming these videos for free on the Web, but it will be a different scenario if you wanted to charge users to view videos in this format or provided technology that decoded or encoded video in these formats. WebM and Ogg, on the other hand, are both open formats, unencumbered by any known patents.

Handling video sources

If you're delivering only one video, the markup is about as easy as placing an image on the page. The video file is supplied in the src attribute. Like img, a width and height are also advisable to set, but make sure it matches the aspect ratio of the video source:

---

[7] Don't lose all faith in the information I'm providing if you launch Google Chrome and find it doesn't run MPEG-4 video. Support has traditionally been included in Chrome, but Google has since pledged to remove support for H.264-encoded video in favor of the other two open formats, so going forward it can't reliably be said to support this format.

[8] There are ways to make Internet Explorer 9 and Safari support at least WebM, but it requires installing additional software that does not ship with the browsers, which is by no means an option to rely on when deciding how to deliver your video content to users in these browsers.

```
<video src="trailer.webm" width="320" height="240"></video>
```

However, this does not provide any fallback content for browsers that don't support the WebM format or for browsers that don't support the video element. To provide multiple source files for the video, another element, the source element, is used to provide alternative content. The source element has three attributes: src, type, and media. The src attribute is where the video file is specified, just like in video. The type attribute is used to supply a video MIME type that gives the web browser a hint as to what video format it is dealing with. Since the video format is a container format, the MIME type is more complicated than with other file types. To address this, the MIME type defines an additional codecs parameter to help narrow down the exact type of video/audio format (container format *and* codecs used). This looks almost like an additional attribute on source, but it is contained inside the type attribute if you look closely at the nested quotes:[9]

```
<video width="320" height="240">
        <source src="trailer.webm" type='video/webm; codecs="vp8, vorbis"' />
</video>
```

This example shows the source video container format (WebM) as well as the video and audio codec used (VP8 and Vorbis). The actual value supplied in the codecs parameter will vary depending on the options set when the video was encoded. Not only is a video a container format that can use a variety of codecs for video and audio, but these codecs also can have their own variations. H.264 in particular has a number of "profiles" that can be chosen for the purposes of using the video in different environments (mobile versus a desktop computer, for instance). Table 5-3 shows common values for the type attribute; the H.264 codecs shown are a profile for mobile devices (baseline), standard-definition digital video broadcasting (main), and high-definition video broadcasting (high).

Table 5-3. WebM, Ogg and MPEG-4 codec parameters for the video type attribute

Video format	MIME types
WebM	video/webm; codecs="vp8, vorbis"
Ogg	video/ogg; codecs="theora, vorbis"
MPEG-4 (baseline) – mobile delivery	video/mp4; codecs="avc1.42E01E, mp4a.40.2"
MPEG-4 (main) – standard-definition video broadcast	video/mp4; codecs="avc1.4D401E, mp4a.40.2"
MPEG-4 (high) – high-definition video broadcast	video/mp4; codecs="avc1.64001E, mp4a.40.2"

The type attribute is not required, but if you do included it (and it is recommended that you do), it will allow the web browser to determine whether it can play a particular video file before it downloads part or all of the file, which will save bandwidth and time from the user's perspective.

---

[9] It is important that the quotes are single quotes surrounding double quotes and not the other way around, because the MIME type's codecs parameter expects its contents to be in double quotes.

▪ **Note** The WHATWG publishes a wiki with a helpful summary of the MIME types needed for the type attribute; it can be found at `http://wiki.whatwg.org/wiki/Video_type_parameters`.

The last attribute, media, specifies the device and/or media the video is optimized for. When set, a user agent can use its value to determine whether the video is intended for one particular type of device (such as a mobile phone). Like with the type attribute, a user agent can inspect this attribute's value to determine whether it should download the video. This is the same attribute that is found on the anchor element (a). It will be discussed in more depth in the "Media queries" section in Chapter 8.

We still haven't quite gotten to providing fallback content, because the last code snippet still provides only one video format. Let's change that. The web browser will parse the content inside the video element in sequential order, moving down the list of source files until it finds one it can play, so under the WebM file in the previous example, we'll add two more lines for the MPEG-4 and Ogg-formatted video:

```
<video width="320" height="240">
        <source src="trailer.webm" type='video/webm; codecs="vp8, vorbis"' />
        <source src="trailer.mp4" type='video/mp4; codecs="avc1.4D401E, mp4a.40.2"' />
        <source src="trailer.ogv" type='video/ogg; codecs="theora, vorbis"' />
</video>
```

▪ **Note** There was a bug in iOS 3.*x* that caused the browser to stop at the first video source instead of moving on down the list. This has been patched, but if it is critical to support older iOS devices, move the MPEG-4 video to the top of the source list.

That's a lot of copies of the same video file! We're aiming for broad compatibility here, but if you wanted to slim this down, you could probably get away with not including the Ogg format. Older versions of Firefox could not handle WebM, so the inclusion of Ogg will help Firefox user who have not updated recently. However, we can instead address those users with additional types of fallback content, which we'll look at next.

After the list of video sources, additional fallback content can be provided to handle cases where the video element itself is not supported. For instance, the object element could be included to provide a fallback to Flash video:

```
<video width="320" height="240">
        <source src="trailer.webm" type='video/webm; codecs="vp8, vorbis"' />
        <source src="trailer.mp4" type='video/mp4; codecs="avc1.4D401E, mp4a.40.2"' />
        <source src="trailer.ogv" type='video/ogg; codecs="theora, vorbis"' />
        <object type="application/x-shockwave-flash" data="videoplayer.swf" width="320"
        height="240">
        </object>
</video>
```

■ **Note** I've simplified the Flash embed code shown here for brevity; in practice this would likely be more verbose, definitely so if you use the HTML wrapper generated by the Adobe Flash IDE, which contains additional parameters and formatting to handle idiosyncrasies across different browsers. Specifically, Internet Explorer is notorious for not handling the `data` attribute like other browsers and instead requires that the SWF be defined in a nested `param` element, like so: `<param name="movie" value="videoplayer.swf" />`.

While an additional SWF file would be included to provide a video player that would handle the Flash video, thankfully a fourth copy of the video file would *not* need to be created. Flash conveniently supports the H.264 video format, so it will be able to play the existing MPEG-4 video.

■ **Note** For a great Flash video player, check out the one provided by the Open Source Media Framework. It can even be configured directly in the browser: www.osmf.org/configurator/fmp/.

Further fallback can be added; for example, a poster image (a still image in place of the video) could be added, followed by a text fallback. For extra accessibility in the text fallback, links can be added to allow the video files to be downloaded. Since `object` can contain fallback content like `video`, this additional fallback content is placed in `object`, but it could be placed below the video source list if `object` were not included:

```
<video width="320" height="240">
        <source src="trailer.webm" type='video/webm; codecs="vp8, vorbis"' />
        <source src="trailer.mp4" type='video/mp4; codecs="avc1.4D401E, mp4a.40.2"' />
        <source src="trailer.ogv" type='video/ogg; codecs="theora, vorbis"' />
        <object type="application/x-shockwave-flash" data="videoplayer.swf" width="320"
        height="240">
        <img src="poster.jpg" width="320" height="240"
        alt="" title="Movie trailer" />
                <p><strong>Movie trailer.</strong><br />
                Download video files as: <a href="trailer.webm">WebM</a>,
                <a href="trailer.mp4">MPEG-4</a>, or <a href="trailer.ogv">Ogg</a>.
                </p>
        </object>
</video>
```

In a browser that didn't support the `video` element and didn't have the Flash Player installed, the browser would display the fallback text (Figure 5-5).

Movie trailer.
Download video files as: <u>WebM</u>, <u>MPEG-4</u>, or <u>Ogg</u>.

Figure 5-5. Fallback content for browsers that don't support the video element might include such things as an image, text, and links to download the video.

Phew! This completes a cascade of fallback content for handling a variety of different user agents. Not the most succinct-looking block of markup, but if access to your video content is essential, it is important to tailor it to the needs of the broadest audience possible.

Video attributes

At this point, if you tested this code, the video would not look any more spectacular than a still image. That's because by default the video will not automatically play, and more importantly it won't have any controls for starting or pausing the video or adjusting the sound. However, as you will see, these and other options are easy to add through the various attributes available on the video element.

Adding video controls

To add control buttons to the video, all that's needed is to add the Boolean controls attribute to video. *Voila*. The browser adds a basic but complete set of controls to the video. An outward difference in HTML5 video that may be a bit of a shock to those used to the consistency of appearance when using Adobe Flash is that the controls for a video look different in each browser, since they are each implementing their own native video player (Figure 5-6).

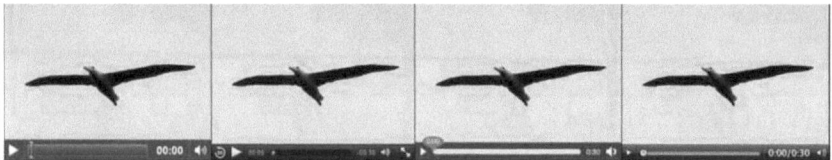

Figure 5-6. Appearance of the video *element controls in different browsers: (L to R) Google Chrome, Safari, Firefox, Opera*

This difference in the appearance of the controls may be a bit of a disappointment if you are design-minded at all, but it is important to remember that since the video is in HTML, a custom set of controls can be created in CSS and JavaScript that provide a consistent appearance across different browsers. That is a topic for another time, however (we'll look at it again in Chapter 7).

Autoplaying and looping video

I mentioned the video will not automatically play when the page loads, but we can change this by using the Boolean autoplay attribute. By adding this attribute…you guessed it…the video begins playing immediately after it loads. Generally it's a bad idea to include this attribute, unless your site works like YouTube or related sites where the user would click a link and be taken to a video page. In such a site, the video is the focus of the page, and the expectation is that the video will be played immediately.

Another Boolean attribute (video has a lot of them) is the loop attribute, which specifies that the video will replay when it has reached the end. Like automatically playing the video, this is usually a good idea only in specific scenarios, such as if the video is part of some sort of background ambience of the page.

Preloading video data

The preload attribute suggests whether any of the video data is preloaded when the page loads, before the user has clicked play on the video. It can take the values none, metadata, or auto. If it's set to an empty string (""), it will map to the auto state. It is a good idea to include this attribute because the default behavior for preloading is not standardized and is up to the web browsers to decide for themselves; however, that being said, it is not a strict instruction and is only an advisory attribute to the web browser. If needed, the web browser can override what is set here based on any user preferences or other factors (such as the autoplay attribute being present). For instance, a user on a mobile phone may not want to preload video to save bandwidth, and a mobile browser may set this as a preference that is then enforced on pages the user visits, despite the value set in the preload attribute.

Because the preload attribute is advisory, the meaning of the different values are not to be taken literally. A value of none suggests that the video should not be preloaded at all (including metadata information). A value of metadata suggests that video data should be loaded up to, but not including, the video itself. Metadata may include the duration, dimensions, and so on. A value of auto suggests anything may be preloaded, which means perhaps only the metadata, but it could mean the entire video itself is preloaded.

Adding a poster image

The poster attribute sets a poster image for the video, which is an image that is shown in place of the video before the video begins playing (Figure 5-7). This image could be anything but it is often the first frame of the video, since the poster image is intended to give the user an idea of what the video looks like. The value given is the location of the image to use, such as this:

```
<video width="320" height="240" controls poster="trailer-poster.jpg"> …
```

This code would use the poster image trailer-poster.jpg, located in the same directory as the HTML page containing this code.

■ **Note** In a production environment, you would want to place images in their own directory to keep your website files organized.

Figure 5-7. A poster image for the flying bird video shown in Figure 5-6

Muting a video

The Boolean `muted` attribute, when added, is meant to set the sound to mute when the video first plays (the user can click the sound icon in the controls to change this). However, at the time of writing, major browsers have not implemented this feature.

Setting cross-origin policy

The attribute `crossorigin` is involved in a specification called Cross-Origin Resource Sharing (CORS), which determines how the video may be shared across separate website domains. It has the values `anonymous` or `use-credentials` (an empty string `""` may also be given, which maps to anonymous). For more information on CORS, see the W3C resource on this specification at `www.w3.org/TR/cors/` or `http://enable-cors.org/`.

Media groups

The `mediagroup` attribute aims to support grouping videos or video tracks together so that they all may be controlled at the same time as a group. It has yet to gain browser support, however when it does, the idea is this: imagine a particular video presentation that also has an accompanying video with a sign language interpretation of the video's audio. When the main video is played, the sign language video should play as well. The `mediagroup` attribute ties these two videos together so the browser knows that if one plays, the other should play at the same time. This could mean the two videos are separate video files embedded on the same page, or it could mean that each video is contained in a video track. Remember that the video format is a container format, meaning it contains at least two types of media: a video track and an audio track. As a container format, additional video and audio tracks can be embedded in a single file. Using the previous example, a particular video may have a video and audio track for the main presentation but have the sign language video as a second video track. In such a scenario, two `video` elements may appear on the page, with each one accessing a different video track on the same video source file. The playback of the two videos is then tied together by having the same name set in their `mediagroup` attribute.

This attribute provides powerful possibilities for video broadcasting on the Web, so keep your eyes on its further development and implementation!

■ **Note** Silvia Pfeiffer, author of *The Definitive Guide to HTML5 Video* (Apress), has a great summary of how this attribute might be used on her blog at this address: `http://blog.gingertech.net/2011/05/01/html5-multi-track-audio-or-video/`.

Audio

Audio in HTML5 admittedly has a fair way to go. Having control over audio on a web page on par with what Adobe Flash is able to do[10] is an active part of development at the moment.[11] Basic audio, allowing the user to start, stop, and adjust the volume of an audio clip, is available using the new audio element. This element is really just the video element without the moving image portion. The controls look like the controls created by the browser; for example, compare Figure 5-8 to Figure 5-7. It has the following attributes, all of which should be familiar from reading the "Video" section: src, preload, autoplay, loop, muted, controls, crossorigin, and mediagroup. Also like the video element, audio supports the source element and fallback content that is nested between its opening and closing tag. An audio element with fallback content would look very similar to its video counterpart:

```
<audio controls>
        <source src="report.oga" type='audio/ogg; codecs="vorbis"' />
        <source src="report.m4a" type='audio/mp4; codecs="mp4a.40.2"' />
        <p>Audio not supported. Download audio files as:
        <a href="report.oga">Ogg</a>, <a href="report.m4v">ACC</a>p>
</audio>
```

■ **Note** If the controls attribute is left off, nothing is shown by default!

The difference here to video is that the audio does not have a width and height (it is possible to adjust the size of the playback bar with CSS), and obviously the format of the source files is different.

Figure 5-8. Appearance of the audio element in Google Chrome

Audio formats

The audio formats will be for the most part familiar from reading the "Video" section. The same browser support discrepancies exist as well, not that that is something to celebrate. Refer to Table 5-2 in the "Video formats" section and look at the audio codecs column. Like with video, the Ogg and MPEG-4 container formats can be used, this time without the video track. Therefore, Ogg audio will work in Google Chrome, Firefox, and Opera, while MPEG-4 audio will work in Safari, Chrome, and Internet Explorer. The Ogg format uses the Vorbis codec (WebM uses this for audio also), so when speaking of just audio, the format is referred to as Ogg Vorbis and has the file extension .oga (or even .ogg). The MPEG-4 container uses Advanced Audio Coding (ACC) for its audio codec. Since it is in the MPEG-4 container, it generally uses the file extension .m4a to differentiate it from .mp4. ACC is the successor to

---

[10] See http://audiotool.com/app as an example. Audiotool is a cloud-based application for creating music that is built on the Adobe Flash Platform.
[11] See the Web Audio API at the W3C: http://dvcs.w3.org/hg/audio/raw-file/tip/webaudio/specification.html.

the MP3 format that is widely used in digital music (for portable music players such as the Apple iPod). ACC-encoded audio may be freely played over the Web (barring any licenses needed for the content itself), but it is not completely patent free. A license is needed for developing tools for encoding and decoding ACC (if you're curious, license fee costs are listed here: `www.vialicensing.com/licensing/aac-fees.aspx`).

> ■ **Note** The WAV audio format can also be used and is sometimes included in the list of fallback content. WAV is an uncompressed audio format, which means the files are relatively large compared to Ogg Vorbis and ACC. MP3 may also be used but MP3 has stricter licensing issues surrounding it than ACC, so it is best avoided in favor of ACC. Both WAV and MP3 are not supported universally across all major browsers either, so there is nothing to gain from their use on that front.

Captions track

HTML5 adds a great new feature that opens up the accessibility of videos. The track element has been added to the HTML specification to define a method of adding subtitles and related timed text tracks to the video and audio elements. By "added," I mean it has been added to the specification, because web browser makers are still working toward implementing the element's functionality. The general idea is that a text file is marked up with textual information that is then loaded with the video or audio and is usually timed to be presented at points throughout the playback of the media resource. The track element would then be placed in the video or audio element and be used to load the timed text file. The track element defines five attributes: kind, src, label, srclang, and default.

> ■ **Note** If you want to provide closed captioning in your video today, check out the Captionator project (`https://github.com/cgiffard/Captionator`). This project uses JavaScript to emulate functionality of the track element so that it can be used while the web browsers catch up with its implementation.

The kind attribute determines what kind of text track is being added (see Table 5-4); if omitted, the default is to identify the loaded text file as being of the subtitles kind. The src attribute defines the address of the text file to load. The actual format for the text file is not defined, but it will likely be a format called Web Video Text Track (WebVTT). The file extension is .vtt. There are other formats, however, such as Timed Text Markup Language (TTML),[12] that may be used instead. The WebVTT format is currently defined only in the WHATWG version of HTML(5),[13] but the W3C has a proposed WebVTT working group charter published.[14]

---

[12] See www.w3.org/TR/2010/REC-ttaf1-dfxp-20101118/
[13] Remember WHATWG uses version-less development, so HTML and HTML5 are one and the same.
[14] See www.w3.org/2011/05/google-webvtt-charter.html

Table 5-4. The different kinds of timed text tracks

Timed text kind	Description
subtitles	Written transcription of the video's dialog only. For situations where the viewer does not understand the speech.
captions	Written transcription of all audio in the video. For situations where the viewer can't hear the audio.
descriptions	Written description of the contents of the video. For situations where the viewer can't see the video (if applicable).
chapters	Chapter titles for media that is broken into subsections, such as might be found on a DVD movie's menu.
metadata	Additional data that can be embedded in the media for use by scripts on the page.

The label attribute gives a human-readable description of the contents of the text track that a web browser could display to a user to change to a different subtitle language, for instance. The Boolean default attribute sets which text track is enabled initially. A particular video could contain subtitles in multiple languages so this attribute could be used to set the default language to use. Speaking of languages, the last attribute, srclang, is for precisely that: defining the language the timed text track is written in.

An example implementation might look like this:

```
<video width="320" height="240">
        <source src="trailer.webm" type='video/webm; codecs="vp8, vorbis"' />
        <source src="trailer.mp4" type='video/mp4; codecs="avc1.4D401E, mp4a.40.2"' />

        <track kind="captions" label="English Captions" srclang="en"
        src="trailer_cc_en.vtt" default />
        <track kind="subtitles" label="English Subtitles" srclang="en"
        src="trailer_st_en.vtt" />
        <track kind="subtitles" label="German Subtitles" srclang="de"
        src="trailer_st_de.vtt" />
        <track kind="subtitles" label="French Subtitles" srclang="fr"
        src="trailer_st_fr.vtt" />
</video>
```

■ **Note** There is a proposal under discussion to allow the track element to include the source element so timed text could be provided in various formats. This would work as a fallback mechanism for the browsers in the same way it works for video and audio media.

Encoding audio and video

Encoding media files is a topic that could easily fill a whole book, so I'll just direct you toward some tools that will help you generate WebM, Ogg, Ogg Vorbis, MPEG-4, and ACC files to work with:

- **HandBrake**: This is an open source transcoder for generating `.mp4` files. See `http://handbrake.fr`.

- **Firefogg**: This is a Firefox extension for performing Ogg encoding. See `http://firefogg.org`.

- **FFmpeg**: This is a very powerful open source suite of tools that includes a command-line tool for converting between different media formats. It's used in other tools, such as Firefogg. See `http://ffmpeg.org`.[15]

- **Miro video converter**: This is an easy-to-use drag-and-drop converter for video formats found on the Web and on mobile devices. It's Mac only, however. See `www.mirovideoconverter.com/`.

- **VLC**: This is a flexible media player that has no problem handling all the web video and audio formats you may deal with. It features an export wizard for converting between different formats. See `http://videolan.org/vlc/`.

- **Adobe Media Encoder**: If you have Adobe software on your computer, you may have a copy of the Adobe Media Encoder, which can import popular video and audio formats and encode them in a variety of different formats. It provides a large set of presets for different video delivery situations.

Last but not least

The new `canvas` element is used to embed a scriptable bitmap into the web page. This essentially means the capability now exists to place a blank image on the page of a certain dimension, which can be drawn upon and graphically manipulated from JavaScript code. Cool! The element itself it quite basic; it just defines two attributes, `width` and `height`, for specifying the dimensions of the canvas. Like prior elements in this chapter, it contains the ability to provide fallback content through placing additional HTML between its opening and closing tags, like so:

```
<canvas width="600" height="300">
        <p>The canvas element is not supported!</p>
</canvas>
```

Like other elements, more fallback content than text could be placed in between the opening and closing tags, but `canvas` is pretty unique, so it may be hard to find suitable alternative content beyond text. Flash could be used as a replacement, so you could, for example, build an interactive application using `canvas` and replicate that functionality in Flash to provide as fallback content. The `object` element (or more rarely, the `embed` element) would then be used inside `canvas`. At any rate, if you tried the previous code on a page, it wouldn't be very exciting because it would just create a blank area in the page

---

[15] Refer to this helpful post for a list of commands when using the ffmpeg command-line tool: www.catswhocode.com/blog/19-ffmpeg-commands-for-all-needs.

layout that was 600 by 300 pixels wide and tall. The real power of canvas comes from dynamically generating imagery using JavaScript, which we will get into in Chapter 7.

Summary

As you have seen, HTML5 has made it easier to include multimedia in your web pages. The semantics are improved too because there are elements dedicated to images, video, and sound, instead of so many types of media relying on a generic object element as has been the case in the past (at least as far as video and audio are concerned). To handle the transition toward richer media in web pages, the new elements (and some of the old) include a consistent and intuitive fallback mechanism. object, iframe, video, audio, canvas, and perhaps soon track all provide the same mechanism for handling alternative content. There is more to look forward to as the specification for timed text moves forward and browsers implement missing features. Perhaps one day one media format will emerge in video (and audio) that all the major web browsers support, as happened with still images, but in the meantime we will have to get used to encoding media two or three times.

CSS3

In this chapter, we'll diverge for the most part from HTML into a totally different language and specification. It's time for Cascading Style Sheets (CSS). CSS may not be HTML, but HTML is not much to look at without CSS, so mastery of one necessitates some degree of mastery of the other.

Since this book is about HTML, we'll spend most of our time in this chapter examining the relationship between HTML and CSS and how the two interact, but we'll explore purely CSS topics as well. The CSS specification is currently in its third iteration, so we'll run through the necessary core CSS concepts you should know and then dive into the details of what is new. There's a bit of technical jargon to cover, but in doing so, we'll set the stage for our exploration of the possibilities of page design. From a usability standpoint, these aspects can be just as important as the semantics of your markup.

The present state: CSS2.1

CSS is broken into levels, which are versions of the specification analogous to the W3C versions of HTML (HTML 3.2, HTML 4.01, HTML5, and so on). The current stable and complete level is CSS level 2 revision 1, otherwise known as CSS2.1. Documents developed by the W3C go through stages of review that are used to identify the stability of a particular specification (Table 6-1).

Table 6-1. W3C maturity levels

Maturity level of specification	Description
W3C Recommendation (REC)	The specification has received endorsement of W3C members and the director and is recommended for widespread adoption.
Proposed Recommendation (PR)	The specification has endured wide review for technical soundness and implementability and has been sent to the W3C Advisory Committee for final endorsement.
Candidate Recommendation (CR)	The specification has been widely reviewed and satisfies the Working Group's technical requirements.
Last Call Working Draft (LC or LCWD)	A Last Call (LC) announcement is used to provide any last review of the specification before it is

	advanced to higher maturity levels.
Working Draft (WD)	The specification has been published for review by the wider community. Working Draft documents might never advance any further.

It often takes years to develop a specification to full maturity, and a particular document might waffle back and forth between different levels of maturity as technological conditions change and new working drafts emerge. For example, CSS2 was a published recommendation in 1998; CSS2.1 (remember, a *revision* on CSS2) took more than a decade to become a W3C Recommendation but finally did so on June 6, 2011! Obviously, this does not mean we had to wait until June 2011 to use features in CSS2.1, but it does mean that the specification potentially could change while it was under review. For comparison, consider this: the W3C's version of HTML5 is currently in Working Draft status! It's not unreasonable to expect that its progression to Recommendation status could take a decade or more. However, as this book has shown, there is so much available for use in HTML5 today. Its availability is not a decade away, but the specification (and subsequent implementations) will evolve over that period. You have also seen features (the track element, for instance) that are yet to be implemented by any major web browser. If the specification were at W3C Recommendation status, unimplemented features would not be found (WHATWG's HTML versionless specification takes a different view to this). So, now that you have an understanding of the state of CSS in the broader picture, what is the state of the next level of CSS, CSS level 3?

CSS3 modules

CSS3 is defined differently than its predecessors. Instead of one monster document covering the entire specification, CSS3 is broken into dozens of modules that are in various states of maturity. This allows self-contained features of CSS to reach maturity quicker and not be held back by being part of a larger draft document. Table 6-2 lists a selection of modules from the W3C. This gives you a taste of some of the features brought into CSS3. You can find the full list of modules at www.w3.org/Style/CSS/current-work.

Table 6-2. A selection of W3C CSS3 modules

Module	Description
Backgrounds and Borders	Covers background and border effects
Multi-column Layout	Covers properties for generating multicolumn layouts within an element
Basic User Interface	Covers styling of interactive, dynamic web page elements
Color	Describes foreground color and opacity
Fonts	Describes font properties and @font-face rule for downloading fonts

Flexible Box Layout	Describes a flexible new layout model that can be used alongside the traditional CSS model
Image Values	Describes what values can be used where an image is expected, which includes CSS-generated gradients
2D Transformations	Describes a property for rotating, moving, skewing, and scaling elements
3D Transformations	Extends 2D transformations into the z-axis
Transitions	Describes animating CSS properties over a certain time period

Using CSS

Now that you have an overview of what CSS3 is from an organizational standpoint, let's run through its proper use. This may well be familiar to you, and if so, feel free to skip ahead to the discussion of specific modules in CSS3, but do at least skim over this section because there are new aspects to using CSS that have been introduced in CSS3.

Attaching a style sheet

Before using CSS with HTML, you need to attach a style sheet to the page so that the CSS styles can access the HTML they are associated with. There are a couple ways of doing this, but the way you should approach it by using the link element. link first came up in Chapter 2, but we did not discuss using it to link style sheets in depth. As you may recall, this element appears in the head section of the page, and the rel attribute is used to indicate the linked document is a style sheet:

```
<!DOCTYPE html>
<html>
        <head>
                <meta charset="utf-8" />
                <title>HTML5 and CSS together</title>
                <link rel="stylesheet" href="css/main.css" type="text/css" />
        </head>
        <body>
                <p>CSS rules!</p>
        </body>
</html>
```

Note As noted in Chapter 2, you can omit the type attribute when linking to a style sheet, as that is what the linked document will be presumed to be by default.

The title attribute has special significance to the link element within the context of style sheets. This attribute is used for differentiating the different possible kinds of style sheets that are linked. You may be asking yourself, "What different kinds of style sheets?" Don't worry, it's all CSS; there isn't another language to learn! The kinds of style sheets determine the priority a particular style sheet has over other style sheets linked on the page. There are three kinds that can be added to a document:

- *Persistent*: Always applied to the document

- *Preferred*: Applied to the document unless an alternative style sheet is applied

- *Alternative*: Alternative to the preferred or persistent style sheet

The main implementation difference between persistent, preferred, and alternative style sheets is that persistent style sheets *do not* have a title attribute, while preferred and alternative style sheets *do*.

All style sheets that are persistent will be applied to the HTML document, regardless of the number that are attached. This is the most common way that style sheets are applied. The style sheet in the preceding code snippet is a persistent style sheet. In contrast, not all preferred and alternate style sheets may be applied. If multiple preferred and alternate style sheets are linked to an HTML document, only one will be selected and used on the page. An alternative style sheet works just like a preferred style sheet, with the additional meaning that it can be used as a replacement for the preferred style sheet specified on the page. Alternative style sheets may be selected by the user for preferential or accessibility reasons.

The following shows a page with a persistent, preferred, and two alternative style sheets attached:

```
...
<head>
    <meta charset="utf-8" />
    <title>HTML5 and CSS together</title>

    <link rel="stylesheet" href="css/main.css" type="text/css" />
    <link rel="stylesheet" href="css/colors-generic.css" type="text/css" title="Generic color
styles" />
    <link rel="alternative stylesheet" href="css/colors-protanopia.css" type="text/css"
title="Protanopia adjusted color styles" />
    <link rel="alternative stylesheet" href="css/colors-deuteranopia.css" type="text/css"
title="Deuteranopia adjusted color styles" />

</head>
...
```

In this example page, main.css is the persistent style sheet and is used to set all the styles for the page, across all situations. colors-generic.css is a preferred style sheet that adds the color-related styles to the page. The two alternative style sheets are given as a choice for users with color blindness in the red-green spectrum: colors-protanopia.css for protanopia and colors-deuteranopia.css for deuteranopia. Presumably, activating these styles would alter the page colors to compensate for areas where color blindness may make the content difficult to view. How these alternative style sheets become available depends on the user agent in use, but some browsers offer a menu option where the user can select alternative styles (Figure 6-1).

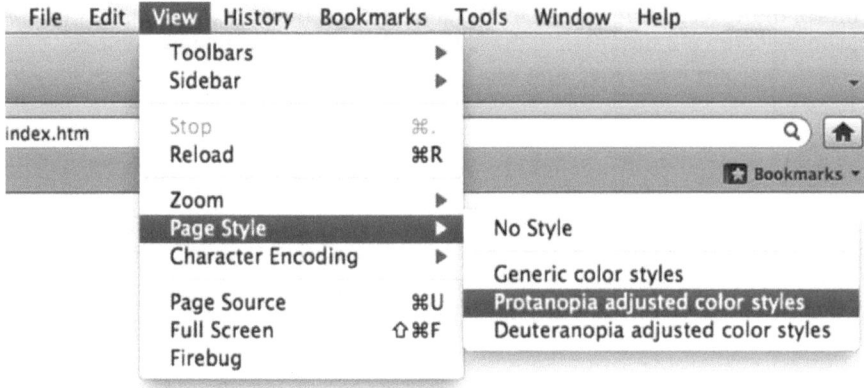

Figure 6-1. *In Firefox, preferred and alternative style sheets can be selected under the View menu.*

You can also set the preferred style sheet using the meta element. The http-equiv="Default-Style" pragma directive may be used to set the preferred style sheet by setting the content attribute to the title of one of the style sheets. For example, the following would set the style sheet with the title "Blue Theme" as the default style sheet:

```
...
<head>
    <meta charset="utf-8" />
    <meta http-equiv="Default-Style" content="Blue Theme" />
    <title>HTML5 and CSS together</title>

    <link rel="stylesheet" href="css/red.css"
    type="text/css" title="Red Theme" />
    <link rel="alternative stylesheet" href="css/green.css"
    type="text/css" title="Green Theme" />
    <link rel="alternative stylesheet" href="css/blue.css"
    type="text/css" title="Blue Theme" />

</head>
...
```

Using the meta element for setting the default style sheet offers a central point at which the preferred styles on the page can be selected. This opens the possibility of changing one value dynamically using a server-side script, for instance, based on user interaction or other variables.

CSS style rules

After attaching a style sheet to a page, you will need to access the HTML elements on the page and style them. A **style rule** is code you will create to style parts of the HTML content. A style rule begins with a **selector**. Selectors will be covered in more detail in the next section, but in short, they are a set of rules for selecting the different components of an HTML page. The selector is followed by curly brackets ({ and }) that enclose all the styling information for a particular style rule. Between the brackets are pairs of CSS properties and values, which taken together are called **declarations**. To provide various styling effects, a

CSS style rule can have one or more declarations, each terminated with a semicolon. They can, and usually do, span multiple lines. Figure 6-2 summarizes the entire style rule syntax and terminology.

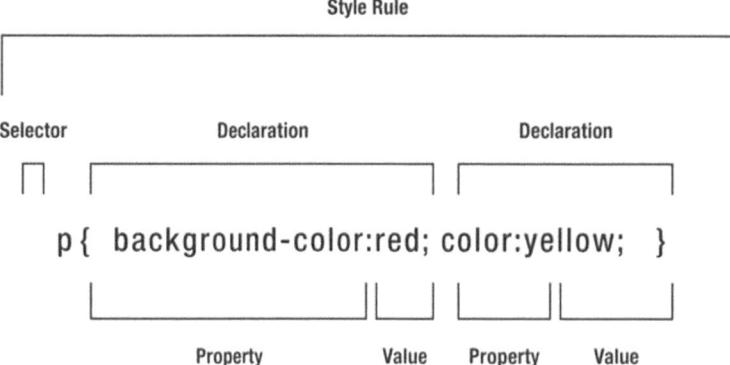

Figure 6-2. *The terminology and syntax of a CSS style rule*

In the example in Figure 6-2, the selector is p, which accesses all the paragraph elements (p) on the page; the style declarations then set their background color to red and the text color to yellow (this is a simple example; we'll get into proper color formatting later).

A CAVEAT: BROWSER CSS3 PROPERTY PREFIXES

As with HTML5, the majority of the CSS3 module specifications are in draft status and being actively refined, which means not all features are implemented across all browsers. And since the specifications are in flux, web browser manufacturers are rightly wary of implementing a particular CSS property in a specification if it could change drastically the next week. The compromise that has been made is to use a convention of prefixes specific to a particular browser that labels a property as a "work in progress." If a web developer sees the prefix, they know that "Ahh, this property could change in the future." Once the property is standardized, the web browsers implement the actual property listed in the specification, and web developers can stop using the prefixed version. The CSS property prefixes for major browsers are as follows:

- -webkit- for Safari and Google Chrome

- -moz- for Firefox

- -o- for Opera

- -ms- for Internet Explorer

For example, there is a CSS property called transform that can be used to, for example, rotate a piece of content, among other effects. The problem is this property is part of a module specification that is in Working Draft status, so the following properties are available to the web developer:

- -webkit-transform

- `-moz-transform`

- `-o-transform`

- `-ms-transform`

When creating a CSS style rule, the web developer would repeat the property with each browser prefix, ending at the end of the list with the actual property as defined in the relevant specification:

```
-webkit-transform: rotate(45deg);
  -moz-transform: rotate(45deg);
    -o-transform: rotate(45deg);
        transform: rotate(45deg);
```

The prefixed versions of the property could then be removed over time as the property is standardized and web browser vendors become compliant with the final specification.

■ **Note** If you encounter a CSS property in this chapter that does not work in a browser you test it in, try adding the appropriate browser prefix and see whether that is the issue.

Essential CSS selector syntax

Selectors are the bridge between your CSS style declarations and the HTML content they need to affect. The majority of selectors you will run into will likely fall into one of three categories: type selectors, ID selectors, and class selectors. There are other categories that we'll get to in due course, but these three are the most common.

Type selectors allow any element to be referenced by its HTML element type name, such as p, article, em, li, blockquote, and so forth. ID selectors allow a specific element to be referenced that has its global id attribute set to some value. Class selectors work the same as ID selectors, except they reference all elements with their class attribute set to some value. These three categories of selectors are termed **simple selectors** and are summarized in Table 6-3.

Table 6-3. Common simple selectors available in CSS

■ NEW in CSS3	Selector	Description	Example CSS	Matching HTML
	*	**Universal selector.** References all elements.	`* { }`	`<p></p>`
	E	**Type selector.** References all elements of type E.	`article { }`	`<article></article>`
	#V	**ID selector.** References an element with an id attribute value of V.	`#logo { }`	`<h1 id="logo"></h1>`
	.V	**Class selector.** References all elements with a class attribute value of V.	`.critical { }`	`<strong class="critical"></strong>`

As you can see in Table 6-3, the ID selector prefixes the value of the ID with a hash sign. Another example might look like this:

```
#company-name { font-weight:bold; }
```

The preceding code would access and bold the text content of an element in the HTML with the id attribute of company-name, such as "The City Press" text in this bit of HTML:

```
<h1 id="company-name">The City Press</h1>
```

The class selector works in a similar way, except that a period is used to reference the class attribute value. The following code would add a border and padding around HTML elements that had their class attribute set to alert:

```
.alert { border:1px solid red; padding:5px; display:inline-block; }
```

■ **Note** You might not be familiar with the code display:inline-block. It has to do will how the styled element is laid out on the page. Exactly what that means will be explained later in the "CSS Box Model" section of this chapter.

The preceding selector might reference the following HTML:

```
<p class="alert">Warning!</p>
```

An advantage with classes is that—unlike IDs—a single element can have more than one class applied to it, so styles can be layered on top of each other inside a single element. For example, the following uses the .alert rule from earlier, plus an additional .critical rule:

```
<p class="alert">
        <span class="critical">Warning!</span> do not feed the kittens, they are
        <span class="alert critical">dangerous</span>
</p>
```

The additional style rule uppercases the text and colors it red:

```
.critical { text-transform:uppercase; color:red; }
```

Taken altogether, this creates an alert box surrounding some text, some of which is merely critical to read and some of which is a critically important alert. The final styled text looks like Figure 6-3.

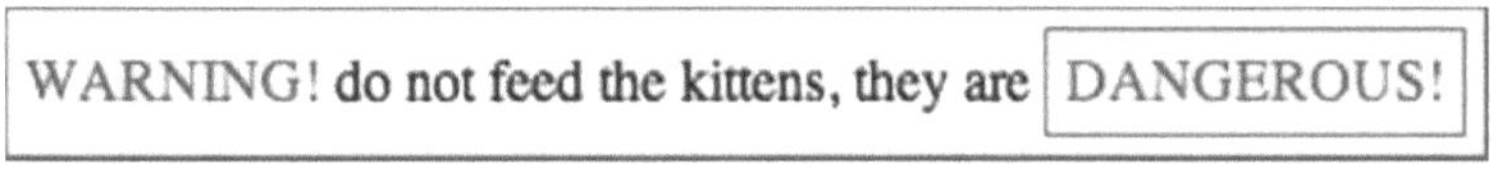

WARNING! do not feed the kittens, they are | DANGEROUS!

Figure 6-3. Class style rules can be "doubled up" on each other by setting more than one styled class attribute value on an element.

Combining selectors

CSS is very flexible in how selectors are defined, and there are plenty of opportunities to save typing if you are careful with your HTML and CSS structures. For example, if a group of selectors have the same CSS declarations they are applying, these style rules can be combined into a comma-separated list, called a **selector list**, which will assign a set of the CSS declarations to all the selectors in the list. For example, the following would change the color of all headers on the page to red:

```
h1,h2,h3,h4,h5,h6 { color:red; }
```

This just saves space and the time of having to type the same CSS declarations over and over; the selectors are still separate entities. It is possible, however, to combine selectors into aggregate selectors, called **compound selectors**, which can be used to match specific content in a web page's structure. Consider a code snippet from earlier:

```
<span class="alert critical">dangerous</span>
```

This element has two classes applied so can be styled using three different selectors:

```
...
span.alert { }
span.critical { }
span.alert.critical { }
...
```

The first two class selectors simply pick out one or the other class—they will reference any span element that has one or the other of the two class values assigned to it. The third chains the two class values together to create a compound selector that will only reference span elements that have both classes applied.

If the type selector is left off (as was done in earlier examples), all elements will be searched for a match. This is equivalent to using the * selector (called the **universal selector**) in combination with another selector (in this case a class selector):

```
.critical { color:red; }      /* match all elements for class 'critical' */
*.critical { color:red; }      /* match all elements for class 'critical' */
p.critical { color:red; }      /* match paragraph elements for class 'critical' */
```

■ **Note** You are likely familiar with this, but if CSS is not something you spend much time with perhaps you don't recognize the purpose of the /* text */ part in the preceding code; that is how you would write a comment in CSS that is ignored by the web browser.

Take a close look at that last line of code, p.critical…; that is two simple selectors placed together, that of a type selector and a class selector. This is where compound selectors get their name, because they are simple selectors that have been compounded together. It's important to note that they always begin with a type selector, a universal selector, or no selector (in which case a universal selector is implied). After the type selector, they can have a long chain of additional simple selectors. Here's an example:

```
em.alert.critical.item { }
```

This selector would only reference an HTML element that was of the correct type and had the correct classes applied, such as the following:

```
<em class="alert critical item">Rocket fuel</em>
```

■ **Note** More than two kinds of selectors can be combined; for example, em.alert.critical#item is a valid compound selector, but in practice this is unnecessarily verbose because there should be only one element with the ID of item on the page, so the inclusion of the class selectors (or even the type selector) would not be necessary.

Compound selectors are powerful, but there are other syntactic options available to match a variety of HTML structures. Let's move on to complex selectors!

Combinators and complex selectors

Table 6-4 lists a set of syntax rules called **combinators**, which determine how the relationship between different HTML elements can be described for the purposes of referencing them with a selector.

Table 6-4. List of combinators in CSS3

■ NEW in CSS3	Selector	Description	Example CSS	Matching HTML

	E F	**Descendant combinator.** Element F nested inside element E.	`div p { }`	`<div>`
				   `<div>`
				      `<p>selected</p>`
				   `</div>`
				`</div>`

	E > F	**Child combinator.** Element F that is a direct child of element E.	`div > p { }`	`<div>`
				   `<p>`
				      selected
				   `</p>`
				`</div>`

	E + F	**Adjacent sibling combinator.** Element F that is immediately preceded by element E.	`strong+em { }`	`<strong></strong>` `<em>selected</em>`

■	E ~ F	**General sibling combinator.** Element F that is preceded by element E. Unlike the adjacent sibling combinator, F does not need to directly precede E.	`strong~em { }`	`<strong></strong>`
				`<p></p>`
				`<em>selected</em>`

Complex selectors combine one or more compound selectors together using a combinator. Because they are composed of compound selectors, they will always use at least a type selector on each side of the combinator. Although both sides of the combinator will include a type selector, the rest of the compound selector can contain any kind of selector chained on to the end. It can even contain mixes of combinators and selectors. For example, imagine a website that allowed guest writers to author content on the site. A section might be created and given a class that designated it as containing guest content:

```
<body>
        <header>
                <h1>Page header</h1>
                <h2>Subtitle</h2>
```

```
        </header>
        <section class="guest">
                <h1>Guest content</h1>
                <div>
                        <article>
                            <h1>Guest article</h1>
                            <footer>Article author</footer>
                        </article>
                </div>
                <footer>Section footer</footer>
        </section>
        <footer>Page footer</footer>
</body>
```

A complex selector might be used to pick out the footer in an article that was the top guest section on the page, for the purpose of emphasizing the author, or what have you:

```
header + section.guest article > footer { border:1px solid red; }
```

Reading right to left, this would add a red border to a footer that was directly contained in an article that was a descendant of a section that has the class guest set. This section must be directly adjacent to a header. Since the header should appear at the top of the page, this would pick out the top section only (if there were multiple sections on the page). To see this demonstrated, create an exact duplicate of the section in the prior code block and paste it below the existing one. If you apply the styles, you will see that only the footer inside the first section's article will have the style applied. To select the footer in any article, the adjacent sibling combinator (+) could be changed to the new general sibling combinator (~), which would match any section with the class guest that was a sibling of the header.

■ **Note** Although it is possible to create long chains of selectors and combinators, you will want to aim to create as concise selectors as possible. Unnecessarily complex selectors can become difficult to comprehend and hard to maintain against changes in the HTML. However, it is important to know that creating such complex selectors is possible, for when you do need them!

Advanced selectors

Beyond the simple type, ID, and class selectors, there are an astounding variety of other selectors available in CSS, which can all be chained on to a type selector if desired. Other types of selectors include the following:

- *Attribute selectors*: Elements can be accessed based on their attributes, attribute values, or parts thereof.

- *Pseudoclasses*: Elements can be selected based on patterns found in their structure, their response to user interaction, their assigned language, or other properties that may not be directly set on an element.

- *Pseudoelements*: Parts of elements that aren't explicitly defined in markup may be accessed, such as the first letter or first line of text in an element.

And more! As you will soon see, ever more so, CSS has powerful logical rules that can be designed to pick out specific chunks of HTML. Let's run through these other selectors so you see what's new.

Attribute selectors

Technically, the ID and class selectors from earlier are attribute selectors, but their syntax is different from the rest of the attribute selectors, so I've separated them. These selectors can reference elements that have certain patterns in their attributes. Table 6-5 summarizes this bunch.

Table 6-5. Attribute selectors in CSS

■ NEW in CSS3	Selector	Description	Example CSS	Matching HTML
	[A]	Elements with an attribute of A	img[alt] { }	<img src="" alt="Dog" />
	[A="V"]	Elements that have an attribute A that equals a value of V	img[alt="Car"] { }	<img src="" alt="Car" />
	[A~="V"]	Elements that have an attribute A that contains space-separated values, one of which equals a value of V	p[accesskey~="q"] { }	<p accesskey="s q"></p>
■	[A^="V"]	Elements that have an attribute A that begins with a value of V	a[type^="text"] { }	<a href="link.html" type="text/html">Link</a>
■	[A$="V"]	Elements that have an attribute A that ends with a value of V	a[type$="css"] { }	<a href="link.css" type="text/css">Link Styles</a>
■	[A*="V"]	Elements that have an attribute A that contains a value of V	img[alt*="man"] { }	<img src="" alt="Germany" />
	E[A|="V"]	Elements that have an attribute A that contains hyphen-separated values, the first of which equals a value of V	p[lang|="en"] { }	<p lang="en-GB-oed"></p>

As you can see, attribute selectors are not new, but a set of three of them are: [A^="V"], [A$="V"], and [A*="V"]. These will allow you to match an element that has an attribute value that starts, ends, or contains a particular piece of text. It's worth pointing out that attribute selectors (any kind), like other selectors, can be chained together into compound selectors:

a[href][rel] { color:orange; }

This selector would match any anchor element (a) that had both the href and rel attributes set. By including a search pattern for a URL in the href attribute, this could be narrowed to a specific subset of hyperlink anchors. For example, on my own site, maybe I want to prefetch pages from my own domain, but I want to style those links differently than others on the page. I might create a rule like this:

```
a[href*="anselmbradford.com"][rel="prefetch"] { color:orange; }
```

This would only match hyperlink anchors that linked to resources that contained "anselmbradford.com" as part of their URL and had their rel attribute set to prefetch, like so:

```
<a href="http://blog.anselmbradford.com" rel="prefetch">Anselm's blog</a>
```

The possibilities of attribute selectors are numerous. Examples include picking specific file types out of a, img, or object source URLs in order to handle styling based on file type. As another example, the polymorphic input element can easily have its different types styled using attribute selectors. For instance:

```
input[type="password"] { border:1px solid red; }
```

This style rule would add a red border around all password input form controls.

When using a class selector on an element, ask yourself whether there is an attribute already present that could be picked out instead. If an existing attribute could be used, adding an additional class attribute solely for styling purposes creates extraneous code that may need to be maintained and updated down the road. For instance, if the preceding style rule were changed to use a class selector instead of an attribute selector, it would mean you would have to remember to add the correct class attribute value to any new password input form controls added to the page instead of relying on their existing type attribute, which they all would need to have anyway.

Styling links and fragment identifier targets

The next group of selectors have to do with the behavior of hyperlinks, called **location pseudoclass selectors** (Table 6-6); this small group deals with referencing unvisited and visited links and fragment identifiers. The :link and :visited selectors are self-explanatory as well as being nothing new, so let's look instead at the new :target selector and how it deals with fragment identifiers.

Table 6-6. Location pseudoclass selectors

■ NEW in CSS3	Selector	Description	Example CSS	Matching HTML
	:link	Hyperlink anchors that have not yet been visited	a:link { }	`<a href="a.html">Link</a>`
	:visited	Hyperlink anchors that have been visited	a:visited { }	`<a href="a.html">Link</a>`

■	:target	An element that is the target of a fragment identifier	p:target { }	`<a href="#target">`
				`    <p id="target">`
				`        selected`
				`    </p>`
				`</a>`

Fragment identifiers were introduced in the "Hyperlinks" section in Chapter 3. In that chapter, an example was given for an anchor element:

`<a href="newpage.html#parttwo">link</a>`

This element links to a specific HTML element on the linked page by matching the fragment identifier #parttwo with the id attribute value partwo, so the page would be scrolled to an element such as this one:

`<h3 id="parttwo">Part Two</h3>`

Since this is using a fragment identifier, this element could be styled using the :target selector. This selector's style rule will apply to any element that is a target of the fragment identifier that appears in the URL (which should be only one element on the page):

:target { text-decoration:overline; }

When the fragment identifier appears in the address bar URL of the page, the element on the page that is being targeted will receive the styling of the :target selector rule. Remove the fragment identifier from the URL, and the style disappears. This is particularly useful in situations where the user could scroll away from the targeted element; by styling it differently, it could be made so that the user wouldn't lose sight of it if they were looking for it again (styles could be added to go so far as to fix the targeted element in place, so it would remain in view even if the page scrolled[1]).

---

[1] This is done using the position:fixed property and value, which will be touched upon later in the chapter.

Selecting elements involved in user interaction

In addition to :link and :visited, the selectors :hover and :active (Table 6-7) are commonly associated with links. However, they can be used to respond to user interaction on any element.

Table 6-7. User interaction pseudoclass selectors

■ NEW in CSS3	Selector	Description	Example CSS	Matching HTML
	:hover	Element that has the user's cursor hovering over it	a:hover { }	`<a href="a.html">Link</a>`
	:active	Element that has been activated by the user, such as by clicking but not yet releasing the mouse button	a:active { }	`<a href="a.html">Link</a>`

For example, the following is a short unordered list:

```
<ul>
        <li>Milk</li>
        <li>Eggs</li>
        <li>Carrots</li>
        <li>Butter</li>
        <li>Almonds</li>
        <li>Flour</li>
</ul>
```

To help the user visually pick out which item they are hovering over, the :hover selector could be used to set up a style rule that changed the background color to light gray:

```
li:hover { background-color:#ccc; }
```

This will be applied only when the user hovers over the items in the list, darkening those rows the user is hovering over (Figure 6-4).

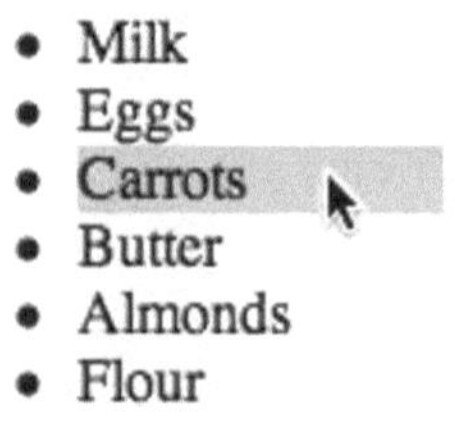

- Milk
- Eggs
- Carrots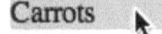
- Butter
- Almonds
- Flour

Figure 6-4. The :hover selector allows a style to be applied only when the mouse cursor is over an element.

The :active selector is for styling an element that is being activated by the user, which, for instance, means the mouse button has been pressed over the element, but it is yet to be released. This selector could be used anywhere the appearance of an element should change when the element is pressed but prior to releasing the element, such as in a drag-and-drop application. It is commonly used on link anchors to flash a different color or other style change when a link is clicked.

Selecting form control elements

Table 6-8 lists a group of selectors used for styling the various states of user interface components, notably, web form controls. Excluding the first four selectors, the selectors from `:indeterminate` onward are part of the CSS3 Basic User Interface Module (the other selectors shown in this chapter are part of the Selectors Level 3 Module).

■ **Note** The WC3's CSS working group published a document on August 12, 2011, that indicates the next iteration of CSS will have all the selectors in this chapter specified in the same module, named Selectors Level 4.

Table 6-8. User interface states pseudoclass selectors

NEW in CSS3	Selector	Description	Example CSS	Matching HTML
	:focus	Element that has focus (accepts keyboard input, such as in a text field).	input:focus { }	<input />[2]
	:enabled	Elements that are in an enabled state.	input:enabled { }	<input />
	:disabled	Elements that are in a disabled state.	input:disabled { }	<input disabled />
■	:required	Elements that require input.	input:required { }	<input required />
■	:optional	Elements where input is optional.	input:optional { }	<input />
■	:read-only	Elements that are in a read-only state.	input:read-only { }	<input readonly />
■	:read-write	Elements that accept input.	input:read-write { }	<input />
■	:valid	Elements that have valid data entered.	input:valid { }	<input />
■	:invalid	Elements that have invalid data entered.	input:invalid { }	<input type="email" />[3]
■	:checked	Elements that are in a checked state.	input:checked { }	<input type="checkbox" checked />
■	:indeterminate	Elements in an indeterminate state.	input:indeterminate { }	<input type="checkbox" />[4]

[2] Applies after user has clicked into the text field.
[3] Input will be invalid until a valid email address is entered.

		It's possible for check boxes to be in a state where they aren't checked or unchecked.		

■	`:default`	Elements in a default state, such as the initially selected radio button on a web form.	`input:default { }`	`<input type="radio" name="rg" />`
				
				`<input type="radio" name="rg" checked />`

■	`:in-range`	Elements with a range limitation, which have a value in the acceptable range.	`input:in-range { }`	`<input type="number" min="1" max="10" value="10" />`
■	`:out-of-range`	Elements with a range limitation, which have a value outside of the acceptable range.	`input:out-of-range { }`	`<input type="number" min="1" max="10" value="11" />`

The `:focus` selector isn't just for forms, but its behavior is easiest to see in the context of web forms. Applied to text fields, the `:focus` selector adds a style when the user clicks in the field and begins to type. When the user clicks another field, the focus moves, and the style rule is applied accordingly. Taking the web form that appeared in Chapter 4, we could add this simple style:

```
input:focus {
        border:5px solid black;
}
```

This style rule will add a prominent black border around any text field the user clicks in to start typing. It will make it clear which text field currently has focus (Figure 6-5).

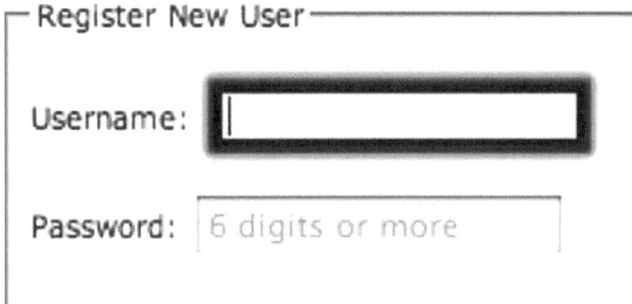

Figure 6-5. *The :focus selector applied to a text field allows styles to be attached when the user selects the field to start typing.*

---

[4] The check box needs to have its indeterminate property set to true in JavaScript.

The :enabled and :disabled selectors both work with the Boolean disabled attribute. The :enabled selector will apply a style to any form element that *does not* have the disabled attribute present, while :disabled will apply a style to any element that *does* have the disabled attribute present.

The :required and :optional selectors are like the :enabled and :disabled selectors, except they are triggered by the presence or absence of the Boolean required attribute.

The :read-only and :read-write selectors work in the presence or absence of the Boolean readonly attribute. Some form controls, such as the file upload control (type="file" as set in input), are read-only by default and will be picked up by the :read-only selector without the addition of the readonly attribute.

The :valid and :invalid selectors work like the :required and :optional selectors, except they aren't tied directly to the required attribute. The :valid selector will pick up any element that has no form validation constraints attached to it (required attribute, pattern attribute, and so on), while :invalid will pick up any element that has constraints, if those constraints are not met.

The :checked and :indeterminate selectors usually apply to check boxes and radio buttons. The :checked selector will apply to these controls when they are in a checked state. :indeterminate is a little more difficult to trigger. It is possible for a check box to be in neither a checked nor unchecked state. Check box controls have a Boolean indeterminate property accessible from JavaScript that can be set, which will then trigger the applicability of this selector. Say you have a check box control:

```
<input id="undecided" type="checkbox" />
```

The id is then accessed from JavaScript to set the state of the check box to indeterminate:

```
function setState() {
        var check = document.getElementById("undecided");
        check.indeterminate = true;
}
window.onload = setState;
```

With this script, the check box will be placed in the indeterminate state (Figure 6-6) and can then have styles applied using the :indeterminate selector.

Figure 6-6. A check box in the indeterminate state

■ **Note** You may find the styles you can apply to check boxes are pretty boring. Safari, Chrome, and Firefox don't support adding borders and background to the check boxes. To see whether your styles are being applied, try setting the height, like height:100px;. Any content around the check box should get pushed out of the way.

The default: style will apply to elements designated as being the default within a given context; for example, the initially checked radio button in a radio button group may be considered the default. This one could be styled, and that style would stay with the initially checked button, even if another radio button was clicked. Another scenario is if there is more than one submit button on a form (which there really shouldn't be—but this is just hypothetical!), one of those buttons will be considered the default submit button for the form. Unfortunately, what gets set to be the default varies from browser to browser. For instance, Opera recognizes the first scenario with the radio buttons, while Safari recognizes the second scenario, but neither recognizes both scenarios.

The last two selectors in this group, :in-range and :out-of-range, are for elements that have a constraint on a range of values that can be input into them. For instance, the number input form control has min and max attributes that set the range of values that can be input into the number field. If the entered value falls into this range between the minimum and maximum range, the :in-range selector style rule will apply, while if it is outside of this range, the :out-of-range selector will apply. The range input form control can use these selectors too, in theory; however, as of this writing, only Opera supports it (and partially so, because the :out-of-range selector is ignored).

Pattern matching selectors

Additional logic can be introduced into a selector by using one of the "nth-" type selectors, part of the **tree-structural pseudoclass** selectors group (see Table 6-9). All but one of these selectors is new in CSS3.

Table 6-9. Tree-structural pseudoclass selectors

▪ NEW in CSS3	Selector	Description	Example CSS	Matching HTML

▪	:root	The root element of the document; will be the html element	html:root { }	`<html>`
				`    <title></title>`
				`</html>`

▪	:nth-child(N)	An element that is the Nth child of its parent	li:nth-child(3) { }	`<ul>`
				`    <li></li>`
				`    <li></li>`
				`    <li>selected</li>`
				`</ul>`

▪	:nth-last-child(N)	An element that is the Nth child of its parent, beginning counting from the last child	li:nth-last-child(3) { }	`<ul>`
				`    <li>selected</li>`
				`    <li></li>`
				`    <li></li>`
				`</ul>`

▪	:nth-of-type(N)	An element that is the Nth sibling of its type	p:nth-of-type(2) { }	`<p></p>`
				`<p>selected</p>`
				`<p></p>`

▪	:nth-last-	An element that is the Nth sibling of its type,	p:nth-last-of-type	`<p></p>`

	of-type(N)	beginning counting from the last sibling	(1) { }	`<p></p>` `<p>selected</p>`
	:first-child	An element that is the first child of its parent	li:first-child { }	`<ul>` `<li>selected</li>` `<li></li>` `<li></li>` `</ul>`
■	:last-child	An element that is the last child of its parent	li:last-child { }	`<ul>` `<li></li>` `<li></li>` `<li>selected</li>` `</ul>`
■	:first-of-type	An element that is the first sibling of its type	p:first-of-type { }	`<p>selected</p>` `<p></p>` `<p></p>`
■	:last-of-type	An element that is the last sibling of its type	p:last-of-type { }	`<p></p>` `<p></p>` `<p>selected</p>`
■	:only-child	An element that is the only child of its parent	li:only-child { }	`<ul>` `<li>selected</li>` `</ul>`
■	:only-of-type	An element that is the only sibling of its parent	footer:only-of-type { }	`<header></header>` `<article></article>` `<footer>selected</footer>`
■	:empty	An element that has no children	p:empty { }	`<p></p>`

These selectors work particularly well with lists, tables, or any other HTML structure that has repeating rows of information. They allow styles to the applied following a repeating pattern, which can be used to zebra stripe a list of items for instance. To begin with, they can be given one of two keywords: even or odd, which apply a style to even or odd counted elements within a particular parent element. For example, the following is a basic HTML list:

```
<ul>
    <li>Row 1</li>
    <li>Row 2</li>
    <li>Row 3</li>
    <li>Row 4</li>
    <li>Row 5</li>
    <li>Row 6</li>
</ul>
```

Odd-numbered rows in this list can be colored gray by adding the following code:

```
li:nth-child(odd) { background-color:#ccc; }
```

Coloring the even rows is as easy as exchanging the keyword odd with even:

```
li:nth-child(even) { background-color:#ccc; }
```

These result in the lists shown in Figure 6-7.

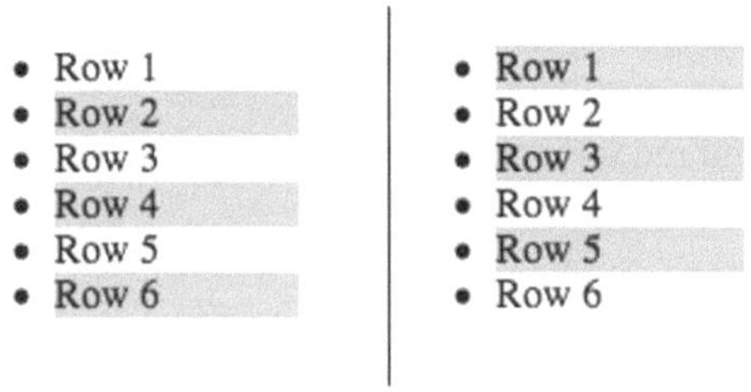

- Row 1
- Row 2
- Row 3
- Row 4
- Row 5
- Row 6

- Row 1
- Row 2
- Row 3
- Row 4
- Row 5
- Row 6

Figure 6-7. Zebra striping on even and odd numbered rows in a list being styled using :nth-child(even) and :nth-child(odd) selectors

Additionally, nth- selectors include a pattern formula that allows different rows from the even or odd ones to be selected. In place of even or odd, the formula *an+b* can be used. The *n* equals the number of child elements to process (six rows in a list in the prior case), with counting beginning at zero. The value of *a* is then multiplied by each value of *n*, and *b* is added to that value. For example, in the formula *3n+1*, the first row processed assigns a value of 0 to *n*, so the formula ends up being $(3 \times 0) + 1$, which equals 1, meaning the style applies to the first row. For the next row, the formula becomes $(3 \times 1) + 1$, which equals 4, meaning the style applies to the fourth row. Next would be $(3 \times 2) + 1$, equaling the seventh row. Figure 6-8 is the appearance of an unordered list that had the following CSS rule applied:

```
li:nth-child(3n+1) { background-color:#cccccc; }
```

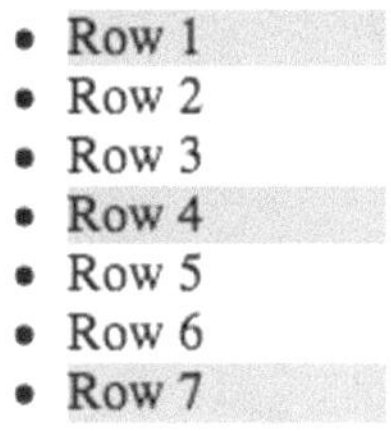

- Row 1
- Row 2
- Row 3
- Row 4
- Row 5
- Row 6
- Row 7

Figure 6-8. Results of the selector :nth-child(3n+1) on an unordered list

The nth- selectors can also be given a concrete value that they should select, such as :nth-child(2) to stylize only the second row, :nth-child(3) to stylize only the third row, and so on.

The nth-of-type selectors, such as :nth-of-type(N), have the ability to pick elements out of a group of elements of a certain type that share the same parent. So, instead of picking the children elements of a particular element, these selectors pick the siblings of a particular element. For example, the following HTML could be the structure of a blog of some sort, with a header and footer section and a number of articles sandwiched between the two:

```
<body>
        <header></header>
        <article><h1>Article 1</h1></article>
        <article><h1>Article 2</h1></article>
        <article><h1>Article 3</h1></article>
        <footer></footer>
</body>
```

Because all these sections share the same parent (the body), the :nth-of-type(N) selector could be combined with a type selector to pick out a particular article while ignoring the header and footer:

```
article:nth-of-type(1){ background-color:#f00; };
```

This would pick out the first article and color its background red (hexadecimal color codes will be discussed later).

■ **Note** If it was just the first item of a particular type that was being selected and that behavior was not going to change, the new :first-of-type selector could be used instead. However, the nth-of-type selectors can use the an+b formula to pick out more than one element.

Pseudoelement selectors

The elements in Table 6-10 are perhaps less common to encounter because their behavior is rather unique among the different selector categories. As you will soon see, they enable styles to be applied to parts of an element that aren't otherwise accessible. While you may recognize the selectors listed in Table 6-10, you may notice that their syntax has changed to include two colons instead of one at the beginning of the selector. See the "What makes a pseudoelement?" sidebar later in this section for more information.

Table 6-10. Pseudoelement selectors

■ NEW in CSS3	Selector	Description	Example CSS	Matching HTML
	::first-line	The first line of an element's content	p::first-line { }	<p>selected not selected</p>
	::first-	The first letter of an	p::first-letter {	<p>Selected</p>

	letter	element's content	}	
	::before	Insert content before an element	p::before { }	`<p>After the content</p>`
	::after	Insert content after an element	p::after { }	`<p>Before the content</p>`

The ::first-line and ::first-letter selectors are self-explanatory, because they select the first line of text and first letter of text within an element. For example, they can be used to create "drop caps" at the beginning of paragraphs and stylistically change the first line of text, as shown in Figure 6-9.

This a paragraph of text used to demonstrate the pseudo-element class selectors. These selectors are used to select parts of the content that isn't otherwise marked up through HTML.

Figure 6-9. The ::first-letter and ::first-line selectors applying styles to a paragraph to create a "drop cap" first letter and bold first line

An effect like that shown in Figure 6-9 could be created by applying the following CSS to a paragraph element (p) filled with text:

```
p::first-line {
        font-weight:bold;
}
p::first-letter {
        margin-top:-0.2em;
        float:left;
        font-size:4em;
        margin-right:0.1em;
}
```

The next two selectors in this group, ::before and ::after, are for generating and inserting content before and after an element. The precise behavior of how this is done is described in the CSS3 Generated and Replaced Content Module,[5] but in brief, images or text may be the inserted around an element. Using CSS to insert text into a page is something that many frown upon, since it is seen as using CSS for something that should be done in HTML. If you do use these pseudoelements, bear in mind that for accessibility reasons the content needs to make sense even if the style sheet is disabled, so any inserted content needs to be frivolous. That being said, let's move on to how you would use these selectors.

Both selectors would generally be used with the CSS content property, which is used to specify the actual content to insert. The content property can take quoted text, url() and attr() notation syntax, and more. The url() notation syntax takes an image file path between its parentheses, like url("images/pic.jpg"). The attr() notation syntax takes an attribute name that is found on the element between its parantheses, which will be replaced with the attribute's value. For example, a link to download a PDF document could be created with the following:

---

[5] See http://www.w3.org/TR/css3-content/

```
<a href="presentation.pdf" type="application/pdf">Download the presentation</a>
```

A selector could then be created to pick out anchor elements on the page that have a type attribute set to the MIME type application/pdf (we'll use a wildcard attribute selector so we don't have to type the whole MIME type). On those elements, the pseudoelements selectors would generate an icon (by linking to an external image) before the link and some text after it that says it's a PDF. Here's an example:

```
a[type*="pdf"]::before
{
        content: url(doc.png);
        margin-right:5px;
}

a[type*="pdf"]::after
{
        content: " (" attr(type) ")";
}
```

Using the content property, the icon is embedded before the anchor element, and the parentheses and value of the type attribute are inserted after the element. Figure 6-10 shows the result.

Download the presentation (application/pdf)

Figure 6-10. The ::before and ::after selectors inserting an icon and file type information around a link

---

WHAT MAKES A PSEUDOELEMENT?

CSS level 1 (CSS1) defined a selector, :first-letter, which has become ::first-letter in CSS3. As you see in Table 6-10, a handful of selectors use the :: prefix, which is syntax that is new in CSS3. This syntax is used to mark these elements as being part of the pseudoelements group of selectors. The prefix is for distinguishing them from other types of selectors. Pseudoelements are unique among the selectors in that they access information that is not specifically marked up by an element in the HTML of the document. For example, looking at the HTML for a paragraph of text, there isn't part that is defined as being the first line of text; instead, the first line is determined by how the content gets laid out in the browser. The ::first-line selector can pick out this part of the HTML, however. From its standpoint, the first line of textual content in an element is inside an ethereal element that it can style (which is why it's called a **pseudoelement**). The same situation arises when using ::first-letter. It is readily apparent to you which character in a paragraph is the first letter, but that isn't explicitly marked up in the HTML, so the ::first-letter selector is used to pick the first letter out from the rest of the content as if it were enclosed in an element.

The ::before and ::after pseudoelement selectors can be used to insert content before or after (respectively) the existing content within an element (note that it works only with elements that can hold content. It won't work with self-closing elements, such as img). Therefore, they are part of this group because they are referring to points in the HTML that are empty. Like the first letter, there is not explicit markup in the HTML that designates the spot between the end of the starting tag and the beginning of the content, or the end of the content and the beginning of the end tag.

Table 6-11 lists a couple pseudoelements that are in the CSS3 Generated and Replaced Content Module specification but have such poor browser support that you are unlikely to be able to use them. We'll see what the future holds for them. Remember that the specification is in draft status, so they could disappear if browser support doesn't materialize.

Table 6-11. Poorly supported pseudoelement selectors

Selector	Description
::outside	Inserts content around an element (to create a second border, for instance)
::alternate	Inserts content at a later, marked location in the document
::marker	Inserts content before the first line of items in a list[6]
::line-marker	Exactly like ::marker, except inserts content before each line of the items in a list

■ **Note** There is a pseudoelement selector named ::selection that allows styles to be applied to text that has been selected by the user. It was originally included in the CSS3 Selectors module, but apparently this behavior was too radical for the W3C, and it has since been removed. However, you will find it has strong browser support. For example, try adding the style rule ::selection { color:#0f0; } to your page and select some text. It will turn it green!

Miscellaneous selectors

Two additional selectors don't fit well into any of the other categories. The :lang(L) selector finds content that is designated as being in a searched-for language (set through its lang attribute or otherwise inherited from the metadata of the page). A language code[7] is placed between the parentheses of the selector. See Table 6-12 for an example.

---

[6] The ::marker selector is explained in greater detail in another specification, *CSS Lists and Counters Module Level 3*, accessible here: http://www.w3.org/TR/css3-lists/#marker-pseudoelement
[7] See http://www.iana.org/assignments/language-subtag-registry for a list of language codes, the "subtags" shown are what you would use.

Table 6-12. Miscellaneous selectors

■ NEW in CSS3	Selector	Description	Example CSS	Matching HTML
	`:lang(L)`	**Language pseudo-class.** Elements that have their language set to a language of L.	`p:lang(fr) { }`	`<p lang="fr"></p>`
■	`:not(S)`	**Negation pseudo-class.** Elements that do not match a selector S.	`p:not(#important)`	`<p id="other"></p>`

The other element in Table 6-12 is the new `:not(S)` selector, which is for finding all elements that *do not* match a certain selector. Combined with other selectors, it can be used to create quite complex matching rules for a style. For example, for the purposes of visually identifying the links on my site that linked to external resources that I did not want to endorse, I might choose to select and style all links that did not contain the "anselmbradford.com" URL in their `href` property and contained the `nofollow` or `noreferrer` attribute values in their `rel` attribute:

```
a[rel^="no"]:not([href*="anselmbradford.com"]) { color:red; }
```

The first part is an attribute selector that works on the `rel` attribute, while the second part contains another attribute selector for working on the `href` attribute, the results of which are negated by the `:not()` selector. Notice that we just search for a value for `rel` that begins with "no" to pick up the two possible values. Applied to the following code snippet, the preceding selector would skip styling the first anchor, style the second and third anchor, and skip the fourth:

```
<a href="http://anselmbradford.com" rel="noreferrer"> Anselm's website </a>
<a href="http://example.com/contact.html" rel="noreferrer"> Example.com contact </a>
<a href="http://example.com/links.html" rel="nofollow"> Example.com links </a>
<a href="http://example.com" rel="bookmark"> Example.com homepage </a>
```

As you can see, the possibilities are virtually endless in regard to the selectors you can construct!

Using selectors effectively

As you saw in the simple selector section earlier, selectors can be generalized to all elements, for example:

```
:only-child { color:blue; }    /* match any element that is the only element contained in its parent element */
::first-letter { font-size:2em; }      /* match the first letter of all elements' content */
```

Depending on the selector, generalizing in this way can become unwieldy because the styles applied may become attached to elements with vastly different purposes and meanings. You will likely see ID selectors generalized in this way, such as in the code snippet `#item {}`. However, this is commonly done because ID selectors will always pick out only one element and so will never generalize out to other elements on the page.

■ **Note** Some professional CSS developers advocate using class selectors in favor of ID selectors. The reason for this essentially boils down to flexibility. ID selectors can be used on only one element on the page, ever. Class selectors can be applied to one element by choice, effectively making them equivalent to ID selectors. However, they can be applied to multiple elements as well, which is an added benefit, if down the road you realize that a particular style rule needs to be applied more than once.

Having said that, going in the other direction and getting too specific with a chain of selectors should be avoided as well. This is termed a selector's **specificity**. And it's a bad thing if a selector's specificity gets too focused. Avoid CSS rules like the following:

```
article section#one ul li.item::first-letter { color:blue;  }
```

Although this will work fine in the situation it's used in, it is brittle. Changes to the HTML could easily cause this rule to no longer be applied, which also means this selector can't be easily moved to another context. By assigning a class to the unordered list (instead of the list item) and picking out the list item by type, the selector could be shortened to the following:

```
ul.toc li::first-letter { color:blue;  }
```

Concise selectors are where you will see your correct application of HTML5's semantic elements coming back to save you time in the long run. Instead of creating complex selectors or relying on classes or IDs to pick out certain kinds of content, you can apply the styles directly to em, strong, article, aside, and so forth, without any deeper specificity needed. Obviously, if you wanted to target a particular kind of article or aside, that is where classes (and possibly IDs) would come into play, but first look at what content can be grouped together using semantic HTML elements, then attributes, and then custom IDs or classes.

CSS Box Model

Now that we've thoroughly covered selectors, you should have a thorough understanding of how to access your HTML from CSS. At this point, there is another fundamental concept that is worth exploring—the CSS Box Model.

As far as CSS is concerned, the HTML elements that make up a web page are contained within a rectangular box that determines its position in relation to the other elements on the page. This paradigm of laying out the page's content in boxes is where the CSS Box Model gets its name. There are three main types of boxes in this model: **block-level**, **line-level**, and **inline-level**. To visualize how these differ, imagine a paragraph of text. By default, a block-level box is constructed around the whole paragraph, a line-level box is constructed around each separate line of text in the paragraph, and an inline-level box is constructed around each word in a single line of text. This is how CSS sees the content and lays it out, but this differs slightly from how you will use the Box Model. You will wrap the content you want to manipulate from CSS in an HTML element, such as a p element for the whole paragraph or an em element for an individual word in the paragraph. You'll then use a selector to stylize these elements. Typically this means you will be dealing with block-level or inline-level boxes. Line-level boxes are not something you get easy access to (although there is the ::first-line selector), so just make a mental note that they are something CSS is using internally to lay out content. You may wrap more than one word in an em, maybe even a whole line, but this will still be viewed as an inline-level box, because it may or may not take up the entire line of text.

Block-level boxes are the most commonly encountered type of box. When styling an element inside a block-level box, you will have access to CSS properties for padding, a margin, and possibly a border sandwiched between the two. Outside the box are positioning properties that can be used to offset the box away from its default position.[8] Inside the box are width and height properties used to set the size of the box. All these properties are shown in Figure 6-11.

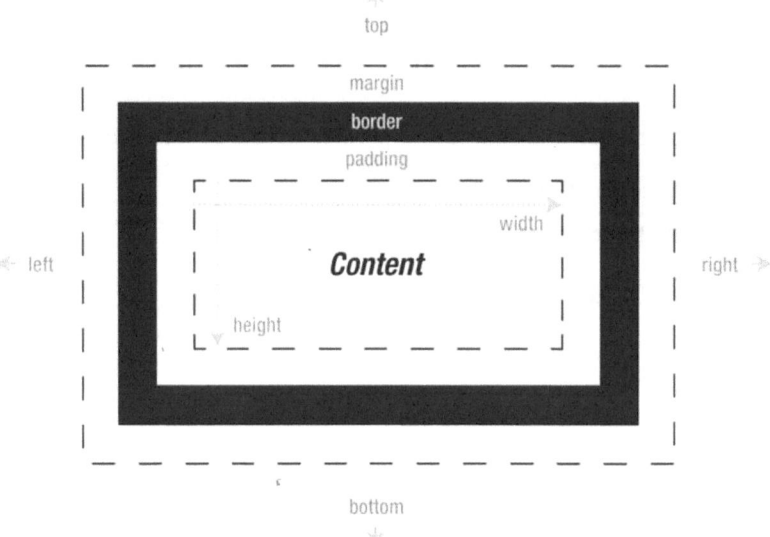

Figure 6-11. A block-level box showing padding, border, margin, width, and height, as well as the positioning properties around an HTML element

A **block-level box** is found most commonly around flow content such as paragraphs, headings, or other elements that provide a division between blocks of content. By default, block-level boxes will expand to fill the width of their containing element and will stack vertically on top of each other.

An **inline-level box** is commonly found around phrasing content such as span, q, em, and so on. By default, inline-level boxes will run horizontally rather than vertically, because they follow the lines of text in the content. The box for an inline level box looks exactly like a block-level box (Figure 6-11) except any margin applied on the top and bottom of the box will be ignored—only margins on the left and right sides have an effect. Additionally, padding applied to the top and bottom will not push away elements above and below the element, as a block-level box would do, but instead will overlap the element's border (if present) over adjacent content. Lastly, inline-level boxes take up only as much space as the content contained within them, plus any padding that is set, meaning they will ignore settings to their width and height properties. Figure 6-12 shows an example of block-level and inline-level boxes and how they interact with each other.

---

[8] The positioning properties (left, top, right, bottom) are used in combination with the position property, which will be discussed later.

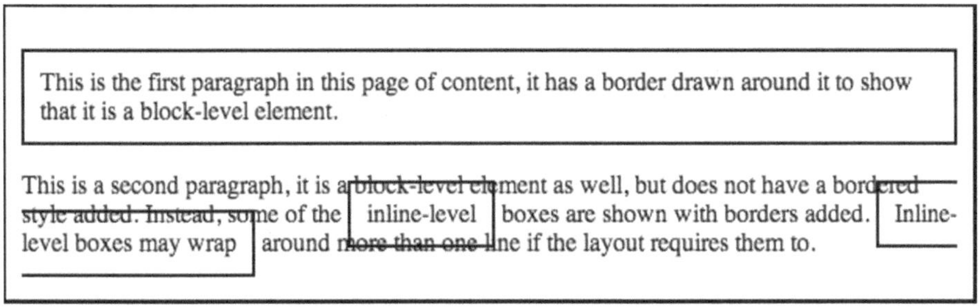

Figure 6-12. Block-level and Inline-level boxes. Note that an inline-level box that extends across two lines will wrap around by default.

In Figure 6-12, there is a border drawn around the entire content and the first paragraph (both block-level boxes), and borders are drawn around a single word and several words. An element that has a block-level box can be referred to as a **block-level** element. The words are contained in inline-level boxes and have 10 pixels (px) of padding applied. As you can see, although the box border has expanded 10px in all directions away from the text, the top and bottom padding does not affect any surrounding elements, and the borders overlap with other content on the page. If you're curious, the following is the HTML to produce the previous:

```
<div class="box">
  <p class="box">
    This is the first paragraph in this page of content, it has a border drawn around it to
    show that it is a block-level element.
  </p>

  <p>
    This is a second paragraph, it is a block-level element as well, but does not have a
    bordered style added. Instead, some of the <span class="box">inline-level</span> boxes are
    shown with borders added. <span class="box">Inline-level boxes may wrap</span> around more
    than one line if the layout requires them to.
  </p>
</div>
```

And the CSS is as follows:

```
.box {
        border:2px solid black;
        padding:10px;
}
```

Setting box type

The type of box used is not set in stone. In fact, there is a CSS property called display for setting the type of box an element is contained in. Setting display:block on an element will treat it as being contained in a block-level box, while setting display:inline will treat it as being contained in an inline-level box. Having the ability to swap between box types is particularly useful with anchor elements (a), which are inline-level elements by default, so they ignore width and height settings.

Consider the following HTML:

```
<a href="#">Link</a>
<a href="#" class="block">Link</a>
```

The preceding code could be styled with the following CSS:

```
a {
        width:200px;                /* set the width */
        height:60px;                /* set the height */
        border:1px solid #000;      /* set a black border */
        background-color:#ccc;      /* set a gray background */
        padding:10px;               /* set 10 pixels of padding */
        text-decoration:none;       /* remove the underline */
        text-align:center;          /* center align the text */
        margin-top:20px;            /* add margin to the top */
}
```

This code produces the appearance of Figure 6-13. The width and height and margin top are ignored because these are two inline-level elements.

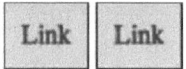

Figure 6-13. Two inline-level elements will line up side by side by default.

Now if an additional style rule is added to convert the second box into a block-level element:

```
a.block {
        display:block;              /* treat as block-level element */
}
```

the appearance of the second link changes to include the width and height (and margin so the elements don't overlap), as shown in Figure 6-14. The whole area of the larger rectangular shape is part of the link's active area, so having an anchor element display as a block-level element offers more flexibility in the size of the linked area. This aspect is particularly useful when creating menus, for instance.

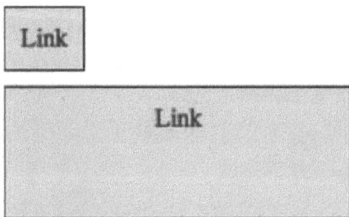

Figure 6-14. Inline-level and block-level boxes. The block-level box moves to its own line.

A problem with setting an inline-level element to display as a block-level element is that the block element will move below the content that came before it, starting a new line of content, as shown in Figure 6-14. There is additional display property that can format the element as being in a block-level box but then treat the formatted box as if it were an inline-level box. Changing the display to display:inline-block produces Figure 6-15.

Figure 6-15. *Inline-level box and block-level box being treated as an inline-level box for layout purposes*

There are several other values for the display property,[9] but block, inline, and inline-block are the three main ones that can be used for changing the default layout behavior of the majority of HTML's elements.

Setting box position

To make adjustments to the position of an element, the position property is used. It has the following values (plus inherit, which just uses its parent element's settings):

- static: The box is in its default position. The positioning properties (left, top, right, and bottom) are ignored.

- relative: The box is offset from its default position by the number of pixels specified in the CSS positioning properties, which are the named left, top, right, and bottom.

- absolute: The box is offset by the number of pixels specified in the positioning properties but is offset from the upper-left corner of the first parent element that has its position property set to a non-static value or to the upper-left corner of the browser's viewing area, whichever comes first.

- fixed: Works like absolute positioning with the added functionality that the box does not scroll with the rest of the content on the page and is instead fixed in the viewing area.

Setting box layering

Since boxes may be positioned relatively and absolutely, that means they may overlap each other (which can be used to create interesting effects!). When two elements overlap each other, the order in which they are layered can be set using the z-index property. There are some caveats with this property, but they are easy to grasp:

- Both elements overlapping each other need to have the same parent element (they need to be contained together in the same HTML block) if the layering is to be changed.

- At least one of the elements needs to have its position property set to relative, absolute, or fixed.

---

[9] See all CSS display property values here: http://www.w3.org/TR/css3-box/#display

- At least one of the elements needs to have its z-index property set. A higher number relative to the other element will bring an element in front of the other one, while a lower number will bring it behind.

Backgrounds and borders

Background and borders used to be pretty limited. The shapes were rectangular with solid-colored backgrounds or a single repeating image. The borders had some variety (solid, dashed, dotted, and so on) but were still stuck in a rectangular shape. Rounded corners, for instance, have been notoriously complex to create. CSS3 has made many effects, including rounded corners, much easier. Rounded corners are part of the CSS3 Backgrounds and Borders Module, which also adds the ability to add multiple backgrounds, clip and repeat backgrounds in new ways, and add drop shadows, to name a few additions.

Basic background color and images

The background-color property sets the color of the background. It will take any color format described in the "Color" section in this chapter. The color is drawn behind any background images so it will show through if the background has images attached that contain transparent areas. The value transparent can be given so that no color shows through.

The background-image property is used to attach images to the background of an element. The syntax url("path/to/bgimage.png") is used to attach the image, where path/to/bgimage.png is the file path to the image to include. The file path may be relative to the location of the style sheet, or it may be absolute (using http:// or similar in the beginning of the path). It's not uncommon to see relative file paths such as url("../images/pic.jpg") since the style sheet is often placed in a different directory from the images. The ../ moves up one directory before going into the images directory.

■ **Note** The quotes around the image's file path are optional if there are no spaces in the filename or file path. If there are spaces, however, quotes around the file path are required.

The background-repeat property determines how a background image (if present) is repeated, if it is repeated. The basic settings are repeat, no-repeat, repeat-x, and repeat-y. These determine, respectively, whether the image is tiled, not tiled (shown only once), tiled horizontally, or tiled vertically. Two new values have been added to this property in CSS3: space and round. Normally when an image is repeated, it will repeat as needed to fill the available space with some portion of the image, even if that means some of the image will be clipped out of view. The space and round properties prevent this clipping from happening. A value of space will fill the available space with the image—without clipping the image—and will then add space between the repeated images as necessary to evenly fill the available area. A value of round works essentially the same way, but instead of filling the excess area with empty space, the image is scaled up to fill the available area. Use the round value with caution, because an image will rapidly degrade in quality as it is scaled up, becoming fuzzy and pixelated. Not good!

▪ **Note** The space and round values of the background-repeat property currently have limited browser support. As of the time of writing, Opera is the only major browser that supports them both. This is a good point to mention that Modernizr (http://modernizr.com), the HTML5 detection library mentioned in Chapter 1, also has detection capabilities for CSS3!

The background-attachment property determines whether a background image or images are scrolled with the content when the page is scrolled. The value fixed fixes a background in place, even if the page scrolls, while scroll allows it to scroll away with the contents. Also, a new value, local, has been added. This value applies only to elements that have their own scrollbar on the page.[10] If this value is set, when the user scrolls the inset scrollbar, the background in that area of the screen will scroll with it.

▪ **Note** For a demonstration of the different values of background-attachment, visit
http://people.opera.com/pepelsbey/experiments/bga.

The background-position property is for offsetting the starting point of the background image. It takes two values that correspond to the horizontal and vertical positioning. You can set specific values or use preset keywords:

```
/* background image is offset 10 pixels left and 25 pixels down */
background-position: -10px 25px;
```

The properties background-clip and background-origin have been introduced in CSS3. Both these properties take the same values, but each has a different function. The background-clip is for specifying the "background painting area," which is the area where the color and images will be rendered. The background-origin specifies the "background positioning area," which is for determining where the point of origin is for the background, meaning the point at which the upper-left corner of a nonrepeated image would begin (the 0,0 point if you are familiar with coordinate spaces). The three values for these properties are as follows:

- border-box: The background painting area/positioning area extends to the outer edge of the border. The border will run over the top of the image, but it can be semitransparent.

- padding-box: The background painting area/positioning area extends to the inner edge of the border. This is the default value.

- content-box: The background painting area/positioning area extends only to edge of the content area, which is the area before any padding is applied.

---

[10] Setting the width and height properties on an element and then setting overflow:auto will cause a scrollbar to appear so the user can get to any overflowing text.

Figure 6-16 illustrates these different values.

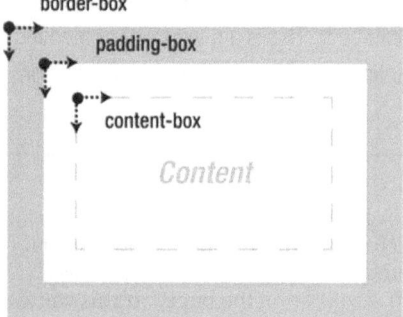

Figure 6-16. *The placement meaning of the three values available values for the* background-clip *and* background-origin *properties.*

To demonstrate these values, we can create two boxes, which we'll apply a background to shortly:

```
<div class="box"></div>
<div class="box no-clip"></div>
```

We'll style both boxes so they have a width, height, padding, margin and a semi-transparent border (the color syntax for the transparent border may look foreign to you; this will be covered in the "Color" section later). One will be clipped to the content area, while the other will be clipped to the border area:

```
.box {
      width:200px;                                  /* set the width to 200 pixels */
      height:200px;                                 /* set the height to 200 pixels */
      padding:20px;                                 /* set the padding to 20 pixels */
      margin:10px;                                  /* set the margin to 10 pixels */
      border:10px solid hsla(0 , 0% , 0% , 0.5 );   /*set a semi-transparent black border */
      background-color: #ccc;                       /* set a gray background color */
      background-image: url(logo.png);              /* attach an image */
      background-repeat:space;                      /* repeat image in available space */
      background-origin:content-box;                /* set image origin to content edge */
      background-clip:content-box;                  /* clip image at content edge */
}

.no-clip {
      background-clip:border-box;                   /* clip image at border edge */
}
```

The boxes will appear like Figure 6-17. The background images will repeat beginning at the same origin but will be clipped at different points.

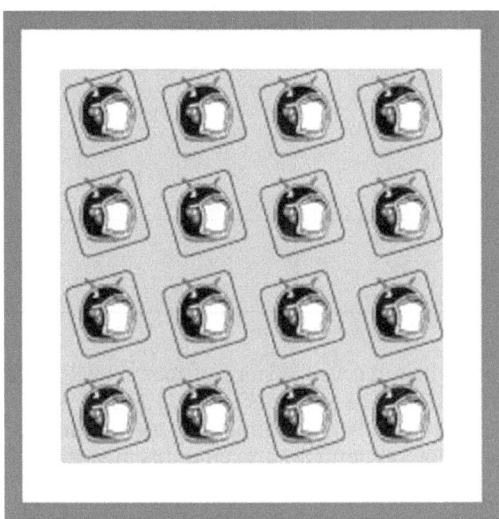

Figure 6-17. *Two treatments of a background using the new background-clip and background-origin properties as well as the space value in the background-repeat property*

Lastly, in backgrounds, the new background-size property can be used to stretch a background over its background area instead of repeating it. This is a useful and needed feature of backgrounds, but be careful your image doesn't get stretched or scaled up too far, or it will begin looking fuzzy, pixelated, and downright awful. The property takes one or two values. One value sets the horizontal and vertical size together, while two values set these independently of each other. The width and height can be set with a percentage, but this risks distorting the image when set for both dimensions of the image. To address this, the keyword auto may be used for one dimension, so the image maintains its aspect ratio. This is the default value for the height when only one value is given:

```
/* Set width to 100% of the available area and height to 50% of the image height */
background-size:100% 50%;
/* Set width to 100% and maintain the aspect ratio of the image */
background-size:100% auto;
/* Set the width 50% and the height to auto */
background-size:50%;
```

■ **Note** The first setting in the previous code will distort the image.

The background-size property also has the keywords contain and cover. A value of contain will scale the image to completely fit in the background area while maintaining its aspect area, even if there is some whitespace on one side. The cover value will scale the image while maintaining the aspect ratio as well, but it will scale the image so that it completely covers the background area, even if this means some of the image will be clipped out of view (Figure 6-18).

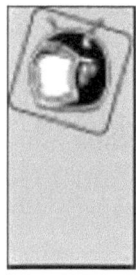 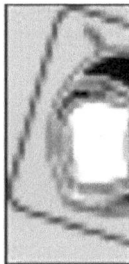

Figure 6-18. *The contain (L) and cover (R) values set on the background-size property. Notice the accentuated pixelation that occurred when the image was scaled up.*

Multiple backgrounds

Added in CSS3 is the ability of the background properties to support having multiple images specified, which will layer on top of each other inside the background area. The syntax is easy—separate each image by a comma. For instance, two images, shown in Figure 6-19, could be combined using the following:

```
background-image: url(logo.png) , url(star.png);
```

Figure 6-19. *Two separate images that will be combined using multiple backgrounds*

Using this technique will result in the combined pattern shown in Figure 6-20.

Figure 6-20. Two separate images layered together in a background

Reversing the order of the images in the backgroud-image property will change their layering. The first image specified will appear on top. The other background properties can be supplied with comma-separated values to set the properties on each image individually; for instance, to only repeat the star image in Figure 6-20, the following could be added:

```
background-repeat: no-repeat , repeat;
```

These values could be set via JavaScript too, which could lead to some pretty interesting dynamic effects!

Rounded corners

The ability to have a property that creates rounded corners on an element is a panacea for web design. This used to be a painful process of slicing up images and placing them into a grid of div elements so the four corners could be isolated. Yuck! The new border-radius property allows borders to be rounded. Borders can be rounded all at once, individually, or even in a nonuniform fashion. Giving the property one length value will set all four corners to that value:

```
border-radius:20px; /* round all corners by 20 pixels */
```

Giving the property four values will set the rounding on each of the four corners:

```
border-radius:100px 50px 25px 0px; /* each corner is rounded by a different amount */
```

Using a forward slash between the values will allow different values to be specified for rounding each side of a corner, leading to a nonuniform corner:

```
border-radius: 100px / 20px; /* round one side of the corner more than the other side */
```

The forward slash in the preceding code breaks the rounding into two values; the first value is the horizontal rounding amount, and the second value is the vertical rounding amount.

The results of the previous three properties applied to an empty `div` with a background color look like Figure 6-21.

Figure 6-21. *Many different shapes can be created by using the* `border-radius` *property.*

Drop shadows

The `box-shadow` property can be used to create a drop shadow around the box. The values it takes are the horizontal distance of the shadow, the vertical distance, the amount of blur to apply, the amount it should spread, and finally the color of the shadow. Here's an example:

```
box-shadow: 10px 15px 20px 5px #999999;
```

This moves the shadow 10 pixels to the right, moves it 15 pixels down, blurs it 20 pixels, spreads it out 5 pixels (this expands the shadow outward in all directions), and sets it to a dark gray color. Figure 6-22 shows this property applied to the shapes created in the "Rounded corners" section.

Figure 6-22. *Shapes with drop shadows applied using* `box-shadow` *property*

Color

If utilized correctly, color can be a powerful addition to a web page's design, improving its structure by visually grouping items together based on their color or separating content in the layout through the use of contrasting colors. It can be abused too, making an otherwise good layout gaudy and, particularly if clashing colors are used, hard to look at. There are accessibility concerns in regard to color too, because certain color choices for the page can make content difficult to read for those with color blindness. Red-green color blindness is most prevalent, so avoid separating content into shades of red and green that are at a similar level of luminosity.

Color on-screen

The colors you see on your screen are defined using combinations of the primary colors red, green, and blue in an additive color model, which means all three combined at full intensity will produce white (Figure 6-23).

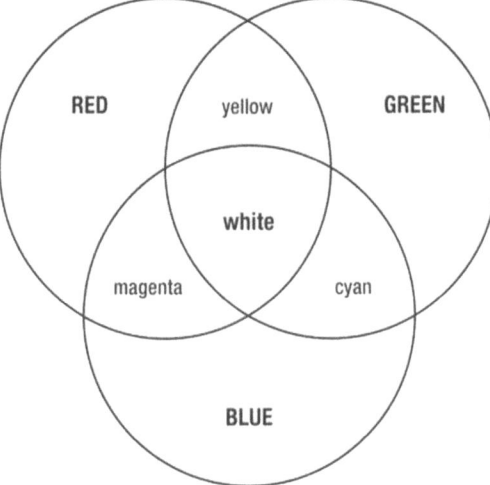

Figure 6-23. *In an additive color model, the primary colors add to the lightness of each other.*

Within CSS, color is commonly defined using **hexadecimal notation**. This notation breaks the red, green, and blue components of a color into two-digit numbers that together result in a six-digit number preceded by a hash sign, in the form #RRGGBB. Called a **hex triplet**, each digit pair has the hexadecimal numerical range of 00–FF. For example, #ff00ff represents full-intensity red and full-intensity blue, without any green. Combined, they produce magenta. If you are unclear of how this sequence of numbers and letters becomes a color, be sure to read the "How web color values are calculated" sidebar for more information.

HOW WEB COLOR VALUES ARE CALCULATED

All the colors you see displayed on your screen are composed of the three primary colors red, green, and blue. As shown in Figure 6-23, it is an additive color model, meaning as the intensity of the primary colors increases, the color becomes lighter and lighter (the lightness is added to) until eventually it becomes white. To define color in a web browser, each primary color is stored in a byte, or 8 bits (8 ones and/or zeros). Each color component (red, green, and blue) then has the possible values in the range of 00000000 to 11111111, which is the range 0–255 in decimal. 0 is complete lack of the color, while 255 is the fullest possible intensity of the color. Decimal is a base-10 counting system, meaning ten digits (including 0) are used before counting moves position. Binary is a base-2 system, meaning only two digits are present (0 or 1). Base-16, hexadecimal, has 16 digits that can be used to compress a binary number, such as 1111, into one digit: F. The following table shows the first 16 digits of each numbering system:

Decimal	0	1 2		3	4 5 6 7				8	9	10	11	12	13	14
Binary	0000	0001 0010		0011	0100 0101 0110 0111				1000	1001	1010	1011	1100	1101	1110
Hexadecimal	0	1 2		3	4 5 6 7				8	9	A	B	C	D	E

The value 255 in decimal can be represented as 11111111 in binary or FF in hexadecimal. Obviously, at two digits long, hexadecimal wins as the most compact representation of the number 255. Pure white, which is the combined full intensity of red, green, and blue, can be represented as red = 255, green = 255, and blue = 255, or in hexadecimal as red = FF, green = FF, and blue = FF. Condensed all together we get FFFFFF. Add a hash sign to the beginning, and this is the hexadecimal notation used for colors on the Web. The range of colors available in this system is $256 \times 256 \times 256$ (or 256^3), which equals 16,777,216 possible colors. (256 is used here instead of 255, because the calculation needs to factor in zero in each color component.)

■ **Note** There is a handy color utility named ColorZilla (www.colorzilla.com) that integrates into Firefox and provides several features such as an in-browser color picker, web page color scheme analyzer, and even a tool for creating CSS gradients!

Hexadecimal notation can also represent color using three digits when a digit is repeated in each of the color components. So, magenta could also be represented as #f0f. White, which is #ffffff in hexadecimal, can be optionally shortened to #fff. #99aaff (a light blue) could be shortened to #9af, and so forth.

It is also possible to use a preset color keyword such as white, black, aquamarine, and so on. While modern web browsers support dozens of keywords for choosing colors, for the sake of consistency stick with precisely defining your colors (through hexadecimal notation or otherwise) to ensure they are the same as what appear in your images and other content. (What exactly does "burlywood" look like? And yes, that is a supported color keyword!)

Color is used in several CSS properties but is most common for setting background and foreground colors. Backgrounds will be covered later in this chapter, so let's first look closer at foreground colors. Foreground colors (for the textual content on a page) are defined using the color property, which is part of the CSS Color Module Level 3. This module is one of the few in CSS3 that is now at W3C Recommendation status. It's a small module, defining color and another property, opacity. In addition to hexadecimal notation, there are other notation systems that can be used in color, which we'll get into next.

Functional notation syntax

Instead of specifying a hexadecimal value, there is another syntax that can be used called **functional notation**. In this form of syntax, the command rgb(R, G, B) is used, where the "R, G, B" are replaced with either the decimal representation or, perhaps more useful, the percentage of a particular color component. So for example, whereas magenta could be written in either of the following hexadecimal notation forms:

```
p { color: #ff00ff; }
p { color: #f0f; }
```

using functional notation this could be rewritten as this:

```
p { color: rgb( 255, 0, 255 ); }
p { color: rgb( 100%, 0% , 100% ); }
```

Functional notation isn't new in CSS3, but the next form of it is: Hue, Saturation, Lightness (HSL).

Hue, saturation, lightness

HSL functional notation uses the form hsl(H, S, L,), where "H, S, L" represents the hue, saturation, and lightness of a color. Before going further with the syntax, you'll need to understand what exactly HSL means.

In an RGB color system, adjusting each of the components of a color to arrive at a shade or tint (darker or lighter version of the same color) is a rather unintuitive process, particularly for inexperienced developers. Depending on the color, more than one of the three RGB components may need to be increased or decreased to achieve a proper shade or tint of the color. Imagine a bright yellow color composed of red and green. A darker yellow cannot be created by only reducing the red component, because that will just result in a greener hue of yellow, not a darker yellow. Both the red and the green components need to be reduced. HSL aims to make this kind of adjustment easier.

In HSL, all the possible colors in an RGB color space are enclosed in a cylinder. The hue is what would commonly be thought of as the actual color (which may be lighter or darker or more or less saturated). Looking down on the HSL cylinder, all colors are visible, and which one is selected is determined by moving around the outside of the cylinder. Because this is a circle in cross section, this movement is given a value between 0° and 360°. The colors are spread around the circle in the order of the colors of a rainbow, beginning and ending at red. So, 0° and 360° are both red.

The saturation is determined by a percentage indicating how far the color is from the center of the cylinder; 0 percent is at the center, which means it would lack all saturation or be grayscale. Conversely, 100 percent means it would be at the edge or at the full possible intensity of a color. Moving down the cylinder darkens the color, ending at black, while moving up the cylinder lightens it, ending at white. This is measured in a percentage too, where 0 percent is black and 100 percent is white, and values in between are darker or lighter shades and tints of the color. Refer to Figure 6-24 for a visual representation of how these values relate to each other.

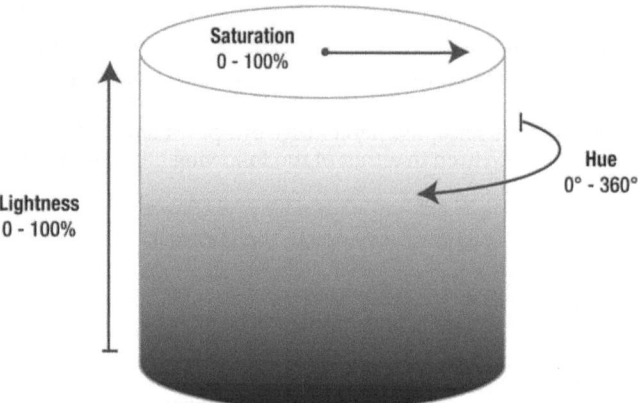

Figure 6-24. Hue, Saturation, and Lightness (HSL) cylinder defining how to adjust RGB colors in a more intuitive fashion

Now that you have an understanding how HSL works, you can use the HSL functional notation syntax where you would have used hexadecimal notation, for example:

```
p { color: hsl(300, 100%, 50%); }        /* magenta */
p { color: hsl(300, 20%, 50%); }         /* pastel magenta - less saturated */
p { color: hsl(300, 20%, 25%); }         /* dark shade - less lightness */
p { color: hsl(115, 20%, 25%); }         /* dark green - different hue */
```

Notice that the lightness is placed in the middle initially (50 percent); if it were at 100 percent or 0 percent, it would make the color pure white or pure black, regardless of the other values.

Opacity

Any element can have its overall opacity adjusted using the opacity property. The possible values are between 0.0 and 1.0 that map to the range 0 percent to 100 percent. The following are all legitimate values:

```
p { opacity:1.0; }          /* totally opaque */
p { opacity:0.0; }          /* totally transparent */
p { opacity:0.5; }          /* 50% transparent */
p { opacity:0.25; }         /* 75% transparent */
```

Opacity can also be added using the functional notation styles outlined earlier by adding an opacity component—called **alpha**—when defining a color. This makes the functional notation styles become rgba(R, G, B, A) and hsla(H, S, L, A), where "A" is an alpha value to add, which has the same value range as the opacity property:

```
p { color: rgba(0, 255, 0 , 0.1); }        /* nearly transparent green */
p { color: hsla(225, 100%, 50%, 0.5); }    /* semi-transparent blue */
```

The difference between setting the color in the color property and the opacity property is that opacity will affect the whole element (including backgrounds and borders), while color will affect only the foreground text (Figure 6-25).

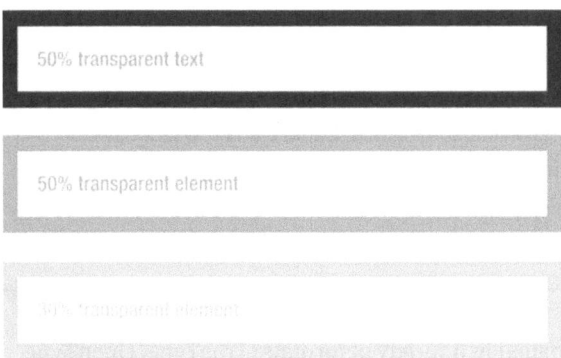

Figure 6-25. *The color property will affect only an element's contents (top), while the opaque property will affect the whole element (middle and bottom).*

Web typography

If there is anything that is more of a disappointment to those coming from the world of print design to web design, typography has got to be it. Or rather, it should be said, "was more of a disappointment," because the ability to control typography has progressed in leaps and bounds in CSS3. The available typeface choices are now potentially limitless, and there are text-level effects that can be applied, such as drop shadows and strokes. With this power comes the need to not abuse typography, to not lose sight of the purpose of typography on the page, and to use these effects to help the user process the content on your page, not to hinder their comprehension.

Web fonts

For years, fonts were something that were referenced in a style sheet, not something that were downloaded for use by a style sheet. If a particular operating system did not have a referenced font installed, the browser would fall back to one of a handful of generic defaults. Practically, this meant Arial, Times New Roman, and Courier New and a few others were the only "safe" typeface choices. Elaborate hacks such as scalable Inman Flash Replacement (sIFR)[11] emerged that replaced text on the page with Adobe Flash content that could display embedded fonts. This effort has since been abandoned in favor of the ability in modern web browsers to download fonts for use on a page. So-called **web fonts** have seen a dramatic rise in availability thanks to the introduction of the @font-face rule, part of the CSS Fonts Module Level 3. This rule allows a font file to be linked into the style sheet for inclusion on the page.

---

[11] sIFR information can be found here: http://novemberborn.net/sifr3, however it is noted that the project is no longer maintained.

■ **Note** Since the typeface definition file needs to be downloaded before it is displayed, using web fonts potentially introduces what front-end developer Paul Irish termed FOUT (Flash Of Unstyled Text),[12] whereby the text on the page flashes with its default font before using the downloaded typeface. Some web browsers have attempted to address this issue, so you may not run into it; however, if you do, there are scripts available such as fout-b-gone (`www.extensis.com/en/WebINK/fout-b-gone/`) that aim to prevent FOUT in browsers where it still occurs.

Depending on the browser, fonts can be downloaded in a variety of formats (TrueType, OpenType, and so on). A newer format that all modern web browsers support is Web Open Font Format (WOFF), which is a lightweight font format developed in 2009 specifically for fonts that will be distributed over the Web. The format is currently undergoing standardization at the W3C.[13]

Google hosts a library of web fonts at `www.google.com/webfonts` that can be linked to remotely for inclusion in your website. Since its launch, this directory has grown exponentially from a handful of fonts to hundreds. This is a good place to start experimenting with web fonts.

The general idea behind downloading fonts is that the `@font-face` directive is placed at the top of your CSS file and specifies the font family and font file source for download:

```
@font-face
{
        font-family: myFont;
        src: url('LunotrobeOutline.woff') format('woff');
}
```

The `font-family` property can then be set to the value of the `font-family` set in the `@font-face` rule:

```
body { font-family: myFont; }
```

This will apply the downloaded font to all elements in the body of the web page.

■ **Caution** You use a variety of typefaces all the time, but like other bodies of work, typefaces were designed by someone! This means you are not necessarily legally allowed to use any font you come across. Be sure you are licensed to use the fonts you choose. For instance, fonts by Adobe Systems can't be used directly as web fonts, even if you have them installed on your computer! However, a subscription-based service such as Typekit (`http://typekit.com`) can be used as an intermediary to allow the use of otherwise restricted fonts.

---

[12] Paul Irish's post on FOUT can be found here: http://paulirish.com/2009/fighting-the-font-face-fout/
[13] See http://www.w3.org/TR/WOFF/

Multiple columns

Creating a text block with multiple columns used to require a lot of different divs for the different columns in the layout. To ease this markup pain, a new property, the columns property, has been added. At its most basic, the property can be set to a value that specifies the number of columns to add, like so:

```
p.col { columns: 3; }
```

This will break the paragraph (with a class attribute set to "col") into three columns within its available area. There are number of related properties for getting more specific with how the columns are displayed; for instance, the gap between columns can be controlled like a border using the column-gap and column-rule properties. There is also a column-count property, which is available just for setting the column count. (The columns property is a shorthand property for these other properties). For example, the following would produce the layout in Figure 6-26:

```
column-count: 3;
column-gap: 2em;
column-rule: 0.35em solid #000;
```

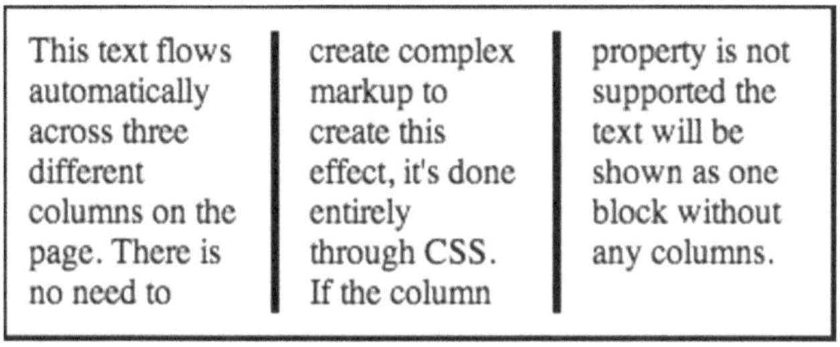

This text flows automatically across three different columns on the page. There is no need to	create complex markup to create this effect, it's done entirely through CSS. If the column	property is not supported the text will be shown as one block without any columns.

Figure 6-26. Multiple columns applied to a paragraph

The column-gap property specifies the width of the gap between the columns, while the column-rule property specifies the width style and color of the vertical rules.

Text effects

The text-shadow property was added back in CSS2, but it was removed in CSS2.1. Well, it's back again in CSS3! Don't let the name fool you; creating a text shadow is probably the least-useful effect possible with this property, but it's the place to start when looking at it. The property uses almost the same format as the box-shadow property shown in the "Backgrounds and borders" section. The only difference is that text-shadow does not have a spread value.

If you play around with the values, you can create effects that appear like indented text, embossed text, and so on. Also, an outline can be added to text this way by offsetting several layered text shadows. To do this, four text shadows can be chained together using commas, each one offset in a different direction:

```
h1 {
        font-size:4em;
        color:#fff;
        text-shadow: -1px 0 0 #000 , 0 -1px 0 #000 , 1px 0 0 #000 , 0 1px 0 #000;
}
```

Remember, the first value is the horizontal offset of the shadow, the second value is the vertical offset, the third value is the blur, and the fourth value is the color. This will create outlined text like Figure 6-27.

Figure 6-27. Outlined text created using the text-shadow property

---

■ **Note** WebKit-based browsers (Safari and Google Chrome) have implemented a property called text-stroke. It is not in any CSS specification at the W3C, so you're best to avoid it until (if) it appears in any of the CSS3 modules. To use it, you need the webkit prefix; the property is -webkit-text-stroke, which takes a width and a color, as in -webkit-text-stroke: 1px #f00.

Rules of typography

There's a rule of composition promoted in Robin William's book *The Non-Designer's Design Book* that states elements on the page that are merely similar should be avoided. If design elements on a layout are different, make them very different in order to create contrast in the layout. Use the contrasting differences among the design elements as a way to help visually organize the page. This fits into typography when you think about the typefaces you choose to use. Fonts fall into two main categories: serif and sans serif. Serif fonts are typefaces with embellishments to the edges of the letters (called **serifs**). These include Times New Roman, Georgia, Palatino, and so on. **Sans serif** (meaning "without serifs") includes Arial, Helvetica, Verdana, and so on. If you start including different serif or different sans serif fonts in the same design, pause for a moment and consider whether it is really necessary to have, for example, Arial and Helvetica together in the same layout. Typefaces that are similar yet distinct enough that their differences are noticeable are best avoided. Along those same lines, it's best to avoid using more than two typefaces overall on the page. There is so much you can do with bolding, italicizing, color, and so on, that even using one typeface offers a plethora of stylistic choices and treatments.

When thinking about the overall organization of textual content, use typography to create a hierarchy of information on the page, clearly identifying what content is more important to read over other content. This is the purpose of headlines, titles, subtitles, and so on; they create a hierarchy your eye can quickly scan to get deeper and deeper into the information on the page. Don't be afraid to size text large when you see it as the top bit of information on the page, but like with your typeface choices, avoid creating typography that is almost the same size but not quite the same, because this will likely be distracting.

The HTML5 outline algorithm discussed in Chapter 3 is particularly useful for helping you organize your page into a hierarchy. You may want to refer to that section when organizing your headings and so forth.

Lastly, the single greatest rule to follow in regard to typography is: if text is meant to be read, make it readable!

Summary

This has been one of the largest chapters in this book, and for good reason! I hope you can appreciate the power of CSS to fine-tune the appearance of elements on your page. This is the tip of the proverbial iceberg; there is plenty not covered that is developing in CSS, such as techniques for creating transitions and animations from CSS without any JavaScript code (the merits of which can be debated!), rotating and otherwise transforming the elements in 2D and 3D space, creating gradients from CSS, applying images to borders, and more! See `www.w3.org/TR/css-2010/#properties` for a list of available CSS properties you can use (because the W3 uses "snapshots," this may not be a complete list until it is updated again). We're not completely done with CSS, because this is a growing area, which, along with HTML5, is paving the path of what is possible on the road ahead, and that is where we will go in the next chapters!

CHAPTER 7

User Interaction and the HTML5 APIs

Included in the HTML5 specification is documentation on how HTML elements, as well as the wider web browser environment, can be accessed from a programmed script. This is a component of the specification that is interwoven throughout the specification. Each component that can be scripted is broken into **application programming interfaces** (APIs) that define how the script can interface with specific elements on the page and specific aspects of the web browser. Some of these APIs are included as part of HTML5, such as the History API for manipulating the browser's forward and back buttons programmatically, while others are part of associated technologies and are covered in separate (but interlinked) specifications to HTML5, such as the geolocation API—which provides web pages with geographic location–aware capabilities. What these APIs are built around is the idea that the page and its environment are represented by a series of objects, such as the geolocation object, which contains location data for the page. In the context of just the page's content, these objects form the means by which a web page's Document Object Model (DOM) may be traversed, as discussed in Chapter 1.

The goal of this chapter is to get you versed in how to explore and use the scripting capabilities defined in the HTML specification so you have the necessary tools to explore on your own beyond what can be shown in this chapter. As examples, we will look at using scripting to interact with the browser's history, as well as the video and canvas elements. Lastly, we'll also look at how to add drag-and-drop support to any element.

Using JavaScript in this chapter

JavaScript has been sprinkled throughout the chapters in this book, but in this chapter we will be working with it more formally, so you'll want to set up a testing environment for JavaScript code. As discussed in Chapter 2, JavaScript can be embedded using the script element, or it can be loaded from an external file, which is the preferable method. Moving it to its own file creates a clearer separation between the markup and scripting on your website.

We're going to create a bare-bones web page to use as a template for the examples in this chapter. Create a directory named jstemplate (on your desktop or wherever is convenient for you to access). You'll use this directory as a starting template for the examples in this chapter. Launch your favorite text editor, and create the following web page:

```
<!DOCTYPE html>
<html>
        <head>
                <meta charset="utf-8" />
                <title>HTML5 Apprentice</title>
                <link rel="stylesheet" type="text/css" href="css/styles.css" />
                <script type="text/javascript" src="js/script.js" defer></script>
```

```
        </head>
        <body>
                    <p>Content goes here!</p>
        </body>
</html>
```

Save this code as a file named index.html in the jstemplate directory you created. Create a second page for the JavaScript named script.js and place it in a directory called js inside the jstemplate directory.

Write the following JavaScript in script.js:

```
// init function runs when page has fully loaded
function init() {
            // code to run
}
window.onload = init;
```

This script will run the function init when the page has fully loaded.

Lastly, create an empty CSS style sheet (just an empty text file at this stage) named styles.css and place it in a directory called css inside the jstemplate directory.

Accessing DOM properties and methods

Chapter 1 provided an overview of the DOM, which describes the elements on a page as a connected tree-like structure (technically an acyclic connected graph), which can be used to gain programmatic access to the page's elements, attributes, and text. What was also mentioned is that the DOM is accessible through a document object, which is contained inside another object—the window object. What wasn't mentioned is that more abstract entities (besides the web page document) can be accessed through the window object. For example, there is programmatic access available to the browsing history, website URL location, screen dimensions, and so forth. Each of these entities is accessible through the window as an object in its own right.

So, what exactly are objects? Objects are merely a collection of **properties** and **methods**. What does that mean? Properties are a series of keys and values, like attributes on HTML elements. They are what an object *has*. For instance, the width of the screen is a property that holds a specific value (the screen width in pixels). Some properties are read-only, while others can have their values overwritten. Properties are also known as variables, depending on the context.

Methods describe what a particular object can *do*. For instance, using JavaScript to pop up an alert window is done through a method. Methods are also known as **functions**. They are self-contained blocks of code that will run only when called, like the function you saw in the template JavaScript code in the previous section.

For instance, the window object has a property called name that can be used to add an identifier to a particular web browser window.[1] This property is not read-only, so it can be read and written to.

As far as methods go, the window object has a method (among many) called alert(), which you've likely seen in use. It pops up a dialog box with a message and an OK button. Using dot notation (described in Chapter 1), these could both be used like so:

----

[1] This may be used in the target attribute of hyperlinks in order to open a linked resource in a specific window.

```
function init() {
        // sets the name of the window
        window.name = "MAIN";
        // shows the name of the window
        window.alert("The name of this window is set to: " + window.name);
}
window.onload = init;
```

The specific usage of this property and method are beside the point at this stage; what is important is the conceptual difference between properties and methods and the knowledge that JavaScript can access settings and behavior in the web browser beyond just the HTML elements on the page.

Logging to the console

Chapter 1 also mentioned the web developer tools available to major web browsers and the code `console.log("message")`. Let's look at these two topics closer. Among the web developer tools in each browser, there will be a means to access a JavaScript console where messages from JavaScript can be logged. In the major web browsers, these are found as shown here:

- *Chrome*: Select View ➤ Developer ➤ JavaScript Console.

- *Firefox*: I recommend using the Console tab in Firebug.

- *Internet Explorer (8 and above)*: There is Script tab in the Internet Explorer Developer Tools, accessible by selecting Tools ➤ Developer Tools.

- *Opera*: Select View ➤ Developer Tools ➤ Error Console. Opera also has a toggle in Opera Dragonfly for showing and hiding a console.

- *Safari*: Select Develop ➤ Show Error Console.

If you modify your template script to log a message, you should see it appear in the JavaScript console when loading the page. Figure 7-1 shows an example in Safari of running the following code:

```
function init() {
        console.log("message");    // log a message to the JavaScript console
}
window.onload = init;
```

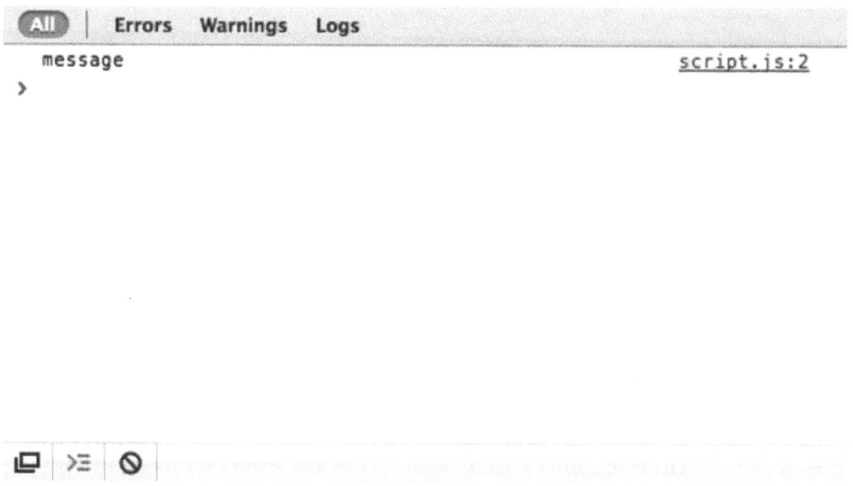

Figure 7-1. Safari's error console showing logged JavaScript output.

■ **Note** Another option for logging JavaScript output is Firebug Lite, a version of Firebug that can be used with Internet Explorer, Firefox, Opera, Safari, and Chrome. Download it here: `http://getfirebug.com/firebuglite`.

Although it is all well and good to log messages to the console, the real power of the console comes from logging parts of the DOM and inspecting the value and existence of objects, properties, and methods. For example, try changing the console message in the prior code snippet to the following, and reload the page:

```
...
console.log(window);    // log the window object to the JavaScript console.
...
```

This will produce (depending on the JavaScript console) a representation of the window object as a collapsible list of properties and methods, as shown in Figure 7-2.

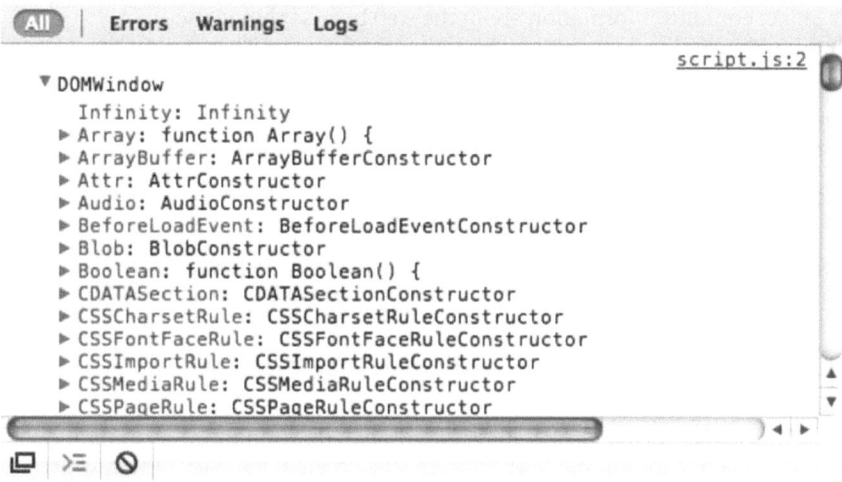

Figure 7-2. The window object as it appears logged in Safari's error console

Scrolling through this list, you will find interesting information about what you can manipulate from JavaScript. For example, you'll see the type of data you can work with from JavaScript, such as Arrays, Booleans, and so on. You'll also see a list of the HTML elements in the form of HTMLAnchorElement, HTMLImageElement, HTMLParagraphElement, and so forth. JavaScript is a prototype-oriented language, meaning it does not have classes (unlike Java or Adobe Flash's ActionScript) but instead utilizes "prototype" objects that provide a basis for other objects. These prototype objects can build on each other, creating a "prototype chain" that allows prototype objects to inherit properties and methods from other prototype objects. This process is analogous to the inheritance capabilities of classes in other object-oriented languages. The HTML element-like entries in the console output shown in Figure 7-2 are the prototype objects that define the properties and methods different HTML elements have when represented in the DOM. For instance, the stop() and play() methods defined for the video element that stop and play a video loaded in that element can be found through exploring the HTMLVideoElement object represented in the DOM (exploring this element, you'll discover it actually inherits these methods from HTMLMediaElement).

■ **Note** When logging HTML elements that appear on the page (by referencing them by their ID, for instance), the error console will normally show the actual HTML code for the element, which will look like a snippet of HTML source code. This behavior doesn't help you discover the properties that a referenced HTML element has, so in cases like this, use the console method console.dir() instead of console.log(). This method will show you the properties of a particular object sent to it.

Other objects of note in the window object include the following:

- The navigator object contains information about the web browser being used such as the plug-ins installed and vendor and version information. Also contained in this object is geolocation information.

- The screen object contains information about the dimensions, color depth, and related information about the display being used to view the current web page.

- The history object contains methods for accessing the browser's forward and back buttons and related functionality programmatically.

- The location object contains information about the web page URL address. The website can be redirected by setting the href property in this object, such as location.href = "http://www.apress.com";.

- The document object contains the DOM representation of all the HTML elements on the web page currently being viewed.

Some information will be buried; for instance, you may not immediately find the alert() method that was used earlier. For this we need to look at the prototype used to create the window object, which is accessible through the following:

```
...
console.log(window.constructor.prototype);    // log the window object's prototype.
...
```

This will reveal the methods defined directly on the window object, as shown in Figure 7-3.

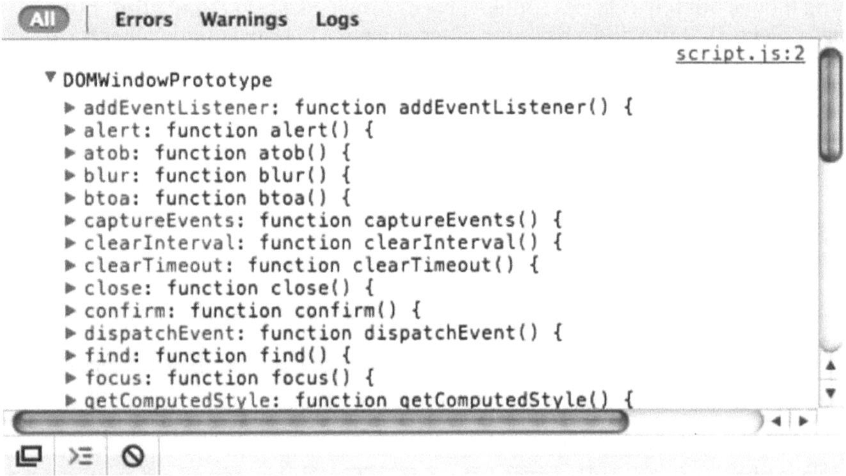

Figure 7-3. The window object's prototype object showing the methods defined for the window object

---

■ **Note** Accessing the object's prototype does not directly reveal the methods inherited by that prototype. For browsers that support it (it's nonstandard), such as Safari, Chrome, and Firefox, you will find a __proto__ property that will give you access to the parent prototype that a particular prototype is built upon. This can be used to inspect the methods inherited from the parent prototype.

Events

Events are the notifications that happen in JavaScript as a result of such things as user input (mouse clicks, keyboard key presses, and so on) or conditions of the page (page has loaded, and so on) that can be "listened to" in order to make something happen when the event occurs. Elsewhere inside the window object you will see a long series of properties that begin with "on," such as onclick, onscroll, onload, and so on. These are the events that the window object can respond to (clicking, scrolling, and loading the page, respectively). These will have values of null for the most part, except for onload, which will be set to function init(), since this was set in the code created earlier at this line:

```
...
window.onload = init;
```

This sets the onload property to our custom event handling init() function, meaning the init() function will run when the window has fully loaded and sent a notification of the onload event.

Each possible event can be associated with a function in this way. For example, the following would associate a function that pops up an alert box when the page is clicked:

```
function windowClickHandler() {
    alert( "Window was clicked" );    // pops up an alert box
}
window.onclick = windowClickHandler;
```

If the function associated with an event is given a parameter, then that parameter holds an object with information about the event that occurred. For instance, the following uses a parameter (named e) that contains a pageX and pageY property, which specifies the location of the mouse cursor on the page:

```
// logs the event object function windowMouseDownHandler(e) {
console.log(e);
// log the mouse location
console.log("Mouse is at: " + e.pageX + ", " + e.pageY);              }
window.onmousedown = windowMouseDownHandler;
```

When this code is run and the page is clicked, the event object (a MouseEvent object in this case) and the mouse location will be logged to the console.

The History API

Let's put all this JavaScript knowledge to use! I mentioned that the window object contains a history object for controlling the browser's forward and back buttons. This is actually not all that can be done with the history object, and HTML5 has built on the History API[2] to allow the actual history record to be updated programmatically. This means pages can be added to the history of the browser, and if the user actually clicks the back button, they will go to the pages that have been added to the history instead of

---

[2] See www.w3.org/TR/html5/history.html.

pages they previously visited. The usefulness of this is evident in pages that use Ajax to load content dynamically. **Asynchronous JavaScript and XML** (Ajax) is a means of loading and injecting content into a page without having to reload the entire page. For instance, websites such as Twitter and Facebook use Ajax to add new posts to their pages.

Really simple Ajax

Ajax uses an object called `XMLHttpRequest` (XHR) to load content from a URL using JavaScript. This content then can be added to the page by using, for instance, the `innerHTML` property of HTML elements.

At its very simplest, using Ajax might look like the following:

```
var xmlhttp = new XMLHttpRequest();
xmlhttp.onreadystatechange = responseReady;
xmlhttp.open("GET","content.txt",true);
xmlhttp.send();
```

The `var` keyword creates a new variable, which is just like a property—it's a container that holds some value that can be read or written to. The new variable in this case holds a new `XMLHttpRequest` object instance (the `new` keyword creates this object). A function is then set to handle the `onreadystatechange` event, which will be fired when the XHR object has retrieved some content. The `open()` method then specifies the kind of method used to retrieve the file, the filename, and whether the request is **asynchronous** (the script continues while the external file loads) or **synchronous** (the script waits for the external file to load before continuing). Setting this to `true` makes it asynchronous and `false` sets it to synchronous. The event handling function might look like this:

```
...
function responseReady() {
          document.body.innerHTML = xmlhttp.responseText;
}
```

This script will set the content on the page to the content that was inside the loaded text file.

As a complete example, we'll create a simple page with a next button and a previous button and a message that loads between the two. Duplicate the `jstemplate` directory from earlier and rename it `ajax`, and then edit `index.html` to look like the following HTML:

```
<!DOCTYPE html>
<html>
        <head>
                <meta charset="utf-8" />
                <title>HTML5 Apprentice</title>
                <link rel="stylesheet" type="text/css" href="css/styles.css" />
                <script type="text/javascript" src="js/script.js"></script>
        </head>
        <body>
                <button id="prevButton">Previous</button>
                <p id="message"></p>
                <button id="nextButton">Next</button>
        </body>
</html>
```

This page contains two buttons and an empty paragraph between the two that we'll fill with content using Ajax. Open `script.js` from the `ajax/js` directory. Add the following script:

```
// create global variables
```

```
var xmlhttp;
var prevbutton;
var nextbutton;
var message;
var messageID = 1;

// initialize variables and add event listening functions
function init() {
            prevbutton = document.getElementById("prevButton");
            nextbutton = document.getElementById("nextButton");
            message = document.getElementById("message");

            prevbutton.onmousedown = prevButtonDown;
            nextbutton.onmousedown = nextButtonDown;

            checkButtons();
            loadFile();
}
// disable previous or next button depending on whether first or last message is displaying
function checkButtons() {
            if ( messageID == 1 ) prevbutton.disabled = true;
            else prevbutton.disabled = false;
            if ( messageID == 3 ) nextbutton.disabled = true;
            else nextbutton.disabled = false;
}
// decrement message ID when previous button is pressed
function prevButtonDown() {
            messageID--;
            if (messageID < 1) messageID = 1;

            checkButtons();
            loadFile();
}
// increment message ID when next button is pressed
function nextButtonDown() {
            messageID++;
            if (messageID > 3) messageID = 3;

            checkButtons();
            loadFile();
}
// load message files using Ajax
function loadFile() {
            var file = "message"+messageID+".txt";

            xmlhttp = new XMLHttpRequest();
            xmlhttp.onreadystatechange = responseReady;
            xmlhttp.open("GET",file,true);
            xmlhttp.send();
}
// add Ajax loaded content to paragraph on the page
function responseReady() {
```

```
                        message.innerHTML=xmlhttp.responseText;
}
window.onload = init;
```

This script uses a variable (messageID) to track which of three messages needs to load when the previous or next button is clicked. You'll need to create three text files to load named message1.txt, message2.txt, and message3.txt and save them in the ajax directory. Add some text to each of these files; just make sure the text is different for each. This text will be injected into the empty paragraph element on the page.

Open index.html in a web browser to test the file. You should be able to click the buttons back and forth and display a different message on each click (Figure 7-4).

(Previous)

Message 3

(Next)

Figure 7-4. The output of a simple Ajax application after two clicks of the next button. The button is disabled when the last of the three messages is displayed.

History-enabled Ajax

If you look at the URL for the page's address in the previous example, you will see it is not updating as the different content is loaded. This isn't ideal because the pages showing the different messages can't be bookmarked, and clicking the browser's back button will not go back to the previously displayed message but instead will go to the previous page viewed. However, the History API can be used to overcome these issues. HTML5 introduces two methods, pushState() and replaceState(), for adding to and editing the browsing history. The first, pushState(), allows a new entry to be added to the page's browsing history, while replaceState() will replace the current browsing location in the history with a new entry.

Let's edit the script in the previous example and include pushState() to add a new entry to the browsing history when the next and previous buttons are clicked. Go back to the previous script and edit the prevButtonDown() and nextButtonDown() methods:

```
...
function prevButtonDown() {
        messageID--;
        if (messageID < 1) messageID = 1;

        var obj = { page: messageID };
        var title = "page"+messageID;
        var url = "#message"+messageID;
        window.history.pushState( obj , title , url );

        checkButtons();
        loadFile();
}
function nextButtonDown() {
```

```
        messageID++;
        if (messageID > 3) messageID = 3;

        var obj = { page: messageID };
        var title = "page"+messageID;
        var url = "#message"+messageID;
        window.history.pushState( obj , title , url );

        checkButtons();
        loadFile();
}
...
```

The pushState() method takes three arguments. The first is a JavaScript object (the curly brackets are shorthand notation for creating an object) that can contain information about the page being added to the history. In this case, it's an object with a single custom property, page, and a value that holds the page ID. Next is the title of the page added to the history (for example, "page1"). Lastly—and most importantly—is the URL of the page to add to the history. The page we'll add is the same page we're on, but we'll add a hashtag to the URL so it becomes ajax.html#message1, ajax.html#message2, and ajax.html#message3 for each click of the next button. We can just add the hashtag without specifying the current page, because the browser will add the current page if no page is specified.

OK, edit the loadFile() function so that it retrieves the message ID from the hashtag in the URL:

```
...
function loadFile() {
        // retrieve the hashtag from the URL using the location object
        var messageHash = window.location.hash;
        if (messageHash == "") messageHash = "#message1";
        var file = messageHash.substr(1)+".txt";      // strip out the "#" from the hashtag

        xmlhttp = new XMLHttpRequest();
        xmlhttp.onreadystatechange = responseReady;
        xmlhttp.open("GET",file,false);
        xmlhttp.send();
}
...
```

Now test the page and use the next and previous buttons. You should see the web page address URL update with the hashtag. This means the individual Ajax-enabled pages of content can be bookmarked, which is great! However, if you click the browser's forward or back button, you will notice the message on the page does not update, even though the URL in the address bar does. The reason for this is that the onload event does not fire again when the user clicks the forward and back buttons. This is because the page has been cached by the browser so that it will load faster as the user navigates through the history. What we need to add is an event that fires when the history has changed, and thankfully there is such an event called onpopstate. At the very end of the script, add the following:

```
...
window.onpopstate = init;
```

This will run the init() function every time the history is navigated. This isn't the most efficient code, because there will be redundant calls to the init() function (for example, twice when first loading the page), but use this simple example to develop from.

Building a custom video controller

Let's look at interacting with the JavaScript methods associated with an HTML element. Earlier I mentioned that the video element has a play() method and a stop() method. We can use these to control video playback from JavaScript, which means we can create a control bar with a custom play and pause button. Say goodbye to a control bar that looks different in every browser! For the graphics we'll use CSS, but more specifically we'll use a concept called **CSS sprites**, which is a technique for using one image file to display two or more images at different points on the page. The idea behind this technique is that a single image file can contain a whole bunch of images, which then can be cropped and positioned in different ways to show the different images. This is kind of like looking through a paper towel tube at cookies spread out on a cookie sheet. You'll be able to see only one cookie at a time, but you can move the sheet around to show different cookies. This technique gives the illusion of multiple images having been downloaded, but in fact only one has, meaning all the images will appear on the page at once and only one request has gone to the server to fetch the image.

On to our example…duplicate the jstemplate directory from earlier and rename it video_player. Create an image for the sprite that contains a play and pause graphic for our video controls (Figure 7-5). Set the size to 80 pixels wide by 30 pixels tall.

Figure 7-5. *An image sprite with two images for the controls on a simple video player*

Update the HTML in index.html to look like the following:

```
<!DOCTYPE html>
<html>
        <head>
                <meta charset="utf-8" />
                <title>HTML5 Apprentice</title>
                <link rel="stylesheet" href="css/styles.css" type="text/css" />
                <script type="text/javascript" src="js/script.js" defer></script>
        </head>
        <body>
        <section>
                <video width="320" height="240" poster="poster.jpg" id="my_video">
                        <source src="trailer.webm" type='video/webm; codecs="vp8, vorbis"' />
                <source src="trailer.mp4" type='video/mp4; codecs="avc1.4D401E, mp4a.40.2"' />
                        <source src="trailer.ogv" type='video/ogg; codecs="theora, vorbis"' />
                        <p>Video playback not supported.</p>
                </video>
                <div class="video_controls">
                        <a href="nojs-player.html" title="Play" id="control_button">
                                <span id="control_graphic" class="play"></span>
                                <label id="control_label">Play</label>
                        </a>
                </div>
        </section>
        </body>
</html>
```

As you can see, this code contains the video element with fallback content[3] followed by a div area for the custom video control. To get this example to work, you will have to include three video files sized to 320 by 240 pixels, which are named trailer.webm, trailer.mp4, and trailer.ogv in the same directory as index.html (it wouldn't be a bad idea to create a video directory or similar for the videos, if you do this be sure to update the HTML).

Next we'll create the JavaScript that will be used to enable this custom control. Open script.js from the video_player/js directory. For the code, first we will create variables to hold a reference to the video, anchor (<a>), span, and label on the page. Next the init() function is updated so that it sets the value of each JavaScript variable to a reference to an HTML element, which can be retrieved through their id attribute using the getElementById() method. Update script.js to look like this:

```
// JavaScript variables used to hold references to HTML elements
var video;
var control_button;
var control_label;
var control_graphic;

// initialization function runs when the page has loaded
function init() {
        video = document.getElementById("my_video");

        control_button = document.getElementById("control_button");
        control_label = document.getElementById("control_label");
        control_graphic = document.getElementById("control_graphic");

        control_button.onclick = playVideo;
}

window.onload = init; // runs the init function when the page has finished loading
```

> ■ **Note** Classes instead of IDs could be used for all the elements, and the document.getElementByClassName() function could have been used to automatically enable functionality for multiple video controls on one page, but this would make the code a bit more complex, so for brevity's sake IDs have been used.

The last line in the init() function calls another function when the button control is clicked. This function is named playVideo(). Go ahead and add it to script.js:

```
...
function playVideo() {
        control_graphic.className = "pause";
        control_button.onclick = pauseVideo;
        control_button.title = "Pause";
```

---

[3] For brevity, the fallback content has been shortened; refer to Chapter 5 for comprehensive fallback content information for the video element.

```
            control_label.textContent = "Pause";

            video.play();

            return false;
}
```

This function sets the class attribute on the control graphic to a CSS class named pause, which positions the CSS sprite over the pause button image. Next, it sets the text content (which is used as fallback content if the CSS style sheet was disabled), and it then plays the video. The return false bit ensures the link (with the ID of control_button) does not go to its linked page when it's clicked; however, if JavaScript is disabled, it'll go to a page called nojs-player.html that would presumably contain a video player that will work without JavaScript (you'll have to build this one on your own). This function also sets a new function for when the button control is clicked again. This new function is called pauseVideo(), and it pauses the video and reverses the changes set in the playVideo() function. Go ahead and add this to your script.js file:

```
...
function pauseVideo() {
            control_graphic.className = "play";
            control_button.onclick = playVideo;
            control_button.title = "Play";
            control_label.textContent = "Play";

            video.pause();

            return false;
}
```

That's all the JavaScript we need; now on to the CSS. First the link anchor element is set to display as a block-level element and has its width and height set. The property overflow is set to hidden so that content that flows outside of the dimensions of the controls does not show up. This is needed to hide the fallback text, because it will be pushed out of the bounds of the control. Open styles.css from the video_player/css directory. Add the following CSS rule:

```
.video_controls a {
    display: block;
    width: 40px;
    height: 40px;
    overflow: hidden;
}
```

Next we add a rule for the span so that it is styled to be a block-level element as well (pushing the other textual content out of the way). This is where the background image sprite (named "controls.png") is attached:

```
...
.video_controls span {
    display: block;
    background-image: url(controls.png);
    background-repeat: no-repeat;
    width: 40px;
    height: 40px;
    background-color: #ccc;
```

```
}
```

Lastly two CSS classes are created that set the position of the background image, moving it to show the play symbol or pause symbol:

```
…
.pause {
    background-position: -45px 5px;
}
.play {
    background-position: 5px 5px;
}
```

That's it! The play and pause buttons are derived from the same image, as shown in Figure 7-6.

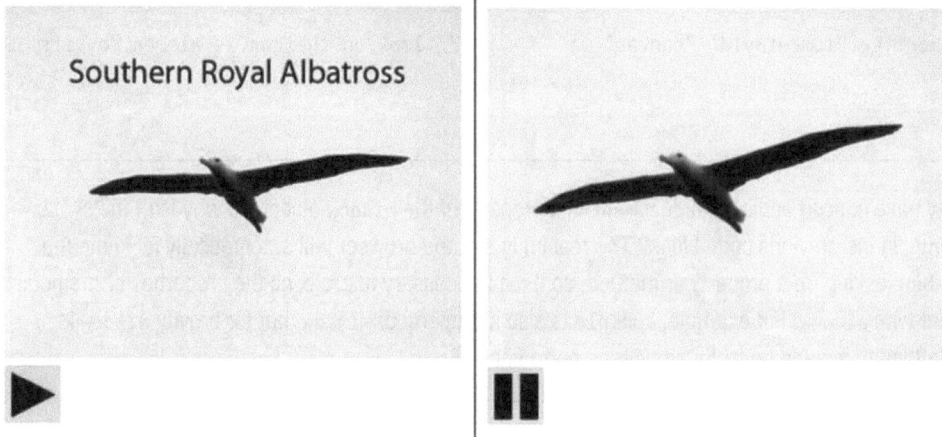

Figure 7-6. The play (L) and pause (R) states of the custom video control using a CSS sprite

Scripted 2D Canvas API

Now let's look at something even more interactive. As you saw in Chapter 5, the canvas element does not have much that can be done to it purely with HTML, because it has only two attributes, which simply specify the width and height of the canvas area. The real power of canvas comes from manipulating the element from JavaScript. Remember, the canvas is a bitmap canvas, meaning it is essentially a blank image that we can manipulate the pixels of through a set of drawing commands.

To work with the canvas, a particular "context" needs to be retrieved from the element, which then can be used as the target of drawing operations. The context specifies what kind of image we are dealing with. There are two choices available: a two-dimensional or three-dimensional image.

Let's begin by hunting down the method for retrieving the context we will draw with.[4] First duplicate the jstemplate directory from the beginning of the chapter and rename it canvas. Modify the HTML in index.html to add a canvas element (and some fallback content) in place of the paragraph of text:

---

[4] For the impatient, the method for retrieving a context is called getContext().

```
...
<body>
        <canvas id="canvas" width="300" height="300">
                <p>The canvas element is not supported!</p>
        </canvas>
</body>
...
```

Now modify script.js in the canvas/js directory to gain access to the canvas element from JavaScript. We'll begin by adding a variable that will hold a reference to the canvas element, which we'll set using the getElementById() method:

```
var canvas;            // variable to hold a reference to the canvas element on the page

function init() {
canvas = document.getElementById( "canvas" );      // look up the canvas element by its ID
}
window.onload = init;
```

■ **Note** You may have noticed earlier that document is a property of the window object, so why isn't the syntax window.document... in the previous code block? The reason is that the browser will automatically look into the window object when looking up a property or method, so it isn't necessary to prefix all the properties or methods of the window object with window. For example, console is also a property of window, but for brevity window is usually left out (although it could be included with no harm caused).

This gets us access to the canvas element from our script. Let's look at what methods are defined for the canvas element by looking at its prototype, like we did with the window object, by accessing constructor.prototype. Edit the script like so:

```
...
function init() {
// look up the canvas element by its ID
canvas = document.getElementById( "canvas" );
// log the canvas element's prototype
console.log( canvas.constructor.prototype );                         }
...
```

This reveals getContext(), which is the method we need to retrieve the context! The other method, toDataURL(), is for converting the canvas image data to a URL that could, for instance, be supplied as the source image data for an image element (img).

As mentioned earlier, the context will tell what type of image we are dealing with, which can be a two-dimensional or three-dimensional image. To retrieve a certain context, a text keyword is given as an argument to the getContext() method.[5] To retrieve a two-dimensional context, the text keyword "2d" is used. To retrieve a three-dimensional context, the text keyword "webgl" is used instead. As you can see, the 3D context uses WebGL for interacting with the image.

■ **Note** WebGL is a 3D rendering specification for web browsers that is overseen by the Khronos group.[6] WebGL is an experimental feature in web browsers, and as such, the webgl keyword may not work for the immediate future. If you experiment with this context and find it does not work, try "experimental"-webgl instead, which is the temporary context keyword being used in supporting browsers until WebGL is further along in its development.

Let's retrieve the 2D context and inspect its properties and methods using the JavaScript console; edit the script to look like the following:

```
var canvas;
var context;            // variable to hold a reference to the canvas context

function init() {
        canvas = document.getElementById("canvas");
        // retrieve the 2D canvas context
context = canvas.getContext("2d");

        // inspect the canvas context
console.log(context);
        // inspect the canvas context prototype
console.log(context.constructor.prototype);
}
window.onload = init;
```

This will log two objects to the console, CanvasRenderingContext2D and CanvasRenderingContext2DPrototype (the actual names may vary by browser). The first will show the properties available on the context, which includes the color of lines and fills added to the canvas. The CanvasRenderingContext2DPrototype shows the available methods, which includes a range of methods for drawing on and transforming the canvas. The graphical capabilities of the canvas encompass the following:

- *Basic drawing*: There are methods for drawing rectangles, lines, curves, and arcs.

- *Fills and strokes*: There are methods for creating solid fills and outlines.

- *Effects*: There are methods for creating shadows, gradients, transparency, and for compositing images on top of each other.

---

[5] The WHATWG runs a wiki at http://wiki.whatwg.org/wiki/CanvasContexts that provides an overview of the canvas context keywords available.
[6] The WebGL specification is available here: www.khronos.org/registry/webgl/specs/latest/.

- *Transformations*: There are methods for scaling, rotating, and translating (moving) the image.

- *Text*: There are methods for adding solid or outlined text.

- *Images*: There are methods for drawing an image (or even a video or another canvas element) onto the canvas, which can then be transformed or otherwise manipulated.

We will explore the first two areas, but be sure to use the console to explore the methods and properties available that are not covered in this chapter. The purpose of many of them is quite self-evident!

Drawing on Canvas

Let's begin by drawing a rectangle on the canvas that covers the available area. The methods related to drawing a rectangle are as follows:

- `fillRect(x,y,w,h)`: Draws a solid rectangle

- `strokeRect(x,y,w,h)`: Outlines a rectangle

Using either of these methods, we can create a rectangle of a given width and height starting at a specified location on the canvas. Before using these methods, you may want to style the rectangle to specify the appearance of the fill and stroke (the outline color). There are a few properties that can be set for this purpose:

- `fillStyle`: The fill color

- `strokeStyle`: The color of the outline

- `lineWidth`: The width of the outline

To set the style properties, set the value equal to a quoted CSS-style color code, such as #00000 for black. The `lineWidth` property takes a number that specifies the width in pixels. To fill the entire canvas with a solid rectangle, you'd specify a starting point of 0, 0 (the upper-left point) and a width and height the same as the canvas width and height. Adding an outlined rectangle on top of that would give us the following:

```
...
canvas = document.getElementById( "canvas" );
context = canvas.getContext( "2d" );
// the color of the fill
context.fillStyle = "#cccccc";
// the color of the outline
context.strokeStyle = "#999999";
// the width of the outline
context.lineWidth = 5;
// fill the canvas area with a rectangle
context.fillRect( 0, 0, canvas.width, canvas.height );
// outline a rectangle inside the canvas borders
context.strokeRect( 30, 30, 200, 100 );
...
```

Add this code to the content of the init() function in script.js in the canvas/js directory to see it in action! The canvas uses a Cartesian coordinate system with an inverted y-coordinate. This means every pixel on the canvas can be specified by an x and y value, where x is the number of pixels from the left side of the canvas area and y is the number of pixels from the top side of the canvas area. For instance, an x, y coordinate of 30, 30, would specify a location 30 pixels from the left side and 30 pixels from the top side of the canvas area (Figure 7-7).

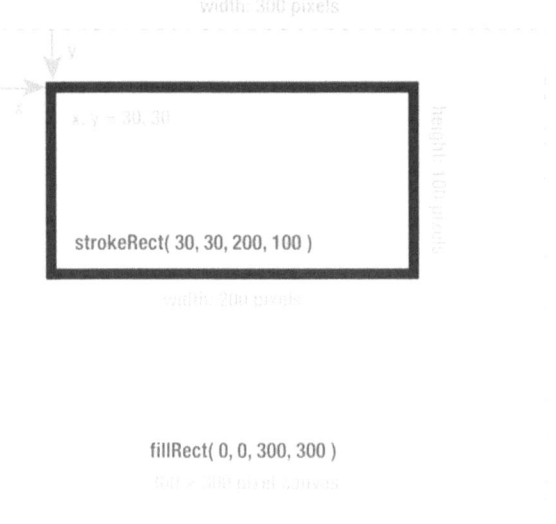

Figure 7-7. The rectangle drawn by strokeRect(30,30,200,100) *in a 300 by 300 pixel canvas*

Drawing more complex shapes than a rectangle is more complicated. A line needs to be created—also known as a **path**—which can be used to build the shape segment by segment. The following are the relevant methods for drawing a simple shape with straight edges:

- beginPath(): Starts a new line
- closePath(): Finishes a new line
- moveTo(x,y): Moves to a coordinate on the canvas
- lineTo(x,y): Draws a line segment to a coordinate on the canvas
- stroke(): Colors the line
- fill(): Fills in the shape created by the line segments

The beginPath() method is first used to tell the canvas that a new shape is being drawn, which consists of line segments. The moveTo() and lineTo() methods are then used to move around the canvas and draw line segments. Lastly, the closePath() method is used to complete a line and connect the beginning and ending points if the line is filled. For example, to create a triangle a path is begun, the drawing point is moved, two lines are drawn, and the path is closed, filled, and outlined:

```
...
context.beginPath();            // start a new line
context.moveTo(50,50);          // move to 50 pixels from the left and top edge of the canvas
context.lineTo(150,50);         // draw a line to 150 and 50 pixels from the left and top edge
context.lineTo(100,150);        // draw a line to 100 and 150 pixels from the left and top edge
context.closePath();            // close the line
context.fill();                 // fill the shape formed by the line with the fill style color
context.stroke();               // outline the line with the stroke style color
...
```

Used in place of the rectangle drawing code earlier, this results in the triangle shown in Figure 7-8.

Figure 7-8. A triangle drawn using the canvas path drawing methods

---

■ **Note** If the `beginPath()` and `closePath()` methods are omitted, the lines won't be automatically closed to form a shape, which may be desired in cases where you just want to have lines without a fill.

In place of the `lineTo()` method, the `arcTo()`, `bezierCurveTo()`, or `quadraticCurveTo()` methods could be used to create shapes with curved edges.

Additionally, the `lineCap` and `lineJoin` properties can be set to affect how the end of line segments and the join points of each segment appear. The `lineCap` property can be set to butt, round, or square to change the end of a line. The `lineJoin` can be set to miter, round, or bevel to affect the shape of the join point of two line segments (Figure 7-9). When set to miter, another property, `miterLimit`, can be used to specify the angle over which a point will be formed.

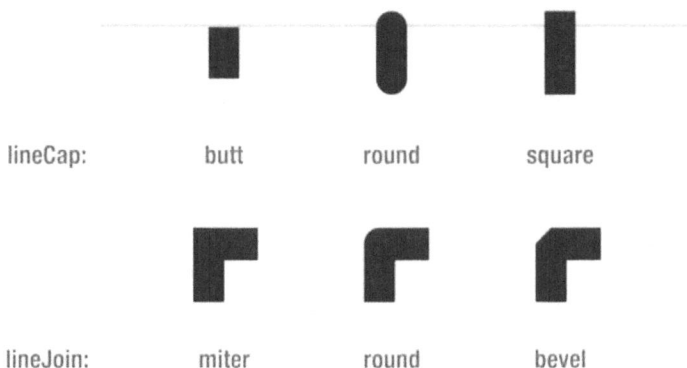

Figure 7-9. The values of the `lineCap` and `lineJoin` properties

TRIGONOMETRY

An area of mathematics that is worth getting your head around when dealing with algorithmically created drawings is trigonometry. Trigonometry is concerned with the study of the angles and sides of triangles, which is critical for drawing specific points around a circle. Since the canvas uses a Cartesian coordinate space made up of rows and columns (the x and y coordinates), finding the x, y coordinates of a point a certain distance away from another point, when the line of sight between them is slanted, is not as straightforward as it would be if they were in a horizontal or vertical line from each other, but finding the point really isn't that much more difficult. All you need is the angle formed inside a triangle drawn between the two. Once you have that, the formulas in Figure 7-10 are all you need.

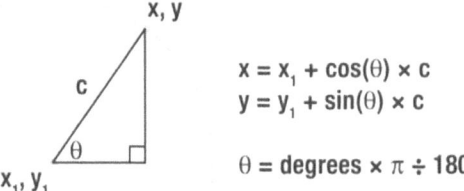

$$x = x_1 + \cos(\theta) \times c$$
$$y = y_1 + \sin(\theta) \times c$$

$$\theta = \text{degrees} \times \pi \div 180$$

Figure 7-10. Determining the point on a circle using trigonometric functions

In Figure 7-10, the angle, theta, needs to be in radians, which equals the angle in degrees times pi divided by 180. Translated into code, the formula in Figure 7-10 might look like this:

```
x = 50 + Math.cos( 45 * Math.PI / 180 ) * 20;
y = 50 + Math.sin( 45 * Math.PI / 180 ) * 20;
```

This would find the x and y coordinates of a point that was at a 45-degree angle and was 20 pixels out from another point at the x, y coordinate of 50, 50 on the canvas.

Let's look at a full example. This example draws a spiral on the canvas, the result of which is shown in Figure 7-11. It runs a loop a number of times that increases the distance from the center ("c" in Figure 7-10) and increases the angle in degrees:

```
// declare the global variables
var canvas;
var context;
var centerX;
var centerY;
var degrees = 0;
var radius = 1;

function init() {
        canvas = document.getElementById( "canvas" );
        context = canvas.getContext("2d");
        centerX = canvas.width/2;
        centerY = canvas.height/2;
        // move to the center of the canvas
        context.moveTo( centerX , centerY );
        // loop two thousand times, drawing a line out further and further from the center
        for (var i=0; i<2000;i++) {
                degrees += 1;
                radius += 0.02;
                context.lineTo(
                        centerX+Math.cos(degrees*Math.PI/180)*radius ,
                        centerY+Math.sin(degrees*Math.PI/180)*radius
                        );
        }
        context.stroke();
}
window.onload = init;
```

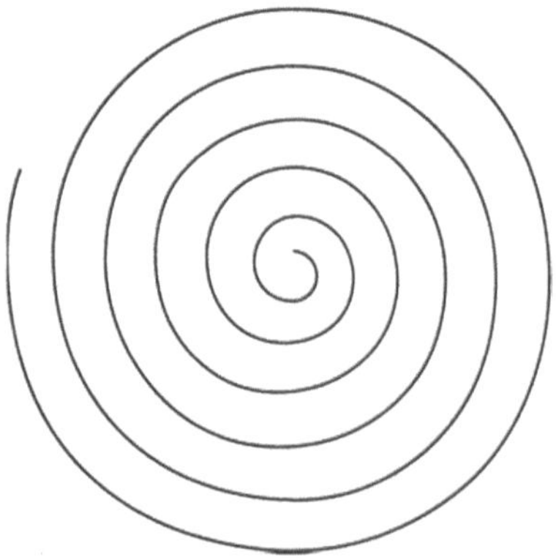

Figure 7-11. Spiral drawn on canvas using trigonometric functions

Canvas state

Setting the fill and stroke style will affect all subsequent graphics created on the current canvas context. To deal with temporarily changing the fill and stroke style, the canvas context has two methods, save() and restore(), which are used to save the styles set and then restore them to the saved state later. When multiple shapes are drawn on the canvas, these two methods are often used to isolate the stylistic changes applied by each shape. For instance, in the following code block, three squares are drawn that are outlined by the colors red, green, and blue, respectively. A border is then drawn around all the boxes. Because save() and restore() are used, the final border does not need a style set because it will be using the original styles:

```
...
context.save();
context.strokeStyle = "#ff0000";
context.strokeRect(0,0,100,100);
context.restore();

context.save();
context.strokeStyle = "#00ff00";
context.strokeRect(50,50,100,100);
context.restore();

context.save();
context.strokeStyle = "#0000ff";
context.strokeRect(100,100,100,100);
context.restore();

// Rectangular outline will be default black, because original style settings were restored
context.strokeRect(0,0,200,200);
...
```

■ **Note** Is canvas a Flash killer? You may have heard this question posed, particularly after Steve Jobs of Apple Inc. famously railed against Adobe Flash in an open letter in 2010, in which he stated that Flash is an antiquated technology that will soon be replaced by HTML5 technologies. This was in part spurred on by the creation of the video element—as video is an area on the Web where Flash dominates—but the canvas element encroaches a bit onto Flash's territory as well, although the overlap is limited. Canvas is a scriptable bitmap image optimized for drawing with pixel data, and it does not include any built-in methods for animation. Canvas uses immediate mode rendering, meaning it does not store the graphics it displays as separate entities. It's like actually painting on a real canvas, where paint can be layered on top of the image, but once on the canvas, it is effectively part of any prior paint that has been applied. Flash content, on the other hand, is traditionally stored as vector imagery (although it handles bitmap data as well), and it includes the concept of a display list for its graphics, which is very much like the DOM for HTML. This means that graphics in Flash are separated into nodes that can be easily accessed from code for interactive and animation purposes. In many respects, SVG, another graphics technology for the Web, is more akin to the traditional space of Flash. Therefore, canvas alone does not replace Flash, but together with other technologies associated with HTML5, it is making the authoring of content traditionally restricted to Flash possible.

Canvas interactivity

Interacting with canvas graphics is a matter of setting an event handler function on one of the mouse-related events of the canvas, such as onmousedown, onmouseover, or onmousemove (use console.log() on the window object to explore the events available) and then doing some drawing on the canvas at the mouse location. For example, the following script records the x, y coordinate of the mouse cursor position and draws a line from the saved to the current position every time the user moves the mouse, creating a simple drawing application (Figure 7-12):

```
// declare global variables
var canvas;                    // reference to canvas element on page
var context;                   // reference to canvas context
var cwidth;                    // reference to canvas width
var cheight;                   // reference to canvas height
var lastX = 0;                 // variable to hold an x coordinate value
var lastY = 0;                 // variable to hold an x coordinate value

// initialize the variables and add event handler
function init() {
        canvas = document.getElementById( "canvas" );
        context = canvas.getContext("2d");
        cwidth = canvas.width;
        cheight = canvas.height;
        context.strokeStyle = "#000000";
        context.strokeRect(0,0,cwidth,cheight);

// call the draw function when the cursor moves over the canvas
        canvas.onmousemove = draw;
}
// draw on the canvas
function draw(e) {
        // update the saved x, y coordinates to the position of the cursor
        // if it is first entering the canvas
        if (lastX == 0) lastX = e.pageX - canvas.offsetLeft;
        if (lastY == 0) lastY = e.pageY - canvas.offsetTop;
        // begin a new line and move to the last saved x, y coordinates
        context.beginPath();
        context.moveTo(lastX, lastY);
        // set the saved x, y coordinates to the position of the mouse cursor
        lastX = e.pageX - canvas.offsetLeft;
        lastY = e.pageY - canvas.offsetTop;

        // draw a line
        context.lineTo(lastX, lastY);
        context.closePath();
        context.stroke();
```

```
}
window.onload = init;
```

Figure 7-12. Doodle made with a simple canvas drawing application

Canvas animation

Animation is just a series of still images, so the basic steps involved in animating are as follows:

1. Clear any existing graphics on the canvas.

2. Draw new graphics on the canvas.

3. Repeat steps 1 and 2

Drawing on canvas uses the drawing methods covered earlier, but clearing the canvas introduces a new method: clearRect(x,y,w,h). This method clears all graphics from the canvas within a rectangular area. For animations, this would usually mean clearing the entire canvas area, unless you could reliably know only one portion of the canvas would be changing throughout the animation.

The global window object contains two methods for repeating a piece of code over time, as is needed in an animation: setInterval(f,t) and setTimeout(f,t). Both of these methods call a custom function (f) after a specified interval (t). The interval is set in milliseconds, so 1000 would be one second in length. The difference between the two is setInterval(f,t) runs continuously, while setTimeout(f,t) executes only once after the set amount of time. We'll use setInterval(f,t) to create a basic animation engine.

■ **Note** Firefox, Chrome, Opera, and Internet Explorer have an experimental method called requestAnimationFrame(), which is used to tell the web browser to repaint the window in order to redraw the frames of an animation. This has advantages over using the setInterval() method because the animation runs only when the browser is available, meaning that, for instance, an animation running in a tab that is hidden will stop because the page is not being shown, saving the computer's processor from consuming resources unnecessarily. You can find more information on this method at https://developer.mozilla.org/en/DOM/window.requestAnimationFrame.

To create a basic animation engine, the following functions are created:

- init() to set up initial variables and start the animation

- invalidate() to specify that the animation frame needs to be redrawn

- clear() to clear the animation frame

- draw() to draw the animation frame

- update() to update variables used when drawing the animation frame

Put together, the code for a basic animation engine looks like the following, which will animate two lines across the canvas (Figure 7-13):

```
// declare global variables
var canvas;
var context;
var cwidth;
var cheight;
var lastX = 0;
var lastY = 0;

// initialize animation
function init() {
        // set variable values
        canvas = document.getElementById( "canvas" );
        context = canvas.getContext("2d");
        cwidth = canvas.width;
        cheight = canvas.height;

        // start animation sequence by calling the update function every 30 milliseconds
        setInterval(update, 30);
}
// clear and redraw the canvas
function invalidate() {
        clear();
        draw();
}
// clear the canvas
function clear() {
        context.clearRect( 0 , 0 , cwidth , cheight );
}
// draw the graphics on the canvas using the saved x, y coordinate values
function draw() {
        context.fillRect(0,lastY,cwidth,5);
        context.fillRect(lastX,0,5,cheight);
}
// update the saved x, y coordinate values. Reset them to zero if they reach the canvas edge
function update() {
        lastY += 1;
        if (lastY > cheight) lastY = 0;

        lastX += 1;
        if (lastX > cwidth) lastX = 0;
```

```
            invalidate(); // call invalidate to redraw the canvas
}
window.onload = init;
```

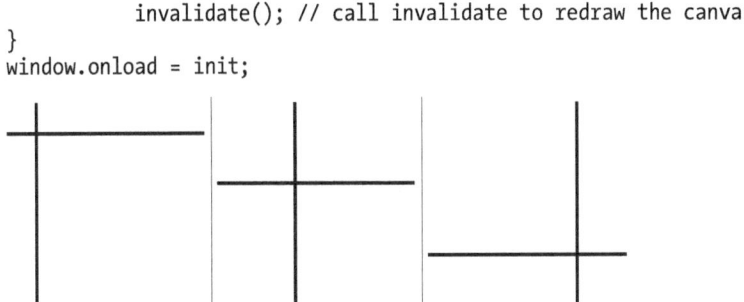

Figure 7-13. Three frames from a basic animation engine that sweeps two lines across a canvas

To see this working, edit `script.js` in the `canvas/js` directory. Obviously, this is just a simple example to show a bare-bones animation engine, but this structure could easily be developed further to create more complex animation sequences.

Drag-and-drop operations

Drag-and-drop functionality as it appears in the HTML5 specification is actually an old Microsoft addition,[7] which was added to Internet Explorer originally more than a decade ago. Since then, the other browsers have caught up and implemented the same functionality—except for Opera, which does not currently support this feature natively. In the supporting browsers, drag-and-drop capability is available to all the elements through the global `draggable` attribute, which has the possible values of `true` or `false`. Most elements will be set to `false` by default, but there are a few exceptions. The image element (`img`) has its `draggable` attribute set to `true` by default, as does the anchor element (`a`), but only if it has its `href` attribute set. Also, although it doesn't have attributes, plain text that has been selected by the user can be dragged by default.

Dragging operations will always have a start and an end, which usually corresponds to something being picked up, moved, and dropped somewhere else. Quite a few events are involved, depending on the complexity of the desired behavior in between the start and end of a drag-and-drop sequence. Table 7-1 describes the relevant events and when they are triggered.

Table 7-1. Events involved in drag-and-drop operations

Event	Description
dragstart	The drag-and-drop operation has begun.
drag	The drag-and-drop operation is occurring.

---

[7] See http://dev.w3.org/html5/spec-author-view/dnd.html for the HTML5 drag-and-drop documentation. Information about the Microsoft implementation it's inspired from can be found here: http://msdn.microsoft.com/en-us/library/ms537658(VS.85).aspx.

dragenter	The dragged item is entering the drop target.
dragover	The dragged item is over the drop target.
dragleave	The dragged item is leaving the drop target.
drop	The dragged item was dropped on the drop target.
dragend	The drag-and-drop operation has ended.

Let's create a file that logs each of these events to the console. Duplicate the jstemplate directory from earlier and rename it dnd. Begin by editing index.html to look like the following:

```
<!DOCTYPE html>
<html>
        <head>
                <meta charset="utf-8" />
                <title>HTML5 Apprentice</title>
                <link rel="stylesheet" type="text/css" href="css/styles.css" />
                <script type="text/javascript" src="js/script.js" defer></script>
        </head>
        <body>
            <section>
                <h1 draggable="true" id="draggable">Draggable</h1>
            </section>
            <section>
                <h1 draggable="false" id="droptarget">Drop Target</h1>
            </section>
        </body>
</html>
```

This HTML page creates two sections, one that has its draggable attribute set to true and one to false (this could be left off, but I included it to explicitly differentiate the two). Each has an ID that will be referenced in the JavaScript for the page.

Now edit the linked CSS file, styles.css (in the dnd/css directory). We will take the sections and create two black-bordered boxes that are arranged side by side:

```
section {
        width:200px;
        padding:10px;
        background-color:#cccccc;
        border:1px solid #000000;
        float:left;
        margin-right:4px;
        text-align:center;
}
```

Lastly, edit script.js (in the dnd/js directory) and write the following script:

```
// global variable to hold reference to the two sections on the page
var draggable;
```

```
var droptarget;

// initialize variable values and set event handling functions
function init() {
          draggable = document.getElementById( "draggable" );
          droptarget = document.getElementById( "droptarget" );

          draggable.ondragstart = dragStartHandler;
          draggable.ondrag = dragHandler;
          draggable.ondragend = dragEndHandler;

          droptarget.ondragenter = dragEnterHandler;
          droptarget.ondragover = dragOverHandler;
          droptarget.ondragleave = dragLeaveHandler;
          droptarget.ondrop = dropHandler;
}
// event handling functions for each of the drag and drop operations
function dragStartHandler(e) { console.log("dragstart"); }
function dragHandler(e) { console.log("drag"); }
function dragEndHandler(e) { console.log("dragend"); }
function dragEnterHandler(e) { console.log("dragenter"); }
function dragOverHandler(e) { console.log("dragover"); }
function dragLeaveHandler(e) { console.log("dragleave"); }
function dropHandler(e) { console.log("drop"); }

window.onload = init;
```

This script will add event handler functions for each of the drag-and-drop events and log a message to the console when the event occurred. If you open this in a web browser and drag the text "Draggable" to "Drop Target," you should see some event messages appear in your JavaScript console.

Depending on the browser you used, you may not see very much. For instance, Google Chrome shows only "dragstart" and "dragend" and appears to ignore all the other events! What's going on here? Well, Chrome expects something called a dataTransfer object to be set, which is essentially a data payload that gets (potentially) delivered to the drop target in a drag-and-drop operation. At its simplest, a drag-and-drop operation involves the following:

- Setting the draggable attribute to true (if it isn't already)

- Setting an event listener function to handle the dragstart event

- Setting the payload of the dataTransfer object in the dragstart event handler function

OK, so we need to add a line of code to the dragStartHandler() function to make this script compatible with browsers such as Google Chrome. Amend the code for the dragStartHandler() function in script.js to look like this:

```
...
function dragStartHandler(e) {
          console.log("dragstart");
          e.dataTransfer.setData("text/plain" , "Payload Landed" );
}
...
```

As you can see, the dataTransfer object has a method named setData() that sets the type and value for the data that is sent along with the dragged item. Now (if you weren't seeing it before), you should see the following events logged to JavaScript console:

```
dragstart
drag
dragenter
dragover
drag
...
dragleave
dragend
```

In the middle, you will see "dragover" and "drag" repeated many times as you drag the item around.

You may notice one event is missing, the all-important drop! The reason for this is the dragover event has the odd behavior of resetting the drag-and-drop operation when you are over the drop target, which has the consequence that the drop event never fires. The dragenter and dragover events could be used to handle the drag-and-drop operation, but in most circumstances you will want to trigger the drop event. What you need to do then is cancel the default behavior of the dragover event. This is a matter of calling the method preventDefault() on the event object that is passed as a parameter into the dragOverHandler() function. Additionally, we will check whether the default behavior has already been prevented, and we'll also return false from the function, which is another way of telling the browser to ignore the default behavior of the event. Both methods can be added in order to ensure the broadest browser support for this instruction. Edit your code and add the following:

```
...
function dragOverHandler(e) {
        console.log("dragover");
        if (e.preventDefault) e.preventDefault();
        return false;
}
...
```

Now when you test the drag-and-drop operation, you should see an entry for "drop" in the JavaScript console. For the last edit, we'll assign the text of the "drop target" to the text in the payload in the dataTransfer object. We'll use the innerHTML property to set the content inside the drop target. Edit the script to make this change:

```
...
function dropHandler(e) {
        console.log("drop");
        droptarget.innerHTML = e.dataTransfer.getData("text/plain");
}
...
```

The getData() method is used to retrieve the contents of the payload set in the dragStartHandler() function, which then assigns that value to the contents of the drop target. Test the page again, and you should see that when you drop the "Draggable" text onto the "Drop Target" text it changes to "Payload Landed."

OK, let's make this a little bit more user friendly. We're going to add a CSS class that creates a dashed black border that we'll make appear and disappear when over the drop target. We'll also add a default border to the h1s that blends into the background so the elements don't shift when the dashed border is added. Edit styles.css, adding the following two rules:

```
h1 {
        border:1px solid #cccccc;
}

.over {
        border:1px dashed #000000;
}
```

Now we'll add the over class when the drag is over the drop target by setting the className property on the drop target. Edit the dragOverHandler() function in script.js to add the class name:

```
...
function dragOverHandler(e) {
        console.log("dragover");
        droptarget.className = "over";
        if (e.preventDefault) e.preventDefault();
        return false;
}
...
```

We need to remove this class in the dragEndHandler() and dragLeaveHandler() functions, so we'll set the className property on those to null, which will remove the CSS class:

```
...
function dragEndHandler(e) {
        console.log("dragend");
        droptarget.className = null;
}
...
function dragLeaveHandler(e) {
        console.log("dragleave");
        droptarget.className = null;
}
...
```

Finally, we need to prevent the default behavior of the dropHandler() function. Some browsers will try to open content that has been dropped. For instance, a link that is dragged and dropped into a browser window may cause the browser to navigate to the link's URL. To prevent this, make the following edit to script.js:

```
...
function dropHandler(e) {
        console.log("drop");
        droptarget.innerHTML = e.dataTransfer.getData("text/plain");
        if (e.preventDefault) e.preventDefault();
        return false;
}
...
```

Now if you test this drag-and-drop operation, you should see the text payload added when the drag-and-drop operation is complete, and the border should appear and disappear during the operation (Figure 7-14).

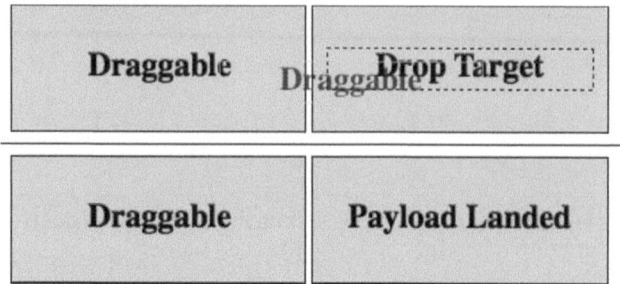

Figure 7-14. A drag-and-drop operation in progress (top) and completed (bottom)

In addition to the draggable attribute, there is the global dropzone attribute. This attribute can in theory be used to specify what kind of data a particular drop target expects to receive as well as what kind of drag-and-drop operation is going on (the specification lists move, link, and copy as its possible values), which in theory could be used to replace any logic introduced in the dragenter and dragleave events. However, at the time of writing, you'll have to wait for this feature to be implemented across the major web browsers.

ADDEVENTLISTENER

The syntax for handling events in this book has looked like the following, for example:

```
window.onload = init;
```

This is an older syntax that I've used because of its wide support, but you should be aware of a newer, more flexible syntax for handling events that you are likely to run into. The addEventListener() method can be added to associate an event handler function with an event. The preceding line of code could be rewritten as follows:

```
window.addEventListener( "load" , init , false );
```

This associates the load event with the function init(), so in this syntax the "on" prefix is left off the event. The advantages of this syntax are as follows:

- The false in the previous code snippet controls exactly when to respond to the event. In short, events can be triggered during two phases: the capture phase and bubbling phase. In the capture phase, a particular element would trigger an event after all its parent elements in the DOM had triggered the event. The bubbling phase is the opposite; a particular element triggers the event before its parent containing elements. A value of true means the event listener responds during the capture phase, and a value of false means it responds during the bubbling phase. The value is usually set to false.

- By adding additional calls to addEventListener(), you can associate more than one function with a single event.

Sorting a list using a drag-and-drop operation

Let's look at another example of a drag-and-drop operation, in the form of a user sortable list. For this example, you'll create an ordered list where the user can—through a drag-and-drop operation— rearrange the order of the list items.

To begin, duplicate the jstemplate directory from earlier and rename it dnd_list. Edit the index.html file to look like this:

```
<!DOCTYPE html>
<html>
        <head>
                <meta charset="utf-8" />
                <title>HTML5 Apprentice</title>
                <link rel="stylesheet" type="text/css" href="css/styles.css" />
                <script type="text/javascript" src="js/script.js" defer></script>
        </head>
        <body>
                <ol>
                    <li>One</li>
                    <li>Two</li>
                    <li>Three</li>
                    <li>Four</li>
                    <li>Five</li>
                </ol>
        </body>
</html>
```

Edit the JavaScript file named script.js in the dnd_list/js directory. This script will use four functions, init(), dragStartHandler(), dragOverHandler(), and dragEndHandler(). First create the global variables and edit the init() function:

```
// define global variables
var dragging;           // the list item being dragged
var dir;                // the direction (up or down) the drag is going in

function init() {
        var li = document.getElementsByTagName("li");
        // loop through list and make items draggable and set the event handler functions
        for ( var i = 0; i < li.length; i++ )
        {
                li[i].draggable = true;
                li[i].ondragover = dragOverHandler;

                li[i].ondragstart = dragStartHandler;
                li[i].ondragend = dragEndHandler;
        }
}
```

This example differs from the previous one in that the draggable attribute value is being added from the script. The script retrieves a reference to all list item elements on the page and adds the ability for them to be swapped around.

Continue with the script:

```
...
function dragStartHandler(e) {
        dragging = e.target;
        e.dataTransfer.setData('text/plain' , null);
        dragging.style.opacity = "0.5";
}
```

The dataTransfer object is set here but to a value of null because we're not using a payload. It just needs to be set to allow the dragover event to fire in Chrome. We're setting the CSS opacity property here too, although it would be advisable to add and remove a CSS class like in the earlier example so that you could easily add more styles in the future. For brevity we'll leave it as is in this example.

The dragOverHandler() function does the real work in this example:

```
...
function dragOverHandler(e) {
        // make sure the item being dragged isn't the same as the one we're dragging over
        // and make sure it hasn't been removed from the page
        if (dragging != e.target && dragging.parentNode != null)
        {
                // determine whether the drag in going up or down
                if ( e.target.previousElementSibling == dragging ) dir = "down";
                else dir = "up";

                // remove the item being dragged from the page
                dragging.parentNode.removeChild(dragging);

                // add item being dragged above or below the item being dragged over
                if (dir == "down"){
                    dragging = e.target.parentNode.appendChild(dragging , e.target);
                }
                else if (dir == "up")
                        dragging = e.target.parentNode.insertBefore(dragging , e.target);
        }
        // prevent the default behavior
        if (e.preventDefault) e.preventDefault();
        return false;
}
```

This function contains the logic for removing the dragged item and adding it back in at a different spot.

Add the final function that resets the styles and, lastly, ensure the script is set to run when the page fully loads:

```
...
function dragEndHandler(e) {
        dragging.style.opacity = "1.0";
}

window.onload = init;
```

That's it! You should have an ordered list that you can drag and drop the items in to change the order (Figure 7-15).

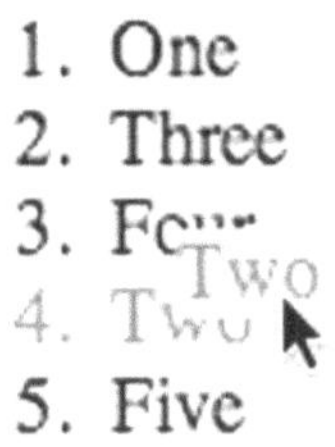

1. One
2. Three
3. Fc~~ur~~
   Two
4. Two
5. Five

Figure 7-15. *A drag-and-drop ordered list allowing for user reordering of the list items*

Summary

My hope it that this chapter has shown you how you can peer into the JavaScript APIs that are sprinkled throughout the HTML5 specification. With scripting, the possibilities are as big as your imagination. The page can be changed in so many ways, dynamically and interactively. For example, an initially uninspiring thing like a blank canvas can be built to include all sorts of interesting effects for generating real-time changes to images. Or drag-and-drop functionality can be used for building all sorts of unique interfaces that might be found on such applications as web forms, games, or administrative interfaces. Using JavaScript, HTML, and CSS together, you could create beautiful skins (controls) for a custom HTML5 video player, which would look the same across all major web browser platforms. You could take the same approach with the audio element as well. The best way to learn how the JavaScript APIs work is to use them; and remember, if something doesn't work, take a step back and use the output in console.log() to help familiarize yourself with what is going on and what is available for you to use.

The Road Ahead

There are many fringes to HTML5, areas that are still being molded and sculpted toward a standard perfection, but to a large degree the road ahead has less to do with HTML5 and more to do with where HTML5 will be used. It is a connected world, and more people are connected via cellular phones than desktop computers. In the years ahead, Internet-enabled smartphones will likely spread to the masses, like low-end "dumb" mobile phones did years ago,[1] and the Web will have visitors who are on the move, surfing web pages on crowded buses, on street corners, in cafés, in restaurants, and, dare I say it, in movie theaters. Mobile devices offer special challenges for you, the web developer/designer. The screen resolution is more complicated, and the screen real estate is more confined, but with a helping hand from CSS3, HTML5 is well supported on contemporary smartphones. What you learned from prior chapters applies here, albeit things may be a little slower and there is a smaller screen area to work with, but those are the design challenges to work around, and they are counterbalanced by the unique possibilities of the mobile space. This chapter will discuss those challenges and possibilities and finish with a discussion of some last corners of the HTML5 specification.

Challenges of the mobile Web

Over the past few years, a host of new Internet-enabled handheld devices have become widely available. While Internet-enabled mobile devices have been around since the 1990s, they arguably first became widely viewed as a viable platform for viewing web pages (as opposed to just using them for e-mail, for instance) with the introduction of the iPhone and its large colorful touchscreen in 2007. What followed was an explosion of large touchscreen devices running iOS, Google's Android OS, Microsoft's Windows Phone 7 platform, and more. Designing for the Web suddenly became a multifaceted process, many times more so than before. A web page might be viewed on a large wide-screen display in a desktop computer environment with loads of processing power, but it may be viewed on a small handheld mobile phone, with processor constraints and a display of just a few inches across. And then there are tablet devices that fall in between the two, such as Apple's iPad or the Samsung Galaxy Tab. However, designing for more than desktop displays is about more than taking differences in screen size and processing power into account. Mobile devices won't have a mouse, and clicking will likely be done with a finger (or stylus if the device is older), so small buttons are best avoided. Then there is the issue of connectivity. Mobile devices may drop their connection as the user is moving about.

---

[1] To appreciate the explosive growth in the worldwide use of cellular devices, take a look at the data collected by the World Bank on mobile cellular subscriptions:
http://data.worldbank.org/indicator/IT.CEL.SETS.P2/countries/1W?display=graph.

Responsive design

Let's consider screen size to begin with, because it is the most obvious difference between desktop computers and handheld devices. There are two broad approaches to mobile design. The first is to essentially develop two different sites, one for a desktop environment and another one for a mobile device. The user is directed to one or the other depending on what browser they view the site in. This may be a viable approach for complex sites that may need lots of effort to accommodate a mobile viewing experience and are better off presenting a simpler version of the site for mobile users. A problem with this approach is the potentially high maintenance involved. If a different site is created for desktops, tablet devices, and mobile phones, what happens if another device with a different form factor becomes popular? For example, Opera has a web browser for the Nintendo Wii game console, and Internet-enabled wristwatches running Android OS have even been developed! The other option is to change the style sheet in use based on the screen size of the viewing device. **Media queries** (discussed a little later) can be used to change the CSS depending on the physical qualities of the viewing device, such as changes based on the display size and resolution. Combine this approach with a fluid layout, and you get what is termed **responsive design**,[2] which aims to accommodate a broad range of screen sizes.

A fixed 960-pixel-wide grid has long been a web design standard that uses CSS to create rows and columns. Developed from this has been responsive grid design, which increases or decreases the amount of columns on the page based on the width and expands the columns visible to the width of the browser viewable area. Development kits such Skeleton (`http://getskeleton.com`) have emerged to help develop flexible layouts of this sort.

■ **Note** Adaptive images (`http://adaptive-images.com`) is a concept related to responsive design that is for handling the scaling of images on a page so they scale down for mobile devices and scale up for desktop displays.

The viewport

On a desktop environment, the **viewport** is the area of a web page visible in a web browser. For instance, if you opened up a web page on your desktop and resized the page down to the physical size of a mobile phone display, the area you see is the viewport. You will likely see scrollbars appear so you can scroll to the rest of the content. You'll also notice the text may wrap to fit in the visible area, if it is not otherwise sized with CSS.

The behavior of the viewport on a mobile device is slightly different. Unlike a desktop environment, in a mobile environment, the web browser covers a fixed area. The viewport defines the area in which text would be wrapped and so forth, which may extend outside the viewable area. The default viewport on iPhone, for instance, is 980 pixels wide (to comfortably accommodate the 960-pixel web page width commonly used in web design), but the page may be scaled down so it fully fits in the 320-pixel viewable area (Figure 8-1).

---

[2] See the seminal article by Ethan Marcotte on responsive web design at `http://alistapart.com/articles/responsive-web-design/`.

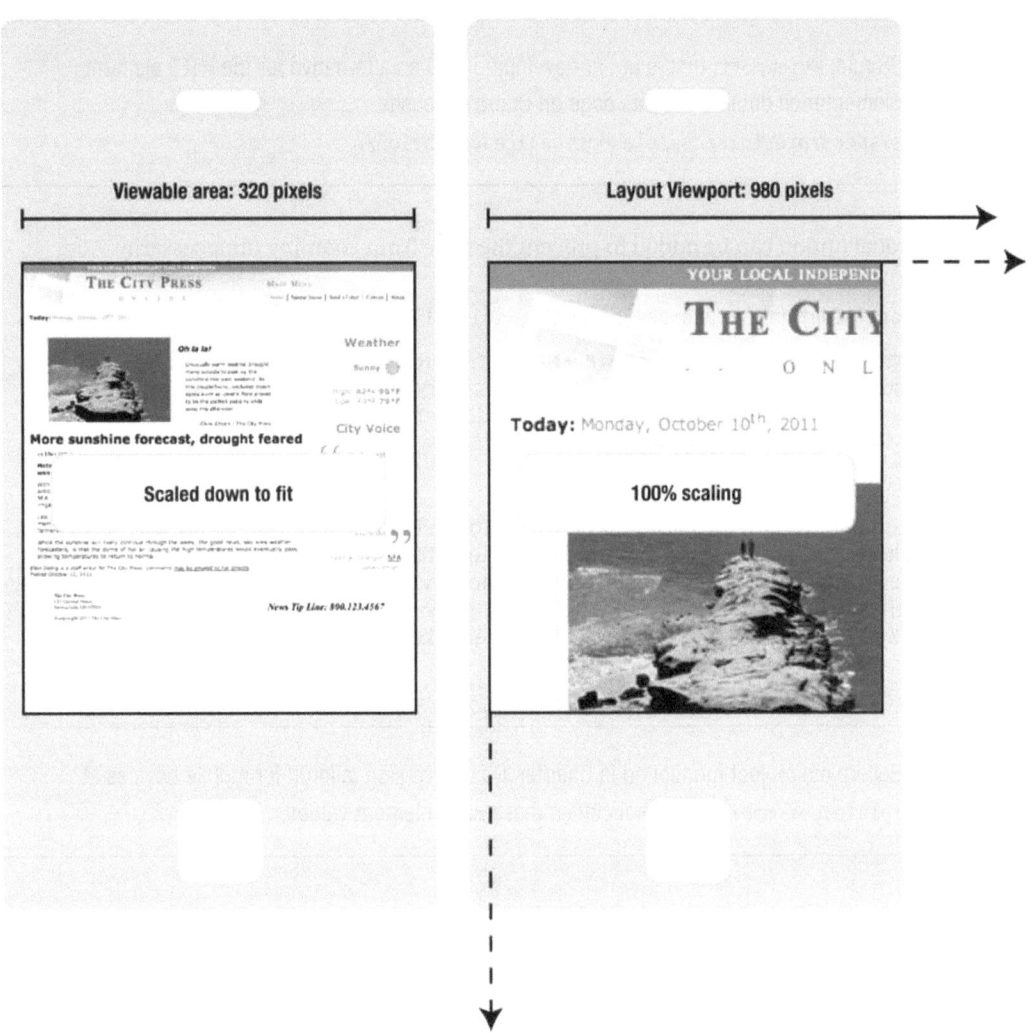

Figure 8-1. *The viewable area on a typical smartphone is 320 pixels, while the viewport the page is laid out in may be much larger, requiring the user to pan to see all content on the page when viewing at actual size.*

Ideally, the web page width would correspond to the viewable area, and this is what can be done to optimize a web page for mobile viewing. To begin with, there is a meta element value that tells a mobile device to set the width of the layout viewport to the width of the viewable area. To do this, the following would be added in the head section of the web page:

```
<meta name="viewport" content="width=device-width" />
```

■ **Note** There is a CSS rule, `@viewport`, that is under development as an alternative for the `meta` element viewport rule. For implementation details, see this page on Opera's website:

`www.opera.com/docs/specs/presto28/css/viewportdeviceadaptation/`.

Next, an additional option can be added to prevent the page from zooming unnecessarily. Add `initial-scale=1.0` to the `meta` element:

```
<meta name="viewport" content="width=device-width, initial-scale=1.0" />
```

The `viewport` meta element value is a fairly recent addition; it was added by Apple for use on the iPhone but has since been incorporated into other contemporary mobile OSs. However, to accommodate older mobile browsers, it is a good idea to add two additional `meta` elements:

```
<meta name="HandheldFriendly" content="true" />
<meta name="MobileOptimized" content="320" />
```

Both these values herald from the earlier days of the mobile Web, so eventually they will no longer be necessary to include, but for now it is a good idea to include them.

Now if the page layout is optimized for a 320-pixel-wide viewing area, it will fit right into the display area of most modern mobile phones, but to actually achieve this width and allow the site to still be comfortably viewable in a desktop environment, you will very likely use media queries, which we'll look at next.

■ **Note** The HTML5 Boilerplate project mentioned in Chapter 1 has a version tailored for mobile devices at `http://html5boilerplate.com/mobile`, which includes these `meta` element values.

Media queries

Media queries are a new addition in CSS3 that allows CSS to inspect the physical characteristics of the viewing device and change the CSS rules accordingly. Media queries grew out of the need to tailor CSS for different media types, such as for print or for screen. A typical media query might look like this:

```
@media only screen and (min-width:480px) and (max-width:767px) {
        body { width:560px; }
}
```

This appears in an external CSS file linked into the page. It specifies both the type of media the enclosed CSS rules will apply to (in this case it's for displaying on a screen) and the minimum and maximum width of the viewing screen on which the enclosed rules would apply. It's not necessary to specify both the minimum and maximum widths. A lot of other values can be selected against as well, such as an exact width, height, orientation, color, resolution, and so on.[3]

■ **Note** Since media types (`screen`, `print`, etc.) are supported in older browsers, the `@media` rule will not necessarily be ignored. The `only` keyword is added at the beginning of the query to hide the enclosed style rules from older browsers, because they will not recognize it, which will cause them to skip past the rest of the media query declaration.

Using media queries in a tiered configuration is useful for accommodating ranges of screen sizes, each fitting the content into a smaller and smaller screen area:

```
@media only screen and (min-width:768) and (max-width:959px) {
        body { width:768px; }
}

@media only screen and (min-width:480) and (max-width:767px) {
        body { width:480px; }
}

@media only screen and (max-width:479px) {
        body { width:340px; }
}
```

These three rules constrain the width of the page through three screen size changes. This example just shows constraining the width, but you will want to style the content all-around for mobile viewing, which would likely mean larger text and larger link areas. For example, the *City Press* news tips form used in Chapter 4 might be altered using media queries to appear in a mobile browser, as shown in Figure 8-2. To tailor the content for the mobile environment, extraneous information has been positioned out of view using CSS, and styles have been added to make the menu more prominent.

---

[3] See www.w3.org/TR/css3-mediaqueries/ for the full list and details.

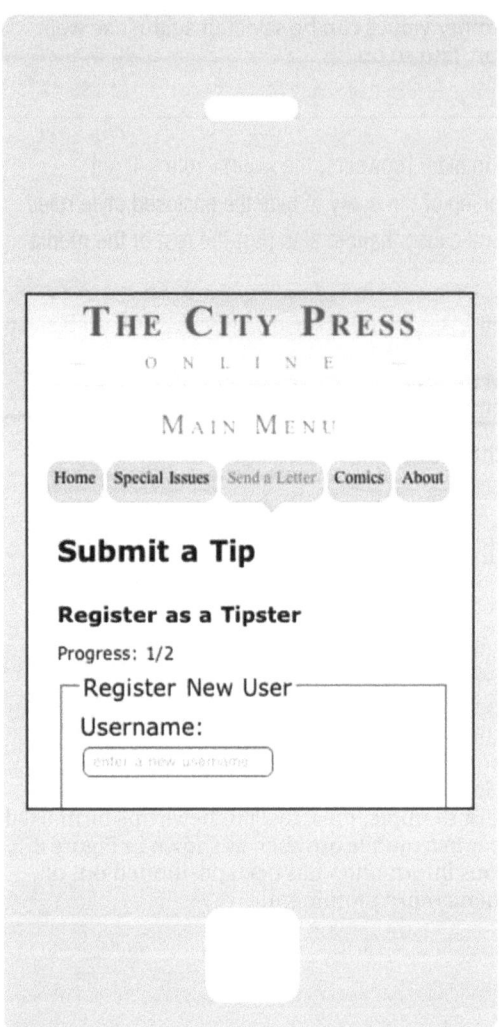

Figure 8-2. The City Press *mobile-optimized news tip submission form page*

TESTING MOBILE WEB PAGES

Testing a web page on an actual mobile device is the best way to know that a mobile page is, in fact, optimized for a mobile device, but it's also possible to quite effectively test web pages on emulated devices running on a desktop computer. Each major platform has its own simulated device that runs on a desktop computer. This is great for checking the layout and basic functionality but is not so great for testing performance, because the simulated device is using the processor of the computer, which is many times more powerful than the processor in the mobile device. At any rate, the following are some resources you may find useful for testing mobile web pages on a desktop computer:

- **Android**: The Android emulator can be downloaded as part of the Android software development kit (SDK) at `http://developer.android.com`, and an assortment of hardware specifics can be emulated and simulated. One caveat of note with Android is that when visiting a page on a local web server, the usual `http://localhost/` address will look for a web server running on the emulator itself. Instead, the special URL `http://10.0.2.2/` needs to be used to access a web server running on the host computer.

- **iOS**: Apple includes a simulator with its Xcode software package, available at `http://developer.apple.com/xcode/`. The simulator can simulate an iPad and an iPhone with and without a Retina display.

- **Windows Phone 7**: The Windows Phone SDK includes an emulator for testing content on the Windows Phone 7 platform. This is downloadable from `http://create.msdn.com`.

- **Opera**: Opera doesn't develop hardware but has a mobile version of its desktop web browser, which has a simulator that may be downloaded from `http://opera.com/developer/tools/mobile`.

In addition to this list, Adobe Device Central is an option for creating generic virtual mobile devices of various configurations and screen sizes. A web page URL can be opened in a virtual device under File ➤ *Open URL....*

It's also possible to test a responsive design in a standard web browser. If the Develop menu is turned on in the advanced preferences of Safari, you will find that there is an option under Develop ➤ User Agent to have the browser masquerade as a mobile browser (or even a browser from another manufacturer!). Open a web page and resize the window, and it'll act like it is being viewed on Safari's mobile version!

Offline application cache

The offline application cache is a way to ensure that critical files are stored on the client so that if the connection is lost and the page is reloaded, the cached files will still be loaded. If all necessary files are cached, the website can be navigated normally even when the user is offline. This may be particularly useful in a mobile web context, where the Internet connection might be intermitted.

The application cache uses the `manifest` attribute found on the root `html` element to associate the web page with a cache manifest file that lists the files to cache (or in some cases, not cache!). The cache manifest file is just a text file with the `.manifest` file extension. It must be served from the web server using the `text/cache-manifest` MIME type. It use a relative or absolute URL but typically looks something like this:

```
<!DOCTYPE html>
<html manifest="/sitecache.manifest">
        <head>
        ...
```

The `sitecache.manifest` file (depending on your configuration; you may name it differently) must begin with the key phrase CACHE MANIFEST and then is followed optionally by three sections. These are the following:

- CACHE: The files to cache.

- NETWORK: The files that always should be retrieved from online.

- FALLBACK: Fallback content for files that were not found in the cache. The file to find is given first, followed by the fallback file's location.

The cache manifest can also contain comments, which are ignored. Comments begins with the hash sign (#). A cache manifest file might look something like this:

```
CACHE MANIFEST

# list of files to cache
CACHE:
index.html
css/styles.css
js/script.js

# files that require a network connection
NETWORK:
userlogin.php

# files to use in place of other files that were not cached
FALLBACK:
images/logo.png images/offline-logo.png
contact.php contact.html
```

This would need to appear on any page that was using the cache. The files listed under the CACHE section will be stored on the client machine and retrieved as necessary to navigate the site. Any files appearing under the NETWORK section will always be fetched from the server. The FALLBACK section maps pairs of files together so that if the first one is not found, the second one will take its place on a page. Using fallbacks, you can provide visual clues to the user that they are surfing a cached version of the page. For example, you could provide alternate images that are branded "offline," which would show up only when the user was viewing the cached images.

Other HTML5 technologies

There are a number of technologies in the HTML5 family that either are not mature enough or are too broad to address within the scope of this book. However, that is no reason you shouldn't be aware of their existence! What follows is a high-level overview of these technologies.

Microdata

Microdata is HTML5 for machines. It's for search engines and other external applications that may want to derive meaning from your content but need more information to understand it. To do this, existing HTML elements can be annotated with attributes that define the type of data on the page to a much finer degree than what is possible with existing semantic HTML elements.

At its most basic level, Microdata uses three attributes: itemscope, itemtype, and itemprop. Consider, for instance, a paragraph about this book:

```
<p>
HTML5 Mastery: Semantics, Standards, and Styling by Anselm Bradford and Paul Haine.
</p>
```

To mark this up using Microdata, first the itemscope property is added to indicate that this paragraph contains a collection of data that is related, a book and authors in this case:

```
<p itemscope>
HTML5 Mastery: Semantics, Standards, and Styling by Anselm Bradford and Paul Haine.
</p>
```

This annotation means that any elements inside the paragraph are related to each other. The itemtype attribute is then used to give a URL of a Microdata vocabulary, which is a defined set of property values for different types of common data, such as people, places, events, and things. The website http://schema.org (which was launched by Microsoft, Google, and Yahoo!) contains a number of vocabularies for an assortment of data. We'll use their documentation on a Book to annotate this paragraph. The itemtype is added with the URL to the vocabulary definition:

```
<p itemscope itemtype="http://schema.org/Book">
HTML5 Mastery: Semantics, Standards, and Styling by Anselm Bradford and Paul Haine.
</p>
```

Visiting the vocabulary address, you will see there are a large number of properties that could be used, many more so than what we need in this simple example. We'll use the itemprop attribute to annotate the content with properties from the documentation. To separate the title from the authors, we'll also need to add span elements for the annotations to attach to:

```
<p itemscope itemtype="http://schema.org/Book">
<span itemprop="name">HTML5 Mastery: Semantics, Standards, and Styling</span> by <span
itemprop="author">Anselm Bradford</span> and <span itemprop="author">Paul Haine</span>.
</p>
```

First the name of the book is annotated, followed by the authors. The authors are a bit of a special case, because they are another object in the Microdata universe, that of a Person, which means they could have their own itemscope property and have additional information marked up about them, such as birth date, address, telephone number, nationality, and so on.

Search engines or other applications could parse this paragraph and be able to pick out where the book title began and ended and who the authors are. This is just a taste, but you should now have an idea of what Microdata is about. The concept is rather simple: keys and values are used to provide detailed metadata for content on a page.

There's some contention over Microdata, because it overlaps with two other formats that existed before it, Microformats and RDFa[4] (Resource Description Framework in attributes). Also, since http://schema.org was launched by several large corporations with vested interests in search engine technology, the neutrality of the syntaxes advocated by this website have been questioned. It is, however, a good starting point to familiarize yourself with the concepts of annotating your page content.

---

[4] Microdata actually evolved from RDFa.

Undo manager API

The undo manager API is a new interface for allowing a web page access to the undo/redo transaction manager inside the web browser. What does this mean? Well, think about when you type some text in the search bar in a web browser; you will likely be able to select Edit ➤ Undo to undo the text that you entered. This is the browser's native undo manager allowing you to undo an operation you have done. However, if you have an interactive web application, such as a rich text editor or drawing application built on canvas, which is controlled by JavaScript, the browser's native undo manager would not pick up the modifications performed by the script. This is where the undo manager API would come in, because it would provide a method to add actions performed via JavaScript to the browser's undo/redo manager. Just as the history API operates by adding URLs to the history "stack," the undo manager allows a particular set of changes to the page (together called a transaction) to be added to the browser's native undo stack. Since this feature is still under development, don't expect it to work in browsers today, but keep it in mind as a capability that will likely arrive in browser implementations in the not-too-distant future.

Upcoming CSS technologies

As you know, this one isn't an HTML5 technology, but it goes hand in hand with HTML. As there are many developments in HTML5, there are also many in CSS3. An interesting area has to do with page layout, and the specifications in this area have yet to fully coalescence into a dominant method(s). Eventually it's expected there will be three main specifications in this area: multicolumn layouts (discussed in Chapter 6); Flexible Box Layouts,[5] or FlexBox, which provides better alignment and positioning of elements within their parent container; and grid/template/region layouts. Currently, grid/template/region layouts are broken into four distinct specifications, but these will likely merge in the future. **Grid positioning and grid layouts** are for handling rows and columns and specifying how elements are positioned in this type of layout (a multicolumn layout can already be thought of as a rowless grid layout). The **template layout** uses a grid as well but defines a template such as "abc" or "bca," where each of the letters corresponds to an element, which can then be rearranged by changing the template lettering order. Lastly, the **region layout** proposes a means by which content would "flow" from one element to another when it overflows its bounds. Positioning in CSS has always been a headache, particularly for novice designers, so these new proposals to the specification will likely empower CSS coders in the same way that HTML5 has provided an explosion of possibilities for HTML coders (and very likely these two people are one and the same, so the creative possibilities will likely be dramatically expanded!).

Lastly, it's worth noting some of the new selectors that are defined in the Selectors Level 4 specification.[6] See Table 8-1 for a list of the upcoming new selectors and a description of their use. Don't expect these to work in the near future, but down the road these will likely be supported by your preferred web browser.

---

[5] See www.w3.org/TR/css3-flexbox/.

[6] See http://dev.w3.org/csswg/selectors4/.

Table 8-1. The new selectors described in the Selectors Level 4 specification

Selector	Description
:matches(S)	Any element that matches one or more compound selectors in a list of selectors (S).
:any-link	Any hyperlink anchors.
:local-link	Any hyperlink anchors that link within a site. Allows internal links to be differentiated from external links that go to other website domains.
:scope	Equivalent to :root unless a contextual reference element set is given. What does that mean? It's a group of elements returned by the querySelector() method in JavaScript, for instance.
:current	In a time-dimensional rendering of the HTML document, such as when text-to-speech is being used to read the document, this selects the element currently being processed.
:past	A previous sibling of the an element selected with :current.
:future	A sibling occurring after an element selected with :current.
:dir(L)	Directional selector selects either left-to-right running text with :dir(ltr) or right-to-left running text with :dir(rtl).
:nth-match(S)	An element that is the Nth sibling before an element that matches a compound selector in a list of selectors (S).
:nth-last-match(S)	An element that is the Nth sibling after an element that matches a compound selector in a list of selectors (S).
:nth-column(N)	An element that is the Nth sibling before a cell element belonging to a column in a grid of rows and columns.
:nth-last-column(N)	An element that is the Nth sibling after a cell element belonging to a column in a grid of rows and columns.
:column(S)	A cell element belonging to a column in a grid of rows and columns that is specified by a selector (S).

Summary

Predicting the future is easy if you assume that the direction things were headed in was wrong and set out to define your own new path. And it seems this has been the way HTML5 has turned out. Web developers disillusioned by the confines of XHTML turned to HTML5 with the hope that it would provide the platform they needed for a new generation of web applications. Now that it has paved its own path forward, the momentum to reinvent the Web has brought a whole new palette of possibilities. There is the flexibility of syntax, the new elements, and the multimedia and richness of JavaScript and CSS features. We've covered a lot, and there is more to come, but for now we've come to the end of this journey. Let this be the beginning of your exploration. There are many roads you can take from here, such as delving deeper into mobile development, CSS3, or the extensive HTML5 APIs. The details of the specifications will no doubt evolve, because that is the nature of the Web, but the fundamentals of what you learned here and the concepts behind the components of HTML5 will continue under the same foundation of knowledge, even if there are changes in the syntax in the future. It is time to play with these technologies and see what is possible in the world of open standards. Go on and craft pages that are semantically sound and rich in content. Go on and make the Web a better place.

Associated Technologies

In addition to CSS3, a number of technologies have been associated with HTML5 but actually are defined in their own specifications. Some were once part of HTML5 but have been spun off into their own documents as they have grown, while others are directly used with HTML5 but were never part of the HTML5 specification. This appendix provides a high-level overview of these different technologies that are commonly associated with HTML5. Additionally, you will also find a list of useful website resources for working with HTML5 at the end of the chapter.

Geolocation

The Geolocation API[1] defines how a web browser can determine a user's geographic location, using their IP or WiFi address or, if they are on a mobile device, the Global Positioning System (GPS) on the device. The location is given as a latitude and longitude coordinate, which may be more or less accurate, depending on the method used in retrieving the location. Determining a user's location with their IP address, for instance, will be far less accurate than using the satellite-based GPS to determine their location.

The implications of retrieving a user's location are quite fascinating, because it enables location-based services to be provided through a web browser. This is perhaps most useful for mobile devices, because information and advertisements can be delivered to a web browser on a device that is on the move.

The JavaScript methods for retrieving a user's location are held in the Geolocation object, which is inside window.navigator.geolocation. The location can be retrieved one time or can be updated continuously. The API defines three methods:

- getCurrentPosition(): Retrieves the current position one time

- watchPosition(): Retrieves and updates the current position as it changes

- clearWatch(): Stops updating a watched position

When attempting to retrieve the user's location, the web browser will typically provide a prompt as to whether using geolocation is allowed.

---

[1] See www.w3.org/TR/geolocation-API/.

Retrieving the current position

The getCurrentPosition() method is given a parameter for the function to call when the position has been successfully obtained (which could take several minutes if GPS is used). Here's an example:

```
function init() {
        // get the current position and call the "locatedSuccess" function when successful
        window.navigator.geolocation.getCurrentPosition(locatedSuccess);
}
function locatedSuccess(geo) {
        // log the returned Geoposition object
        console.log(geo);
}
window.onload = init;
```

▪ **Note** Depending on the web browser used, this code will likely work only on a live web server (one running locally is fine). If it is not working, first check that the URL address of the page includes http:// at the beginning.

This script will attempt to obtain the current location and then call the locatedSuccess() function when it has done so. The location query is done asynchronously so that other processes can continue to function on the page. The function is handed a parameter that contains a Geoposition object that contains information about the location. The Geoposition object contains a timestamp property and coords property, which contains yet another object, a Coordinates object. The Coordinate object contains the following properties, which may contain null values depending on the hardware capabilities of your viewing device (for instance, if your device does not have GPS capabilities, these values will be limited):

- latitude: The north-south position on the earth

- longitude: The west-east position on the earth

- altitude: The height of the position, gathered if the viewing device has the capability to measure altitude

- accuracy and altitudeAccuracy: The accuracy of the position as measured in meters

- heading: The direction of travel as measured in degrees around a circle

- speed: The speed of travel in a certain heading in meters per second

▪ **Note** In addition to the timestamp and coords properties, Firefox includes an address property for retrieving address information such as city, country, and even street information!

Update the preceding locatedSuccess() function to print the location data on-screen:

```
function locatedSuccess(geo) {
        var lat = geo.coords.latitude;
        var long = geo.coords.longitude;

        document.body.innerHTML = "<ul><li>lat:"+lat+"</li><li>long:"+long+"</li></ul>";
}
```

An additional function name can be given to the getCurrentPosition() method to specify a function to run when the request for the user's location has failed. Edit the init() code and add a locatedFailed() function:

```
function init() {
        // get the current position
        //and call the "locatedSuccess" or "locatedFailed" if
successful or not
        window.navigator.geolocation.getCurrentPosition
(locatedSuccess, locatedFailed);
}
function locatedFailed(e) {
        // log the error code and message
        console.log(e.code , e.message);
}
```

The locatedFailed() function will run when the location was unable to be obtained. The parameter handed to it is a PositionError object that contains an error code and a message. The following are possible errors:

- *Error code 1, permission denied*: The user didn't authorize using geolocation.

- *Error code 2, position unavailable*: The position can't be determined.

- *Error code 3, position retrieval timed out*: Retrieving the position took too long.

If you want to test this function, the easiest way is to deny the geolocation request from the browser. Depending on the browser and whether you accepted the previous request for geolocation information, the browser will remember your choice and won't ask you again. Google Chrome, for instance, will require you to click the "target" icon in right of the address bar where you will have the option to clear the geolocation settings (the page will need to be reloaded for the settings to take effect). Figure A-1 shows what this dialog looks like. For Firefox, the geolocation permissions are found under Tools ➤ Page Info, which will open a dialog box with information about the page currently being viewed. Selecting the Permissions tab will allow you to set the preferences for sharing location information with a particular page. Safari has location settings set in its Privacy tab in the browser's Preferences pane. If you are unsure of where to clear geolocation information in your preferred browser, check in the application's preferences or the right side of the address bar, because these are the usual locations for the geolocation permission settings.

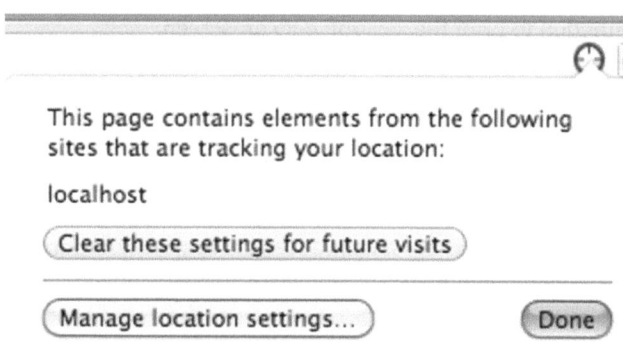

Figure A-1. Dialog for clearing geolocation settings for a page being viewed in Google Chrome

Lastly, the getCurrentPosition() method can be handed a custom object that can be used to set various options used in retrieving the location. This object can be set up with the following properties and values:

- enableHighAccuracy: Set to true or false. If enabled, the highest accuracy method for determining the location is used, such as GPS. Be aware that this will increase battery usage and the length of time for retrieving the location.

- timeout: How long to wait (in milliseconds) when retrieving the location before throwing a position unavailable error.

- maximumAge: How long (in milliseconds) a particular position should be considered the current position.

These options may be added to the getCurrentPosition() method using shorthand object creation notation, like so:

```
var options = {
        enableHighAccuracy: true,
        timeout: 120000,
        maximumAge: 1000
};
window.navigator.geolocation.getCurrentPosition(locatedSuccess, locatedFailed, options);
```

This will enable high-accuracy positioning (which is dependent on the hardware available), set the timeout to two minutes, and set the maximum age of the location to one second.

Watching the current position

Getting the location once is fine for a stationary device, such as a desktop computer, but for a mobile device, the location would have to be continually retrieved to be accurate. The watchPosition() method is used to continually poll the location (this is where the maximum age option is useful) to update the location information. It takes the same arguments as the getCurrentPosition() method, but it should be set to a variable that can later be referenced and handed to the clearWatch() method if updating the location continuously is stopped. Here's an example:

```
var geoWatchID = window.navigator.geolocation.watchPosition(locatedSuccess, locatedFailed,
options);
```

Later in the code, geoWatchID can be passed as an argument to clearWatch() to stop the position from updating:

```
clearWatch(geoWatchID);
```

SVG and MathML

SVG and MathML have two totally different purposes, but they have one thing in common: they are both XML-based languages that can be embedded in HTML5. Scalable Vector Graphics (SVG) is for describing vector shapes, while Mathematical Markup Language (MathML) is for describing mathematical notation.

SVG is one half, along with canvas, of the Web's standard imaging options. While canvas deals well with bitmaps, SVG deals well with vector shapes. It also has built-in animation capabilities, which would need to be built from scratch in canvas.

The syntax of both is beyond what can be covered here, but being XML-based, they both look very much like HTML, except with a different set of elements. For example, the following code shows an HTML page that includes both MathML and SVG to describe and diagram the trigonometric functions shown in Chapter 7.

```
<!DOCTYPE html>

<html>
        <head>
                <meta charset="utf-8" />
                <title>SVG and MathML Demo</title>
        </head>
        <body>
                <h1>SVG and MathML embedded in an HTML5 page</h1>
                <p>
                <math>
                        <mi>x</mi>
                        <mo>=</mo>
                        <mrow>
                                <msub><mi>x</mi><mn>1</mn></msub>
                                <mo>&plus;</mo>
                                <mi>cos</mi>
                                <mfenced><mi>&#x3B8;</mi></mfenced>
                                <mo>&InvisibleTimes;</mo>
                                <mi>c</mi>
                        </mrow>
                </math>
                </p><p>
                <math>
                        <mi>y</mi>
                        <mo>=</mo>
                        <mrow>
                                <msub><mi>y</mi><mn>1</mn></msub>
                                <mo>&plus;</mo>
                                <mi>sin</mi>
                                <mfenced><mi>&#x3B8;</mi></mfenced>
                                <mo>&InvisibleTimes;</mo>
                                <mi>c</mi>
```

```
                                    </mrow>
                        </math>
                        </p><p>
                        <svg>
                                <circle r="100" cx="101" cy="101" fill="white" stroke="black"/>
                                <polygon points="101,101 171.710678,30.2893219 171.710678,101"
style="fill:white;stroke:black;" />
                                <rect width="10" height="10" x="161.710678" y="91"
style="fill:white;stroke:black;" />
                                <text x="71" y="101" fill="black" font-family="sans-serif"
font-size="16">x, y</text>
                                <text x="126" y="61" fill="black" font-family="sans-serif"
font-size="16">c</text>
                                <text x="121" y="96" fill="black" font-family="sans-serif"
font-size="16">&#x3B8;</text>
                                <text x="175" y="27" fill="black" font-family="sans-serif"
font-size="16">x<tspan font-size="11" baseline-shift="sub">1</tspan>, y<tspan font-size="11"
baseline-shift ="sub">1</tspan></text>
                        </svg>
                        </p>
        </body>
        </html>
```

The preceding code creates the notation and diagram in Figure A-2.

SVG and MathML embedded in an HTML5 page

$x = x_1 + cos(\theta)c$

$y = y_1 + sin(\theta)c$

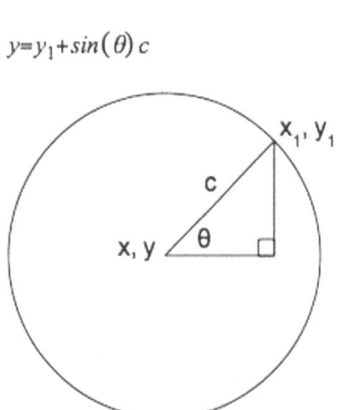

Figure A-2. A diagram created from markup using HTML, MathML, and SVG

Client-side storage

Imagine a web application that could save data the user had worked on in a client-side database and then sync that with a server-based database when the user connected online. Such offline functionality would be tremendously useful for improving the latency of the application, since the user's data would not need to be sent back and forth over the network as frequently, and it would also help in situations where connectivity may be spotty, such as in a mobile environment.

Web storage

Cookies have long been the method for storing data on the client-side browser. A problem with cookies has been that they are small, allowing only 4 kilobytes of storage each, which is minuscule by the standard of today's data-rich web pages/applications. In response to this, a new generation of client-side storage solutions have emerged. The most stable solution, and the one that can be seen as a replacement for cookies, is the Web Storage API,[2] which allows up to 5 megabytes of storage. Web storage is actually broken into two options, the localStorage object and sessionStorage object, both of which are properties of the window object. The difference between the two is that data stored in localStorage is persistent, while data stored in sessionStorage is lost when the browser session ends (such as when quitting the browser), but otherwise they are used in the same manner. Each is just a series of key/value pairs, so a key is set with some data, and then the key is used to retrieve the data later.

Using web storage

Using web storage is really quite straightforward. To add data to the storage, use either of the following syntaxes:

```
window.localStorage.setItem("key","value");
window.localStorage["key"] = "value";
```

In this code, the "key" and "value" can be any string of text. To retrieve the data from the storage, use either of the following:

```
var val = window.localStorage.getItem("key");
var val = window.localStorage["key"];
```

To remove data, either remove a specific key or clear the whole storage:

```
window.localStorage.removeItem("key");
window.localStorage.clear();
```

WEB STORAGE EXAMPLE

Using the contenteditable attribute, you can create a simple text editor that saves changes on the client. For this example, create a new HTML file named edit.html and fill it with the following code:

```
<!DOCTYPE html>
```

---

[2] See http://dev.w3.org/html5/webstorage/.

```
<html>
        <head>
                <meta charset=utf-8 />
                <title>Contenteditable and localStorage demo</title>
                <script type="text/javascript" src="js/script.js"></script>
        </head>
        <body>
                <section id="editable">This text may be edited and the changes will
                be saved locally.</section>
                <button id="startEditBtn">Turn editing on</button>
                <button id="stopEditBtn">Turn editing off and save changes</button>
                <button id="clearBtn">Clear changes!</button>
        </body>
</html>
```

Now create a new JavaScript file named script.js and place it in a directory named js that is in the same location as edit.html. Fill it with the following script:

```
var editable; // variable for editable area

// initialize the variables and add event handlers
function init()
{
        editable = document.getElementById('editable');
        var startEditBtn = document.getElementById('startEditBtn');
        var stopEditBtn = document.getElementById('stopEditBtn');
        var clearBtn = document.getElementById('clearBtn');

        startEditBtn.onmousedown = startEdit;
        stopEditBtn.onmousedown = stopEdit;
        clearBtn.onmousedown = clear;

        // update text with data in local storage
        if (localStorage.getItem("savedtext")) editable.innerHTML =
        localStorage.getItem("savedtext");
}

function startEdit()
{
    // add the contenteditable attribute
    editable.setAttribute("contenteditable", true);
}

function stopEdit()
{
    // disable the contenteditable attribute
    editable.setAttribute("contenteditable", false);
    // save the text
    localStorage.setItem("savedtext", editable.innerHTML);
}

function clear()
{
```

```
    // clear the local storage
    localStorage.clear();
    // reload the page
    window.location.href = "";
}
window.onload = init;
```

Open the HTML page in a web browser, and you will be able to turn on editing (which adds the contenteditable attribute), save the edits, and see those edits stick because they will be stored in the local storage (Figure A-3).

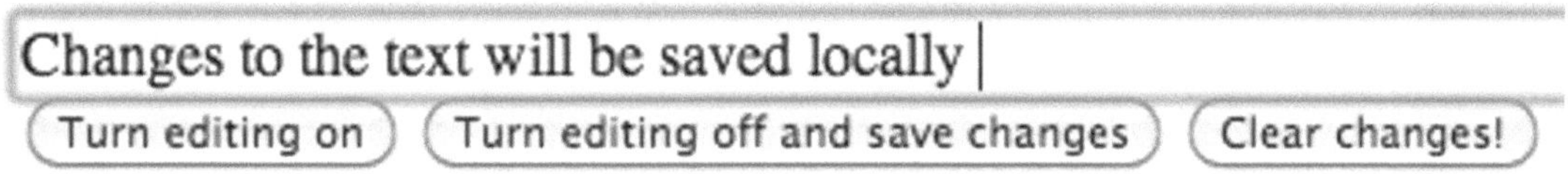

Changes to the text will be saved locally |

(Turn editing on) (Turn editing off and save changes) (Clear changes!)

Figure A-3. A simple application using local storage

Other storage options

Local storage is easy to use, but with that ease comes limits on its capabilities. It's really not comparable to a database you would find on the back-end web server, which likely describes the relationship between the stored data and provides methods for ensuring data integrity. Since web technologies are moving toward enabling the creation of web applications, having a fully capable database on the client end is a desirable option. One such option is Web SQL, which essentially embeds an SQLite[3] database into the web browser. This means **Structured Query Language** (SQL) commands can be used directly from JavaScript. Pretty cool! Unfortunately, the future of Web SQL has darkened considerably, because disagreements over standardizing the use of SQLite as the embedded database has led to support being dropped for the initiative by the W3C. Because of this, Mozilla has said it will drop support in Firefox, which means support is spotty and not reliable going forward. Too bad.

Another option, which is currently supported only in Firefox but has planned support from other major web browsers, is the Indexed Database API,[4] also known as IndexedDB. This database solution stores key/value pairs, like web storage, but includes more sophisticated features, such as transactions for ensuring data is successfully committed to the database, which helps guarantee data integrity. IndexedDB is not as sophisticated as Web SQL (it's not a relational database), but it is more capable than web storage and is looking like it will be the option to use in the future for handling client-side data storage that is more complex than what web storage will accommodate.

Web workers

Web workers are making computationally intensive tasks on the Web a little less painful. JavaScript is a single-threaded language, meaning a script that takes a lot of processing power could completely paralyze any user-interactive scripts that may be running. Using a web worker, a new thread can be spawned that runs a script without interrupting the processing of UI interactions or other events in the main script. Web workers come in two flavors: dedicated workers and shared workers. Shared workers

---

[3] See http://sqlite.org.
[4] See www.w3.org/TR/IndexedDB/.

are more powerful than dedicated workers because they can communicate with multiple scripts, while a dedicated worker responds only to the script that spawned it in the first place.

Web Sockets API

The Web Sockets API[5] is a specification that defines a protocol for providing two-way communication with a remote host. The Web's roots have traditionally been essentially one-way. A server sends a page to a client web browser, and then nothing happens between the two until the user clicks a link and requests another page. What a web socket provides is an open connection over which data can be sent from the client to the server at any time after the page has loaded, and vice versa. This could be used , for example, to create multiplayer online games or applications, because data can be sent to the server from one client and distributed to all other clients connected to the same server.

Video conferencing and peer-to-peer communication

A project is underway to create a specification for video conferencing between two web browsers. This is a major area of difference between the W3C HTML5 and WHATWG HTML specifications, because it is included in the WHATWG version but omitted from the W3C specification. Instead, the W3C has a separate specification named "WebRTC 1.0: Web Real-time Communication Between Browsers."[6] Since both specifications are in draft status, it is not inconceivable that the version included in the WHATWG HTML draft may well be spun off into a separate specification in the future, as has happened at the W3C.

Anyway, administration issues aside, the actual technology for enabling video conferencing requires that two separate web browsers gather video and audio and stream it over a peer-to-peer connection to each other. Specifically, the following steps need to happen:

1. Gain access to a webcam or other video/audio input device.

2. Record the video/audio locally so that it can be streamed to a remote web browser.

3. Connect and send the video/audio to a remote web browser.

4. Display a video/audio stream in a video or audio element on the local and remote web browsers.

An API called the Stream API, which defines an interface called `MediaStream`, would be used with JavaScript to handle parsing and displaying of the streaming media. In terms of sending the media stream, another API, called the Peer-to-peer Connections API, would be used. This API describes a `PeerConnection` JavaScript interface that defines methods for connecting and sending a media stream to a remote peer.

---

[5] See http://dev.w3.org/html5/websockets/.
[6] See http://dev.w3.org/2011/webrtc/editor/webrtc.html.

WAI-ARIA

WAI-ARIA,[7] the Accessible Rich Internet Applications specification (the WAI stands for Web Accessibility Initiative), aims to provide a syntax for making modern dynamic web applications accessible to people with disabilities. WAI-ARIA uses attributes to mark up user interaction of the page's content and describe how page elements relate to each other. WAI-ARIA defines a `role` attribute with a large set of values for describing how a web feature is presented and how the page is structured. There are also a large number of "aria-*" prefixed attributes for describing the state of web page features. These attributes can be used to annotate, for example, whether a menu has a submenu or what actions a dragged object can perform when being dropped on a target. The WAI-ARIA specification is a large specification in its own right; for further information on it, visit the WAI's WAI-ARIA overview page: `www.w3.org/WAI/intro/aria`.

File API

There are three specifications under development related to reading, browsing, and writing to files on the file system of a client machine. The main one is the File API,[8] which includes interfaces called `File`, `FileList`, `FileReader`, and `FileError` that define methods that, for instance, can be used to read the name and last modification date of files or groups of files. The specification also defines a `Blob` for interfacing with raw binary data, which may be inspected for size and type and sliced into chunks. The File API deals with files that could appear in the web browser through a web form's file input type or even through dragging and dropping a file from the user's system to the web browser window. Extending the File API are the Directories and System[9] and Writer[10] APIs. Directories and Systems is what describes methods of interacting directly with the user's local file system. Obviously, this has security implications, so the file system exposed is sandboxed so web applications don't have unrestrained power to intrude into a user's computer. The Writer API does what you would expect; it defines how files or blobs of raw data can be written to the file system. It also defines a `FileWriterSync` interface for working with writing files in conjunction with the Web Workers API.

Useful web resources

The following websites are resources you may find useful when developing with HTML5:

- *W3C's Working Draft HTML5 specification*: `http://w3.org/TR/html5/`

- *WHATWG "living" HTML specification*: `www.whatwg.org/specs/web-apps/current-work/`

- *Html5.org*: Includes a HTML5 validator and a tracker for changes to the WHATWG specification: `http://html5.org`

- *Html5rocks.com*: Includes an online code editor playground and slide presentation made entirely with HTML5 technologies: `http://html5rocks.com`

---

[7] See `www.w3.org/TR/wai-aria/`.

[8] See `www.w3.org/TR/FileAPI/`.

[9] See `www.w3.org/TR/file-system-api/`.

[10] See `www.w3.org/TR/file-writer-api/`.

- *Html5doctor.com*: Contains informative articles about HTML5 as well as a comprehensive element reference; `http://html5doctor.com`

- *Caniuse.com*: Compatibility tables for HTML5, CSS3, and related technologies: `http://caniuse.com`

- *Html5test.com*: Browser score for HTML5 and related feature support: `http://html5test.com`

- *CSS3 Selectors Test*: Browser test for support of a wide range of CSS selectors: `http://www.css3.info/selectors-test/`

- *Mobilehtml5.org*: HTML5 feature compatibility tables for mobile and tablet browsers: `http://mobilehtml5.org`

- *HTML5boilerplate.com*: Starting template for HTML5 pages: `http://html5boilerplate.com`

- *Modernizr*: JavaScript library for testing browser support of HTML5, CSS3, and related features: `http://modernizr.com/`

- *Google Chrome Frame*: Method of enabling modern web technology capabilities in older browsers: `http://code.google.com/chrome/chromeframe/`

- *Html5pattern.com*: Regex patterns for client-side validation in web forms: `http://html5pattern.com`

- *Mozilla Developer Network (MDN)*: Great, easy-to-follow resource on HTML5 and other web technologies: `https://developer.mozilla.org/en/HTML/HTML5/`

- *Html5gallery.com*: A showcase of sites using HTML5 technologies: `http://html5gallery.com`

- *Mediaqueri.es*: A showcase of sites using media queries: `http://mediaqueri.es`

Index